Mary Margaret McBride

ENCYCLOPEDIA OF COOKING

Mary Margaret McBride

Encyclopedia of

America's
Most Complete
Cookbook
Edited by

HOMEMAKERS
RESEARCH
INSTITUTE

COOKING

Volume

5

Published by Homemakers Research Institute
Evanston, Illinois

ANNE LONDON, *Director*

Editor-In-Chief

ANNE LONDON
Director, Homemakers Research Institute

Test Kitchen Director

ESTHER BURNS
Assistant Director, Homemakers Research Institute

Associate Editors

BERTHA K. BISHOV   FREDA C. DeKNIGHT
VIVIAN J. MALONE   EUGENIA J. WHITE

Assistant Editors

LEONA SHAPIRO   ETHEL I. UGELOW
DOROTHY KAHN   RUTH SHEFER

Testing and Research Assistants

ESTHER B. GALLER   HARRIET MILLER
DEBORAH WINER   CAROLE P. ROSENBERG
CAROLE OLDERSHAW   MARSHA LISITZA
JACQUELINE KUCERA   LESLIE ANN WINER
RHODA SLITT   ESTELLE FISHER
SYBIL B. GRUCCI   MARGARET MASI
ROSE AXELROD   ROSLYN BAKER
ANITA SHERMAN   JEAN HIRSH
SYLVIA POPUCH   OLGA SHERMAN
STEVE LEE   JEFFREY ALAN

Art Director

BEN BURNS

Associate Art Director

BEN ROSEN

Illustrators

HENRY R. MARTIN   PASCHA PHILLIPS
PAUL PINSON

What the Complete Encyclopedia of Cooking Contains

CONTENTS OF VOLUME 5

Complete Index of Entire Encyclopedia in Volume 12

FISH AND SHELLFISH COOKBOOK

Variety is one of the keys to successful meal planning. Very few people realize how many varieties of fish are available on the market. Only about seven species of fish are well known to the average consumer from coast to coast, although there are actually about 160 varieties sold in the United States. Modern refrigeration, quick-freezing, and rapid transportation make it possible for inlanders as well as those living on the shores to enjoy the great variety of fish all the year round.

Fish is frequently less costly than meat and, like meat, it is a primary source of protein and the essential vitamins and minerals. Fish dishes, very often, are time-savers for the busy homemaker, inasmuch as the cooking time for most fish is short. Fish, then, should always be kept in mind as an alternate, not a substitute, for meat in the daily menu. The flavor of fish is delicate. When properly cooked and skillfully combined with other foods it soon becomes a favorite dish several times a week.

BASIC FISH COOKERY HINTS

Although the flavor, texture, appearance, and size vary according to the species, the fundamental rules for cooking most fish are few and easy to follow. For this reason, the use of basic recipes, such as frying, broiling, planking, boiling, and steaming are emphasized through this section.

General Cookery Rules

The principal differentiation in types of fish, as related to fish cookery, is the variation in fat content.

As a rule, fat fish, such as salmon or shad, are most desirable for baking, broiling, and planking because their fat content will keep them from becoming dry.

Lean fish, such as cod and haddock, are preferred by some for boiling and steaming as their flesh is firm, and will not easily fall apart while cooking. Both fat and lean fish are suitable for frying.

There are, however, so many exceptions to these rules that actually all fish may be cooked by any of the basic methods with excellent results if allowances are made for the fat content. For example, lean fish, such as halibut, may be broiled or baked if basted frequently with melted fat; otherwise they will have a tendency to become dry.

Most Important Cookery Rule: The most important thing to remember in cooking fish is that it is too often overcooked. Just enough cooking to enable the flesh to be flaked easily from the bones will leave the fish moist and tender and bring out its delicate flavor.

HOW TO BUY FRESH FISH

Most varieties of fish, like many other types of food products, are particularly abundant fresh during some one season of the year. Local fish dealers will gladly furnish information concerning seasonal offerings, and indicate those varieties that can be used to the best advantage, including the less familiar varieties. If it is desired to save time in preparation and cooking, fish should be purchased as fillets, steaks, or dressed.

How to Select Fresh Fish

In buying fish in the round, the following points should be observed to insure freshness:

Eyes: Bright, clear, full, and bulging.

Gills: Reddish-pink, free from slime or odor.

Scales: Adhering tightly to the skin, bright colored with characteristic sheen.

Flesh: Firm and elastic, springing back when pressed, not separating from the bones.

Odor: Fresh, free from objectionable odors.

Quantity to Buy

Servings of fish are generally based on 1/3 to 1/2 pound of the edible flesh per person. When serving steaks, fillets, or sticks, allow 1/3 pound per person or 2 pounds for 6 people. For dressed fish, allow 1/2 pound per person or 3 pounds for 6 people. For whole fish, allow about 1 pound per person or 5 pounds for 6 people.

MARKET FORMS OF FRESH AND FROZEN FISH

Fish is marketed in various forms for different uses. Knowing these forms or "cuts" is important in buying fish. The best known forms of fish are given below.

Whole or Round Fish

Whole or round fish are those marketed just as they come from the water. Before cooking, they must be scaled and eviscerated (which means removing the entrails). The head, tail, and fins may be removed if desired, and the fish either split or cut into serving-size portions, except in fish intended for baking. Some small fish, like smelt, are frequently cooked with only the entrails removed.

Drawn Fish

Drawn fish are marketed with only the entrails removed. In preparation for cooking, they generally are scaled. Head, tail, and fins are removed, if desired, and the fish split or cut into serving-size portions. Small drawn fish, or larger sizes intended for baking, may be cooked in the form purchased after being scaled.

Dressed or Pan-Dressed Fish

Dressed fish are scaled and eviscerated, usually with the head, tails, and fins removed. The smaller sizes are ready for cooking as purchased (pan-dressed). The larger sizes of dressed fish may be baked as purchased but frequently are cut into steaks or serving-size portions.

Steaks

Steaks are cross-section slices of the larger sizes of dressed fish. They are ready to cook as purchased, except for dividing the very largest into serving-size portions. A cross-section of the backbone is usually the only bone in the steak.

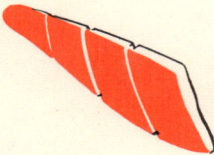

Sticks

Sticks are pieces of fish cut lengthwise or crosswise from fillets or steaks into portions of uniform width and length.

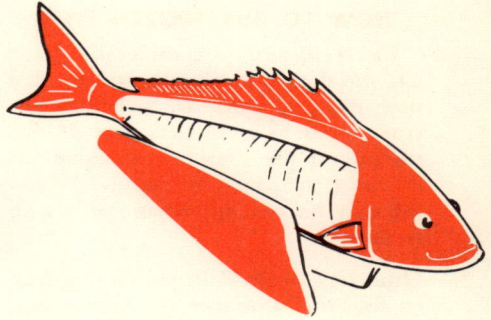

Fillets

The sides of the fish, cut lengthwise away from the backbone, are called fillets. They are practically boneless and require no preparation for cooking. Sometimes the skin, with the scales removed, is left on the fillets; others are skinned. A fillet cut from one side of a fish is called a single fillet. This is the type of fillet most generally seen in the market.

Butterfly Fillets

Butterfly fillets are the two sides of the fish corresponding to two single fillets held together by uncut flesh and the skin.

STORING OF FRESH FISH

Fish, like many other food products, will spoil easily if not handled with care. When fish is received from the market, it should be wrapped in moisture-proof paper or placed in a tightly covered dish and stored immediately in the refrigerator. Stored in this manner, the odor of fish will not penetrate other foods. If fish cannot be thoroughly refrigerated, it should be cooked at once and reheated for serving.

HOW TO BUY FROZEN FISH

In recent years a considerable trade has developed in frozen fish, so that now most varieties are available the year round to consumers both in the interior of the country and those living near the source of supply. Frozen fish may be used interchangeably with fresh fish.

Quantity to Buy: In purchasing frozen fish, the allowance for each person is the same as for fresh fish: 1/3 to 1/2 pound of the edible flesh per person.

CARE AND STORAGE OF FROZEN FISH

When frozen fish which is wrapped in parchment paper or cellophane is to be used shortly after purchasing, it should be enclosed in another wrapping of paper before being placed in the refrigerator. The additional wrapping prevents the absorption of odors by other foods as the fish thaws. Packaged frozen fish should remain in the unopened package until time to use.

If you wish to keep the fish frozen for several days, place the unopened package in the freezing unit or frozen foods compartment of your refrigerator. Fish will keep as long as it remains solidly frozen, but once it thaws, it should be used immediately. Never refreeze fish after it thaws.

THAWING FROZEN FISH

Fillets, steaks, and dressed fish may be cooked as if they were in the unfrozen form; however, additional cooking must be allowed. When fish are to be breaded or stuffed, it is more convenient to thaw them first to permit easier handling. Thawing is necessary for the cleaning and dressing of whole or drawn fish.

Thawing fish in the refrigerator at a temperature of 37° to 40° has become the accepted practice. The fish should be held at this temperature only long enough to permit ease in preparation. Whole or drawn fish may be thawed more readily by immersing them in cold running water. Thawing at room temperature, although sometimes practiced, is not recommended since a considerable amount of drip usually results.

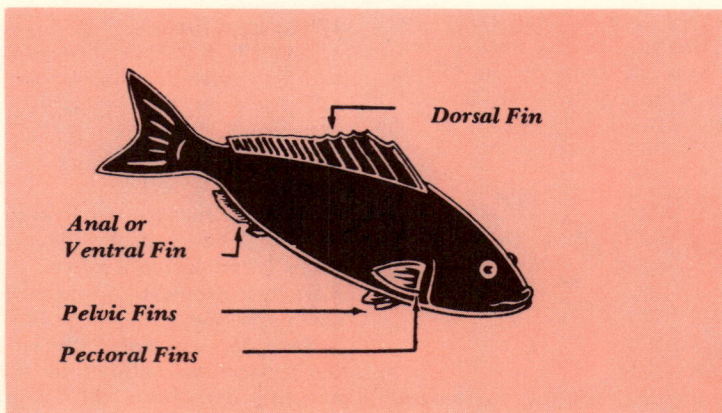

Fish Fins

CLEANING AND DRESSING FISH

Today the homemaker can obtain almost any variety of fish—fresh or frozen—already cleaned and dressed, filleted or steaked. Therefore, most of the time, there will be no need for cleaning and dressing fish for cooking.

However, freshly caught fish may be available at times, so information on cleaning and preparing fish for cooking is presented here.

Scaling: Lay the fish on the table and with one hand hold the fish firmly by the head. Holding a knife almost vertical, scrape off the scales, working from tail toward head. A scaler may be used instead of a knife. Since scales are more easily removed from a wet fish, it is advisable to soak the fish in cold water for a few minutes before scaling. Take care to remove all the scales near the base of the fins and head.

Cleaning: Remove the entrails after cutting the entire length of the belly from the vent (anal opening) to the head. Cut around the pelvic fins and remove them. Remove the head, including the pectoral fins, by cutting above the collarbone. If the backbone is large, cut down to it on each side of the fish, and then snap the backbone by bending it over the edge of the cutting board or table. Cut any remaining flesh which holds the head attached to the body. Cut off the tail.

Removing Head

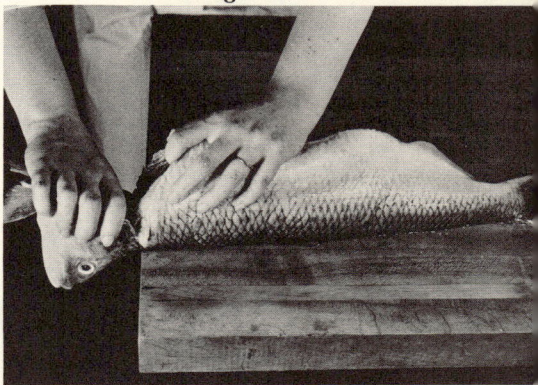

Breaking Backbone

Cutting to Remove Dorsal Fin

Removing Fin

Scaling Fish

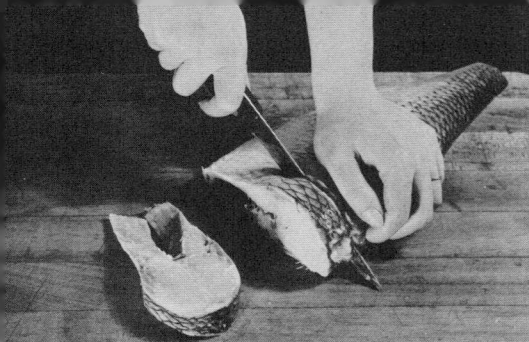

Cutting a Steak

Cutting Fillet from Tail to Head

*Cutting Along Backbone
to Remove Fillets*

Freeing Fillet at the Tail

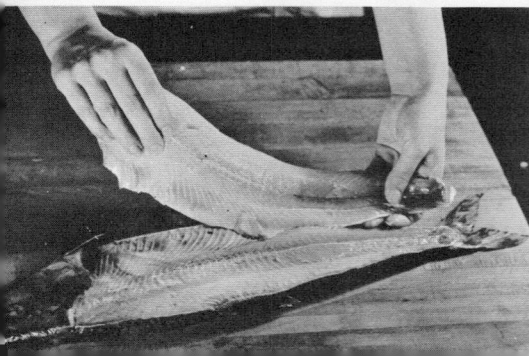

Fish Fins: Remove the dorsal or large back fin by cutting the flesh along both sides of the fin. Then, giving a quick pull forward toward the head of the fish, remove the fin with the root bones attached. Remove the other fins in the same manner. Never trim the fins off with shears or a knife since the bones at the base will be left in the fish. Wash the fish in cold running water, removing the blood, any remaining viscera, and membranes. The fish is now dressed or pan dressed, depending on its size, and is ready for cooking. Large fish may be cut crosswise into steaks.

Filleting: With a sharp knife, cut through the flesh along the back from the tail to just behind the head. Then cut down to the backbone just above the collarbone. Turn the knife flat and cut the flesh along the backbone to the tail, allowing the knife to run over the rib bones. Lift off the entire side of the fish in one piece. Turn the fish over and repeat the operation on the other side.

Skinning: If you wish, you may skin the fillets. Lay the fillets flat on the cutting board or table, skin side down. Hold the tail end with your fingers, and with a knife cut through the flesh to the skin about one-half inch from the end of the fillet. Flatten the knife on the skin and cut the flesh away from the skin by pushing the knife forward while holding the free end of the skin firmly between your fingers.

Removing the Skin from a Fillet

USUAL MARKET FORMS, SIZES, AND PRODUCING AREAS OF FISH AND SHELLFISH

Species	Fat or Lean	Usual market range of round fish	Usual market forms	Main production areas [1]
SALT-WATER FISH				
Bluefish	Lean	1 to 7 pounds	Whole and drawn	Middle and South Atlantic
Butterfish	Fat	1/4 to 1 pound	Whole and dressed	North and Middle Atlantic
Cod	Lean	3 to 20 pounds	Drawn, dressed, steaks, and fillets	North Atlantic; North Pacific
Croaker	Lean	1/2 to 2 1/2 pounds	Whole, dressed, and fillets	Middle and South Atlantic
Eel	Fat	2 to 4 pounds	Alive	Atlantic, Maine to Gulf
Flounder	Lean	1/4 to 5 pounds	Whole, dressed, and fillets	All Coastal Areas
Fluke	Lean	1 to 5 pounds	Whole, dressed, and fillets	North Atlantic
Grouper	Lean	5 to 15 pounds	Whole, drawn, dressed, steaks, and fillets	South Atlantic; Gulf
Haddock	Lean	1 1/2 to 7 pounds	Drawn and fillets	North Atlantic
Hake	Lean	2 to 5 pounds	Whole, drawn, dressed, and fillets	North and Middle Atlantic
Halibut	Lean	8 to 75 pounds	Dressed and steaks	Pacific
Herring, sea	Fat	1/4 to 1 pound	Whole	North Atlantic; North Pacific
Kingfish	Fat	15 to 30 pounds	Whole, dressed, and steaks	South Atlantic and the Gulf
Lingcod	Lean	5 to 20 pounds	Dressed, steaks, and fillets	Pacific
Mackerel	Fat	3/4 to 3 pounds	Whole, drawn, and fillets	North and Middle Atlantic; California
Mullet	Lean	1/2 to 3 pounds	Whole	South Atlantic; Gulf
Pilchard	Fat	1 1/2 to 2 ounces	Whole, canned	Atlantic and Pacific
Pollock	Lean	3 to 14 pounds	Drawn, dressed, steaks, and fillets	North Atlantic
Pompano	Fat	1 1/2 pounds	Whole, dressed, and fillets	South Atlantic and Gulf
Rockfish	Lean	2 to 5 pounds	Dressed and fillets	Pacific
Rosefish	Lean	1/2 to 1 1/4 pounds	Fillets	North Atlantic
Salmon	Fat	3 to 30 pounds	Drawn, dressed, steaks, and fillets	Pacific
Scup (Porgy)	Lean	1/2 to 2 pounds	Whole and dressed	North and Middle Atlantic
Sea bass	Lean	1/4 to 4 pounds	Whole, dressed, and fillets	Middle and South Atlantic; California

1 North Atlantic area includes the Coastal States from Maine to Connecticut; Middle Atlantic area, New York to Virginia; South Atlantic area, North Carolina to Florida; Gulf area, Alabama to Texas; Pacific area, Washington to California (North Pacific, Washington, Oregon, and Alaska); and Midwest area, Central and Inland States.

USUAL MARKET FORMS, SIZES, AND PRODUCING AREAS OF FISH AND SHELLFISH

Sea trout	Lean	1 to 6 pounds	Whole, drawn, dressed, and fillets	Middle and South Atlantic; Gulf
Shad	Fat	1½ to 7 pounds	Whole, drawn, and fillets	Middle and South Atlantic; Pacific
Snapper, red	Lean	2 to 15 pounds	Drawn, dressed, steaks, and fillets	South Atlantic; Gulf
Sole, Lemon	Lean	2 pounds	Whole, dressed, and fillets	North Atlantic; North and South Pacific
Spanish mackerel	Fat	1 to 4 pounds	Whole, drawn, dressed, and fillets	South Atlantic; Gulf
Spot	Lean	¼ to 1¼ pounds	Whole and dressed	Middle and South Atlantic
Swordfish	Fat	200 to 600 pounds	Steaks	Atlantic and Pacific oceans
Whiting	Lean	½ to 1½ pounds	Whole, drawn, dressed, and fillets	North and Middle Atlantic
FRESH-WATER FISH				
Bass	Lean	¾ to 1 pound	Whole and drawn, also reserved as game fishes	Great Lakes, Lakes, and Rivers
Buffalo fish	Lean	5 to 15 pounds	Whole, drawn, dressed, and steaks	Mississippi Valley
Carp	Lean	2 to 8 pounds	Whole and fillets	Lakes and Rivers
Catfish	Fat	1 to 10 pounds	Whole, dressed, and skinned	Lakes and Rivers
Crappie	Lean	1 to 4 pounds	Reserved as game fishes	Lakes and Rivers, Ponds and Creeks
Lake herring	Lean	½ to 1 pound	Whole, drawn, and fillets	Great Lakes
Lake trout	Fat	1½ to 10 pounds	Drawn, dressed, and fillets	Great Lakes and Lakes
Muskellunge (Musky)	Lean	3 to 10 pounds	Reserved as game fishes	Great Lakes, Lakes, and Rivers
Sheepshead	Lean	½ to 3 pounds	Whole, drawn, dressed, and fillets	Lakes and Rivers
Suckers	Lean	½ to 4 pounds	Whole, drawn, dressed, and fillets	Lakes and Rivers
Smelt	Lean	2 ounces	Whole	Great Lakes and Tributary streams
Trout, Brook	Lean	1 to 2 pounds	Reserved as game fishes	Mountain streams of eastern, northern, western states

	Fat/Lean	Market Forms	Form	Where Found
Whitefish	Fat	2 to 6 pounds	Whole, drawn, dressed, and fillets	Great Lakes
Yellow perch	Lean	½ to 1 pound	Whole and fillets	Great Lakes, Lakes and Rivers
Yellow pike	Lean	1½ to 10 pounds	Whole, dressed, and fillets	Great Lakes and Lakes
SHELLFISH				
Abalone	Lean		In the shell	Pacific coastal areas
Clams	Lean		In the shell, shucked	All Coastal Areas
Crabs	Lean		Live, cooked meat	All Coastal Areas
Crayfish, American	Lean		In the shell	Fresh waters, Pacific states
Crayfish: Rock or Spiny Lobster Tails	Lean		Headless	Florida and South African coasts
Lobsters	Lean		Live, cooked meat	North and Middle Atlantic
Oysters	Lean		In the shell, shucked	All Coastal Areas
Mussels	Lean		In the shell	Middle Atlantic
Shrimp	Lean		Headless, cooked meat	South Atlantic; Gulf and Pacific

Baked and Planked Fish

BAKED FISH FILLETS OR STEAKS

2 pounds fish fillets or steaks
1 teaspoon salt
⅛ teaspoon pepper
2 tablespoons lemon juice
1 teaspoon grated onion
4 tablespoons butter or other fat, melted
Paprika

Cut fish into serving-size portions. Sprinkle both sides with salt and pepper. Add lemon juice and onion to melted fat.

Dip each piece of fish into this mixture and place in a greased baking pan. Pour rest of fat over fish.

Bake in moderate oven (350°F.) 25 to 30 minutes or until fish flakes easily when tested with a fork. Sprinkle with paprika. Serve immediately on a hot platter. Serves 6.

BAKED STUFFED FILLETS OR STEAKS

2 fillets or steaks, about 1 pound each
1 teaspoon salt
⅛ teaspoon pepper
Bread stuffing (½ recipe, below)
4 tablespoons butter or other fat, melted
3 slices bacon (optional)

Remove skins from fillets, if skins have not been removed. Sprinkle both sides with salt and pepper.

Place one fillet or steak in well greased baking pan. Place stuffing on fish and cover with remaining fillet or steak. Fasten together with toothpicks or skewers. Brush top with melted fat and lay slices of bacon on top.

Bake in moderate oven (350°F.) 30 to 40 minutes or until fish flakes easily when tested with a fork. Remove carefully to hot platter, take out fasteners, garnish and serve hot with a sauce. Serves 6.

Planked Whole Fish

PLANKED WHOLE FISH

3 or 4 pound fish, dressed
1½ teaspoons salt
⅛ teaspoon pepper
4 tablespoons butter or other fat
Seasoned mashed potatoes
Seasoned cooked vegetables (peas, carrots, cauliflower, tomatoes, or onions)

If hardwood plank is used, oil well and place in a cold oven and heat thoroughly as oven preheats.

Clean, wash, and dry fish. Sprinkle inside and out with salt and pepper. Brush with melted fat.

Place fish on the hot oiled plank or on a greased oven glass or metal platter. Bake in a hot oven (400°F.) 35 to 45 minutes or until fish flakes easily when tested with a fork.

Remove from oven and quickly arrange a border of hot mashed potatoes around fish. Place in preheated broiler until potatoes are slightly browned, about 5 minutes.

Remove and arrange two or more hot vegetables around fish. Garnish with parsley and lemon or tomato wedges. Serve immediately on the plank. Serves 6.

BREAD STUFFING FOR FISH

3 tablespoons chopped onions
¾ cup chopped celery
6 tablespoons butter or other fat, melted
1 teaspoon salt
⅛ teaspoon pepper
1 teaspoon thyme, sage, or savory seasoning
4 cups day-old breadcrumbs

Cook celery and onions in melted fat for about 10 minutes, or until tender. Add cooked vegetables and seasonings to breadcrumbs; mix thoroughly.

If dressing seems very dry, add 2 tablespoons water, milk, or fish stock to moisten.

SPENCER METHOD FOR FISH FILLETS

2 pounds fish fillets
1 cup milk
2 teaspoons salt
¾ cup fine, dry breadcrumbs

Cut fillets in individual portions, and soak 3 minutes in milk to which salt has been added. Drain, and roll in dry breadcrumbs.

Place fish on a greased baking dish and dot with butter.

Bake in very hot oven (500°F.), allowing 10 minutes per inch thickness of fish. Heat may be reduced for larger fish, towards end of cooking time. Serves 6.

BAKED STUFFED WHOLE FISH

3   or 4 pound fish, dressed
1½ teaspoons salt
Bread stuffing (see Index)
4   tablespoons butter or other fat,
      melted
3   slices of bacon (optional)

Clean, wash, and dry fish. Sprinkle inside and out with salt.

Stuff fish loosely, and sew opening with needle and string, or close with skewers.

Place fish in greased baking pan. Brush with melted fat. Lay slices of bacon over top. Bake in moderate oven (350°F.) 40 to 60 minutes or until fish flakes easily when tested with a fork. If fish seems dry while baking, baste occasionally with drippings or melted fat.

Remove string or skewers and serve immediately on hot platter, plain or with a sauce. Serves 6.

FILLET OF FISH MARGUERY

3   tablespoons butter or margarine
1   onion, minced
6   cooked or canned shrimp
1   cup hot medium white sauce
2   egg yolks
½   cup cream
1   tablespoon minced parsley
Dash of nutmeg
Juice of ½ lemon
¼   cup sherry
2   pounds fish fillets

Sauté onion and shrimp about 5 minutes in 2 tablespoons melted butter.

Beat egg yolks with cream and slowly pour hot white sauce into egg-cream mixture, stirring constantly. Return to heat and cook 1 minute. Add remaining butter, parsley, nutmeg, and lemon juice; mix well. Remove from heat and add wine.

Place fish fillets in greased casserole. Arrange sautéed onion and seafood on fillets. Cover with sauce.

Bake in moderate oven (350°F.) about 20 minutes. Serves 6.

Note: Oysters and mushrooms may be added to shrimp.

Baked Stuffed Whole Fish

STRIPED BASS CREOLE

Clean 4-pound striped bass; rub with oil or fat, and season with salt and pepper.

Place fish in greased baking pan. Add 1/2 cup tomato juice and sprinkle 1 tablespoon finely chopped onion over fish.

Bake in moderate oven (350°F.) about 30 minutes, basting occasionally. Remove from oven.

Pour 1 cup Creole sauce (below) over fish. Sprinkle top with bread-crumbs; dot with butter. Place in oven until browned. Serves 5.

Creole Sauce for Bass: Simmer together for about 10 minutes 1 1/2 cups canned tomatoes, 1 green pepper, thinly sliced, and 1/2 cup mushrooms, thinly sliced.

In a separate saucepan, melt 1 tablespoon butter; gradually add 1 tablespoon flour, cooking and stirring over low heat until well blended.

Stir 1 cup fish stock or hot water into blended flour and fat. When thoroughly mixed, add to first mixture and cook 2 minutes longer.

FISH COOKED IN ALUMINUM FOIL

Use small or medium fish such as porgies, trout, sunfish, or yellow perch.

Clean and wash fish; remove heads and tails, if desired. Wipe dry and sprinkle inside and out with salt and pepper.

Cut sheets of foil large enough to wrap each fish separately. Spread center of each sheet with 1 tablespoon butter or margarine. Wrap up fish and fold over foil to seal edges.

To Cook Indoors: Put wrapped fish on baking sheet. Bake in moderate oven (375°F.) about 30 minutes.

To Cook Outdoors: Put wrapped fish directly on hot coals and cover with more coals. Cook 10 to 15 minutes, depending on size of fish.

Striped Bass Creole

COD OR HADDOCK— ITALIAN STYLE

1 pound cod or haddock
1/2 teaspoon salt
1 cup tomato sauce
1 tablespoon lemon juice
1/2 cup grated American or 1/4 cup grated Parmesan cheese
2 tablespoons butter or margarine

Cut fish into 3 servings; sprinkle with salt. Place in greased oven-glass pie pan.

Pour tomato sauce (the better its flavor the better the dish) and lemon juice over fish. Sprinkle with cheese and dot with bits of butter.

Bake in hot oven (400°F.) until fish flakes and cheese has browned lightly, about 25 minutes. Serves 3.

FISH BAKED IN ENVELOPES (En Papillotes)

Use small fish weighing about 1/2 pound each. Brook trout are especially good prepared this way.

Clean and draw fish. Season inside and out with salt and pepper. Rub with bacon fat, oil, or butter.

Cut brown wrapping paper in squares big enough to completely wrap each fish. Grease the paper well. Place fish in center of paper. Put a slice of onion and a slice of bacon on each. Fold edges of paper together and tie securely at each end with string.

Bake in hot oven (400°F.) 20 to 25 minutes.

STUFFED FILLETS IN CHEESE SAUCE

2   pounds fish fillets
2   tablespoons lemon juice
Salt and pepper
¼ cup melted butter or margarine
Bread stuffing (below)
Cheese sauce (below)

Dip the fillets in melted butter. Stuff them with bread stuffing, roll up, and fasten with toothpicks.

Place in a 12 inch rectangular baking dish. Pour the lemon juice over them and sprinkle with salt and pepper.

Pour the cheese sauce into the dish, and bake in slow oven (325°F.) for 30 minutes. Serves 6.

Bread Stuffing:

1   cup fine, dry breadcrumbs
½ cup melted butter or margarine
¼ teaspoon salt
⅛ teaspoon pepper
2   tablespoons chopped parsley

Combine ingredients in the order given and mix well.

Cheese Sauce:

2   tablespoons butter or margarine
2   tablespoons flour
1½ cups milk
2   cups grated sharp Cheddar cheese
½ teaspoon salt
⅛ teaspoon paprika
½ teaspoon dry mustard

Melt butter, add flour and mix well. Slowly add milk, grated cheese, and seasonings and stir until thickened.

BAKED FISH PARMIGIANA

4 servings any fish fillets or steak
Salt and pepper
1 cup tomato sauce
½ cup grated Parmesan cheese
2 tablespoons melted butter or margarine (optional)

Place fish (thawed, if frozen) in shallow baking dish. Season lightly with salt and pepper.

Spread tomato sauce over each fillet; sprinkle with cheese. For a more attractive appearance, sprinkle with melted butter or margarine.

Bake in hot oven (425°F.) until fish flakes easily, 15 to 20 minutes. Serves 4.

Stuffed Fillets in Cheese Sauce

Baked Stuffed Fresh Salmon

BAKED STUFFED FRESH SALMON

Remove head, tail, and fins from 8- to 10-pound fresh or frozen whole salmon.

Sprinkle Ac'cent lightly inside cavity; fill with stuffing (below), being careful to fill loosely.

Skewer or truss fish to shape. Brush with oil; place on strip of foil (for easy removal later) in shallow roasting pan.

Bake in moderate oven (350°F.), allowing 12 minutes per pound.

Garnish with parsley and lemon slices. Slice and serve with egg sauce accompanied by boiled new potatoes and peas.

Savory Stuffing for Salmon:

¼ cup minced onion
2 tablespoons butter or margarine
¼ teaspoon dried savory, crumbled
¼ teaspoon powdered marjoram
⅛ teaspoon powdered thyme
1 teaspoon finely chopped parsley
1 teaspoon finely grated lemon rind
1 teaspoon salt
⅛ teaspoon pepper
1 teaspoon Ac'cent
2 cups soft breadcrumbs, toasted

1 slightly beaten egg

Brown onion lightly in butter or margarine. Add herbs, lemon rind, salt, pepper, and Ac'cent. Blend well. Lightly stir in breadcrumbs and egg.

Fill cavity of fish; skewer or truss closed.

Makes enough for 8- to 10-pound dressed fish.

FISH CREOLE

1½ pounds fish fillets
2 tablespoons butter or margarine
1 cup chopped onion
½ cup chopped green pepper
1½ teaspoons salt
¼ teaspoon pepper
¼ teaspoon paprika
2 cups canned tomatoes, drained

Haddock, flounder, red snapper, ocean perch, cod, halibut, pollack, blue pike may be used. If desired, 2 pounds whole fish may be used.

Arrange fish in greased shallow baking pan or casserole.

Sauté onion and green pepper in butter. Add seasonings and tomatoes. Pour over fish.

Bake in moderate oven (375°F.) 30 minutes. Serves 4 to 5.

RED SNAPPER À LA CREOLE

1 3-pound red snapper
1/2 teaspoon salt
Dash of pepper
1 large onion, chopped
1 bay leaf, crumbled
3 sprigs parsley, chopped
1 sprig thyme, chopped
1 cup white wine
3 tablespoons butter or margarine
2 tablespoons flour
1/2 cup chopped mushrooms
6 tomatoes, chopped fine
1/2 cup cracker crumbs

Clean and wash fish. Season with salt and pepper.

Mix onion, bay leaf, parsley, and thyme. Spread evenly over bottom of baking pan. Put fish in pan. Pour wine over fish.

Bake in moderate oven (350°F.) 20 minutes.

Melt 2 tablespoons butter in a saucepan. Sprinkle in flour, and when browned add mushrooms and tomatoes. Simmer 10 minutes. Pour over fish. Cover with crumbs. Dot with remaining butter. Bake 10 minutes longer. Serves 6.

Variations: Flounder, haddock, pompano, or redfish may be prepared in the same manner.

RED SNAPPER WITH TOMATO SAUCE

1 3-pound red snapper (or other large fish)
Seasoned flour
6 tablespoons butter or margarine
1/2 cup chopped onion
2 cups chopped celery
1/4 cup chopped green pepper
3 cups canned tomatoes
1 tablespoon Worcestershire sauce
1 tablespoon ketchup
1 teaspoon chili powder
1/2 lemon, finely sliced
2 bay leaves
1 clove garlic, minced
1 teaspoon salt

Few grains red pepper

Sprinkle fish inside and out with seasoned flour. Place in baking pan lined with greased paper.

Melt butter; add onion, celery, and green pepper; simmer 15 minutes.

Add tomatoes, Worcestershire sauce, ketchup, chili powder, lemon, bay leaves, garlic, salt, and red pepper. Simmer until celery is very tender, then put the mixture through a potato ricer or food mill.

Pour the sauce around fish.

Bake in slow oven (325°F.) about 45 minutes.

Baste frequently with sauce. Serves 6.

BAKED OR PLANKED SHAD

Clean and split shad. Place skin side down on hot buttered plank or in greased shallow baking dish.

Sprinkle with salt and pepper. Brush with melted butter.

Bake in hot oven (400°F.) 20 to 25 minutes, basting frequently with melted butter. Garnish with parsley. Serve at once.

With Creamed Roe: After baking, spread creamed roe (below) over fish. Sprinkle with 1/2 cup buttered breadcrumbs. Brown under broiler.

Creamed Roe:

1 shad roe, parboiled
2 tablespoons butter or margarine
1 teaspoon grated onion
2 tablespoons flour
1/2 cup light cream
2 slightly beaten egg yolks
1 tablespoon lemon juice

Discard outer membrane of roe. Mash the roe. Melt butter in a saucepan.

Add onion and blend in flour. Slowly stir in cream and cook over low heat until thickened, about 5 minutes. Slowly add to beaten egg yolks, stirring constantly. Add lemon juice and roe. Season to taste with salt and pepper.

Baked Ocean Perch

BAKED OCEAN PERCH

Place two 1-pound packages ocean perch in glass baking dish. Season with salt and pepper.

Melt 1/4 pound butter (1/2 cup) and mix in 2 1/4 cups cracker meal. Cover fillets with butter-crumb mixture. Sprinkle with chopped parsley, if desired.

Bake in moderate oven (350°F.) 30 minutes, or until fish is tender and crumbs browned.

Serve with pickled onions and beets, if desired. Serves 6.

Variations: Haddock or flounder fillets may be substituted for ocean perch.

BAKED CHICKEN HALIBUT, DUTCH STYLE

1 2 1/2-pound chicken halibut
Lemon juice
Salt, pepper, nutmeg
3/4 cup breadcrumbs
2 tablespoons minced parsley
1 teaspoon minced chives
Butter or margarine
Fine dry breadcrumbs
3 beaten eggs
1/2 cup milk

Rub fish inside and out with lemon juice. Season with salt and pepper.

Fill opening with stuffing: Combine 3/4 cup breadcrumbs, parsley, chives, 1/2 cup butter, and salt, black pepper, and nutmeg to taste. Sew or skewer opening.

Brush generously with butter, roll in fine dry breadcrumbs. Place in a buttered baking dish. Bake in hot oven (400°F.) 15 minutes.

Meanwhile prepare a soft custard sauce: beat together eggs, milk, 2 tablespoons butter, salt, pepper, and nutmeg to taste.

Pour this custard over fish; reduce heat to moderate (350°F.). Cover with a buttered paper; bake 15 to 20 minutes or until custard is set. Serve with Dutch fish sauce (below).

Dutch Fish Sauce:

4 1/2 tablespoons butter or margarine
4 teaspoons minced onion
1 tablespoon flour
1 cup fish stock (or strained canned clam juice)
2 tablespoons tarragon vinegar
3/4 cup heated sour cream
1/2 cup minced sweet gherkins
1 tablespoon minced parsley
Salt, pepper, nutmeg

Heat 1 1/2 tablespoons butter in saucepan. Add minced onion and cook only until limp. Sprinkle over flour. Blend in fish stock; add vinegar. When mixture thickens, add heated sour cream. When hot, add sweet gherkins, parsley, and salt, pepper, and nutmeg to taste.

Now beat the sauce, add 3 tablespoons butter gradually, or enough to make it foamy.

Serve the fish from the baking dish, passing this sauce.

BAKED BROOK TROUT

Wipe the cleaned trout and wrap each in a strip of bacon. Place in baking pan.

Bake in moderate oven (350°F.) 20 minutes without turning.

POMPANO

This fish is found in the warmer coastal waters of the South Atlantic and Gulf of Mexico.

The Florida pompano is regarded as one of the most delicately flavored fish. Fillets may be broiled, poached, or sautéed.

ROYAL POINCIANA POMPANO

1 large pompano
2 cups cooked cleaned shrimp
2 eggs
1 cup heavy cream
½ cup chopped mushrooms
¼ cup sherry
About ½ teaspoon salt
Pepper and paprika, to taste

Split and bone the fish. Place half in a well buttered baking dish.

Grind or chop shrimp fine.

Beat eggs and half the cream together. Mix with shrimp, mushrooms, wine, and seasonings. Spread over half of fish. Cover with the other half. Pour remaining cream over fish.

Bake in moderate oven (350°F.) 45 minutes. Serve garnished with sliced cucumbers marinated in French dressing or sprinkled with lemon juice. Serves 4 to 6.

POMPANO EN PAPILLOTTE

3 medium-sized pompano
3 cups water
1 chopped shallot or 2 tablespoons chopped onion
6 tablespoons butter or margarine
2¼ cups white wine
1 cup crabmeat
1 cup diced cooked shrimp
½ clove garlic, minced
1½ cups chopped onions
Pinch of thyme
1 bay leaf
2 cups fish stock
2 tablespoons flour
2 egg yolks
Salt and pepper

Clean pompano and cut into 6 fillets, removing heads and backbones.

Combine heads, bones, and water. Simmer until there are 2 cups stock.

Sauté shallot and fillets in 2 table-spoons butter. Add 2 cups wine; cover and simmer gently until fillets are tender, 5 to 8 minutes.

Sauté crabmeat, shrimp, and ¼ clove garlic in 1 tablespoon butter. Add onions and remaining ¼ clove garlic and cook 10 minutes. Add thyme, bay leaf, and 1¾ cups fish stock; simmer 10 minutes.

Blend together 2 tablespoons butter and flour and gradually add remaining ¼ cup fish stock. Add to crabmeat mixture with stock drained from fillets. Cook, stirring constantly, until thickened.

Beat egg yolks and add hot sauce and ¼ cup wine. Mix thoroughly. Place in refrigerator to chill until firm.

Cut 6 parchment-shaped hearts 8 inches long and 12 inches wide. Oil well and place spoonfuls of sauce on side of each heart. Lay poached fillet on sauce and fold over. Seal edges.

Lay sealed hearts on an oiled baking sheet. Bake in very hot oven (450°F.) 15 minutes, or until paper hearts are browned. Serve at once in paper hearts. Serves 6.

Variations: Sea trout, striped bass, or fresh salmon may be substituted for pompano.

BAKED HADDOCK AU GRATIN

1 whole or filleted haddock, about 3 pounds
1 No. 2 can tomatoes
1 clove garlic, chopped fine
4 tablespoons American or Parmesan cheese, cut in bits
Salt and pepper, to taste
1 tablespoon chopped thyme

Place fillets in greased baking dish. Add remaining ingredients.

Bake in moderate oven (350°F.) until fish flakes when pierced with fork, about 1 hour. Serves 6.

Note: Flounder, cod, or ocean perch fillets may be substituted for haddock. Cut down baking time to 35 minutes.

BAKED FILIPINO FISH, MANILA HOTEL STYLE

1 red snapper, or whitefish (3 to 5 pounds)
Lime juice

Stuffing:

1 cup grated very mild American cheese
1 clove garlic, minced fine
3 cups minced cashew (or pine) nuts
1 cup fine dry breadcrumbs
½ teaspoon grated nutmeg
1 small onion, scraped to pulp
2 crumbled bay leaves
6 tablespoons butter
½ cup Madeira or sherry
Additional 6 tablespoons melted butter

Prepare the fish for stuffing and brush inside and out liberally with lime juice.

Stuff with a mixture of the cheese, garlic, nuts, breadcrumbs, nutmeg, onion, bay leaves, and the 6 tablespoons butter.

Lay in well oiled pan or earthenware baking dish; put into hot oven (425°F.) for 15 minutes. Reduce heat to moderate (350°F.) and baste frequently with a mixture of the wine and butter.

Note: Chopped almonds, Brazil nuts, hazelnuts, pine nuts, or pecans do equally well, but the cashew is traditional in the Philippines.

SUNSET SCALLOP

1 cup tomatoes
½ cup water
4 whole cloves
1 tablespoon sugar
1 teaspoon salt
2 tablespoons butter or margarine
2 tablespoons flour
2 tablespoons fat
¼ cup minced onion
2 pounds fish fillets

Cook tomatoes, water, cloves, sugar,

and salt for 5 minutes. Strain.

Melt butter in top of double boiler; add flour and stir until well blended. Cook 1 minute.

Slowly add the hot strained tomato mixture and stir until thickened. Cook 2 minutes longer.

Melt fat and cook onions until clear. Place cooked onions in a greased casserole.

Wipe fillets with a damp cloth and place on onions. Pour hot sauce over fish.

Bake in very hot oven (450°F.), allowing 10 minutes per inch thickness of fish.

If frozen fillets are used, increase time to 20 minutes for each inch thickness of fish. Serves 6.

BAKED FISH IN SOUR CREAM

3 pounds frozen fish fillets
½ teaspoon salt
⅛ teaspoon pepper
1½ teaspoons Ac'cent
Onion rings
1 cup thick sour cream

Thaw fish; place in buttered or oiled flat baking dish or oven-glass platter. Sprinkle both sides of fillets with salt, pepper, and Ac'cent; let stand 10 minutes.

Cover fish with onion rings (slice onions thin; separate into rings); pour or spoon sour cream over onions.

Bake uncovered in moderate oven (350°F.) until fish flakes easily when tested with a fork, about 30 to 35 minutes.

Baste fish occasionally with the cream and if liquid evaporates too fast, or fish seems dry, add a tablespoon or two hot water.

Serve from baking dish, adding watercress or any other fresh green garnish, at the last moment just before serving. Serves 6.

Broiled Fish

Broiled Fish
California

BROILED FISH FILLETS OR STEAKS

2 pounds fillets or steaks
1 teaspoon salt
1/8 teaspoon pepper
4 tablespoons butter or other fat, melted

Cut fish into serving-size portions. Sprinkle both sides with salt and pepper.

Place fish on a preheated greased broiler pan about 2 inches from the heat, skin side up, if skin has not been removed from fillets.

Brush fish with melted fat. Broil for 5 to 8 minutes or until slightly brown, baste with melted fat, and turn carefully. Brush other side with melted fat and cook 5 to 8 minutes or until fish flakes easily when tested with a fork.

Remove carefully to a hot platter, garnish, and serve immediately plain or with a sauce. Serves 6.

BROILED EEL

Skin and clean eel, remove backbone and cut in individual pieces. Rub with salt and let stand 10 minutes.

Wipe to remove salt, brush with melted butter or oil, and place on oiled broiler 4 inches from heat.

Broil in moderately hot oven (400°F.) 10 minutes, or until golden brown.

The flesh should flake easily with a fork. Sprinkle with salt and pepper and minced parsley. Serve with maître d'hôtel sauce or lemon juice.

BROILED FISH CALIFORNIA

2 to 4 small whole fish
1/4 cup lemon juice
1/2 teaspoon Ac'cent
1/2 teaspoon salt
Few grains pepper
Melted butter or margarine

Remove heads from fish and clean; do not split. Rub inside with lemon juice, Ac'cent, salt, and pepper.

Place on broiler rack; brush with melted butter. Broil, with surface of fish 3 to 4 inches below source of heat 8 minutes; turn; brush with melted butter; broil 5 to 8 minutes longer, depending on size of fish, or until fish flakes easily with fork.

Serve with California sauce (below); garnish with lemon wedges and fresh mint. Serves 4.

California Sauce:

2 tablespoons butter or margarine
2 tablespoons flour
1/2 teaspoon salt
1/2 teaspoon Ac'cent
4 tablespoons brown sugar
1/2 cup lemon juice
1/2 cup water
1/2 cup golden seedless raisins

Melt butter or margarine; blend in flour, salt, Ac'cent, and brown sugar.

Combine lemon juice and water; add and stir over low heat until smooth and thickened. Add raisins; simmer 5 minutes. Makes about 2 cups.

Broiled Stuffed Fillets

BROILED SCROD

A true scrod is a young codfish, weight between 1 to 2 pounds. When it is split down the back, has the head, tail, and bones removed, it is referred to as a "scrod." Fillets of other fish, however, are frequently referred to incorrectly by this name.

To broil a scrod, brush with melted butter or dip in olive oil, then in fine breadcrumbs. Sprinkle with salt and pepper.

Broil on a preheated greased broiler pan about 2 inches from heat, skin side up, until browned, about 5 minutes or until fish flakes easily when tested by a fork.

Baste with melted butter or olive oil, turn and broil other side.

BROILED SMELTS

Clean as for deep fried smelts. Dip in olive oil, then in breadcrumbs. Dust with paprika.

Broil quickly until golden brown.

Put on hot platter. Sprinkle with melted butter.

BROILED STUFFED FILLETS

1 medium onion, grated
6 flounder fillets (about 2 pounds)
1 teaspoon salt
1/8 teaspoon pepper
2 teaspoons Ac'cent
1/2 cup finely chopped celery
1/3 cup melted butter or margarine
1 teaspoon savory
4 cups soft breadcrumbs
Creole sauce

Grate onion over surface of fish fillets; sprinkle with salt, pepper, and Ac'cent.

Combine celery, melted butter, savory and breadcrumbs; spread over fillets. Roll up and tie or secure with wooden picks.

Broil with surface of fish 4 inches below source of heat for 15 to 20 minutes. Do not turn. Serve with Creole sauce. Serves 6.

BROILED SWORDFISH STEAKS

2 swordfish steaks about 1-inch thick
    (2 pounds)
1 teaspoon Ac'cent
Salt and pepper
Melted butter or margarine

Sprinkle surface of fish with Ac'cent, following the rule of $\frac{1}{2}$ teaspoon per pound. Let stand 5 minutes.

Sprinkle with salt and pepper. Brush with melted butter or margarine. Place on greased broiler rack in broiler, with surface of fish about 3-inches below heat.

Broil about 8 minutes on each side, brushing frequently with melted butter or margarine. Serves 6.

BROILED SALMON STEAKS
WITH MAYONNAISE SAUCE

4 salmon steaks, about $\frac{3}{4}$ inch thick
$\frac{1}{4}$ cup mayonnaise
2 tablespoons chopped parsley
2 tablespoons chili sauce

Preheat broiler at (550°F.) for 10 minutes.

Arrange salmon steaks on greased baking sheet. Place under broiler and broil about 8 minutes or until lightly browned.

Combine mayonnaise, parsley, and chili sauce; blend well. Spread broiled salmon steaks generously with mixture. Broil 2 to 3 minutes longer or until sauce is delicately browned.

Serve with romaine or lettuce on a large platter. Garnish with slices of tomato and cucumber. Serves 4.

TROUT BROILED WITH BACON

Have trout cleaned and ready for the pan. Wrap each trout in bacon strip, fastening bacon with a wooden pick.

Lay them flat in broiler pan and cook with moderate heat until bacon is crisp on side next to heat source. Turn and crisp the other side.

BROILED BROOK TROUT
(Or Other Small, Fresh-Water Fish)

Line baking sheet with aluminum foil, or grease thoroughly.

Brush whole, cleaned fish, inside and out with melted fat. Sprinkle inside and out with salt, pepper, and Ac'cent. Place on foil.

Broil, with surface or fish 3 inches below source of heat 5 minutes. Turn; broil 4 to 5 minutes longer. Brush with melted butter or margarine several times during broiling. Serve with cucumber sauce.

Broiled Swordfish Steaks

Fried Fish

Oven Fried Fillets

PAN-FRIED FISH

2 pounds fillets, steaks or pan-dressed fish
1 teaspoon salt
⅛ teaspoon pepper
1 egg
1 tablespoon milk or water
1 cup breadcrumbs, cracker crumbs, corn meal, or flour

Cut fish into serving-size portions. Sprinkle both sides with salt and pepper.

Beat egg slightly, and blend in the milk. Dip fish in the egg and roll in crumbs.

Place fish in a heavy frying pan which contains about ⅛ inch melted fat, hot but not smoking. Fry at a moderate heat. When fish is brown on one side, turn carefully and brown the other side. Cooking time about 10 minutes, depending on the thickness of the fish. Drain on absorbent paper.

Serve immediately on a hot platter, plain or with a sauce. Serves 6.

OVEN FRIED FILLETS

2 pounds fish fillets
1 teaspoon salt
1 tablespoon paprika
¼ teaspoon pepper
1 cup milk
1 cup breadcrumbs
4 tablespoons butter or other fat

Cut fillets into serving pieces. Season with salt, pepper, and paprika. (If frozen fillets are used, let them thaw before cutting.)

Dip the fish in milk and roll in crumbs. Place in a well greased baking pan. Pour melted fat over fish.

Place pan on shelf near the top of a very hot oven (500°F.) and bake 10 to 12 minutes, or until fish flakes easily when tested with a fork. Serve immediately on a hot platter, plain or with a sauce. Serves 6.

DEEP FAT FRIED FISH

Prepare 2 pounds fish as for pan-fried fish.

Use a deep kettle with a frying basket and enough fat to cover the fish, but do not have the kettle more than half full of fat. Heat the fat to 375°F.

Place a layer of fish in the frying basket and cook to an even golden brown, about 3 to 5 minutes. Raise basket, remove fish, and drain on absorbent paper.

Serve immediately on a hot platter, plain or with a sauce. Serves 6.

Fried Fish

SAUTEED BROOK TROUT

Wipe the cleaned trout. Sprinkle with salt. Roll in corn meal or flour. Sauté in butter until delicately brown. Remove trout to hot platter.

To the drippings in pan add additional butter, salt, and lemon juice. Let it brown slightly and pour over fish. Sprinkle with chopped parsley.

FISH FILLETS MEUNIERE

Season and dredge fish fillets with flour. Fry in butter. When done, remove from pan.

Place a little sweet butter in the same pan and cook it until nut-brown in color. Pour over the fish. Sprinkle with chopped parsley and a little lemon juice.

With Almonds: Sprinkle fish fillets meunière with slivered almonds, sautéed in butter.

FILLETS IN WINE, PORTUGUESE STYLE

Crush or chop 3 cloves garlic. Add 1 teaspoon salt, $\frac{1}{4}$ teaspoon red pepper, 1 cup wine vinegar, and $1\frac{1}{2}$ cups water.

Pour over 2 pounds fish fillets and leave overnight. Drain from liquid, fry in deep fat, or sauté until delicately browned. Serves 6.

DEEP FRIED SMELTS

Remove small scales with a sharp knife. Slit fish along the underside and remove entrails. Then remove silver lining from stomach by grasping with thumb and index finger. Rinse and dry.

Dip fish in egg beaten with a little milk. Roll in corn meal or fine cracker crumbs. Or use a combination of corn meal and cracker crumbs.

Fry in hot deep fat (370°F.) until golden brown, 3 to 5 minutes. Drain on absorbent paper. Sprinkle with salt, pepper, and lemon juice. Serve with tartar sauce or ketchup and lemon wedges.

Note: Smelt fanciers usually like these fish fried whole and the bones are eaten.

PAN-FRIED OR SAUTÉED SMELTS

Clean as for deep fried smelts. For best results use a half inch of bacon fat in a heavy skillet. Brown until crisp on one side. Turn and brown other side.

Smelts may also be sautéed in butter until brown on both sides.

Smelts Meunière: Sauté smelts in butter. Remove to hot platter. Sprinkle with chopped parsley. Melt additional butter in pan. Pour over smelts. Serve with lemon wedges.

Smelts Amandine: Sauté smelts in olive oil. To serve, sprinkle with slivered almonds sautéed in oil.

Smelts Au Beurre Noir (With Black Butter): Serve sautéed smelts with black butter (See Index) poured over fish.

FILIPINO FISH EN ADOBE

1½ pounds fish
Salt
1   tablespoon hot fat
1½ tablespoons minced garlic
½   cup minced onion
2   bay leaves
2   green peppers, cut in ½-inch
        strips
5   tablespoons vinegar
⅓   cup water

Clean fish (any kind); cut it cross-wise into individual servings. Rub with salt.

Sauté fish in hot fat until brown. Remove fish and reserve.

Add garlic and onion to pan, adding more fat; brown well; add bay leaves, green peppers, and vinegar. Cook slowly until peppers are tender.

Add fish with water. Let simmer 5 minutes. Serve hot. Serves 6.

EELS

Eels should be alive when bought and will be skinned, cut up, and cleaned on request.

To prepare at home, cut off the head and slit the skin lengthwise. Peel off, cut open and remove entrails. Wash in salt water and cut into convenient lengths.

FRIED EEL

Cut eel in 2-inch lengths. Wash and dry thoroughly. Season with salt and pepper.

Dip in crumbs, then in egg, and again in crumbs. Brown quickly in a small amount of fat. Cover, reduce heat, and cook slowly until tender.

Serve with tomato sauce or other desired sauce.

Poached or "Boiled" Fish

LIQUIDS USED FOR BOILING FISH

Boiled fish may be improved in flavor by cooking in one of the following liquids: **Acid Water, Fish Stock,** or **Court Bouillon.**

ACID WATER

To each quart of water add 1½ tablespoons of salt and 3 tablespoons of lemon juice or vinegar.

FISH STOCK (Fumet)

To each quart of cold water add 1 pound of fish trimmings (head, bones, skin, and tail) and 1½ tablespoons of salt, bring to a boil and simmer for 30 minutes. Strain.

COURT BOUILLON

⅓ cup diced carrots
⅓ cup chopped onion
⅓ cup chopped celery
2 sprigs parsley
2 tablespoons butter or other fat,
      melted
2 quarts water
6 whole black peppers
2 whole cloves
1 bay leaf
2 tablespoons salt
2 tablespoons vinegar

Cook the vegetables in fat about 5 minutes to brown slightly.

Add water, spices (tied in a bag), and vinegar; simmer 30 minutes. Strain.

STEAMED FILLETS

2   pounds fillets
1½ teaspoons salt

Salt fish on both sides. Place fish in a well greased steamer pan, and cook over boiling water for 10 to 12 minutes or until fish flakes easily when tested with a fork.

Remove fish carefully to a hot platter, and serve hot with a rich brightly colored sauce. Serves 6.

Poached Salmon with Herb Dressing

POACHED SALMON WITH HERB DRESSING

Select salmon steaks of even thickness, buying 1 steak for 2 servings.

Place piece of aluminum foil in bottom of frying basket. Place 1 steak on foil, top with another piece of foil; continue until all the steaks are added.

Place basket in kettle; add 1 or 2 slices of onion, 3 slices of lemon, 3 or 4 whole black peppers, a piece of bay leaf, 1 to 2 teaspoons salt, and 1/2 teaspoon Ac'cent per pound of fish.

Add enough boiling water to cover fish. Set over low heat; simmer 15 to 20 minutes depending on amount of fish.

Lift out basket. Remove steaks by lifting foil under each. Cool; then chill.

To serve, top with chilled cooked asparagus and herb dressing. Garnish with cucumber slices, watercress, and capers.

Herb Salad Dressing:

1 1/2 tablespoons sugar
1 teaspoon salt
1/4 teaspoon Ac'cent
2 teaspoons prepared mustard
1/4 teaspoon rosemary
1/8 teaspoon thyme
1/4 teaspoon savory
2 tablespoons flour
1 slightly beaten egg
3/4 cup milk
1/4 cup lemon juice
1 tablespoon butter or margarine

In top of double boiler combine sugar, salt, Ac'cent, mustard, herbs, and flour. Add egg; blend well.

Add milk slowly, blending well. Add lemon juice.

Cook over hot water, stirring constantly, until thickened. Add butter or margarine; stir until melted. Cool, then chill.

Add 1/4 to 1/2 cup light cream if a thinner dressing is desired. Makes about 1 cup dressing.

French Rolled Fillets

POACHED OR "BOILED" FISH

2 pounds fillets
2 quarts water
3 tablespoons salt

Cut fillets into serving-size portions.
Place fish in a wire basket or on a plate. The plate if used should be tied in a piece of cheesecloth. Lower the fish into the salted, boiling water and simmer (never boil), about 10 minutes or until fish flakes easily when tested with a fork.

Remove fish carefully to a hot platter. Garnish and serve hot with a rich, bright colored sauce. Serves 6.

FRENCH ROLLED FILLETS

1 tablespoon butter or margarine
2 tablespoons minced onion
1½ pounds fish fillets
1½ teaspoons salt
Speck of pepper
4 peeled, quartered small tomatoes
¼ pound mushrooms, sliced
½ cup dry wine
½ cup cold water

Grease a large frying pan with butter. Strew onion over it.

Roll each fillet like a jelly roll, place in frying pan, seam side down. Sprinkle salt and pepper over fillets.

Arrange tomatoes around and place mushrooms over top. Pour over wine and water. Cover and simmer 10 minutes, or until fish is tender.

Remove fish to hot platter, keeping warm while preparing sauce.

Sauce: To prepare sauce cook liquid left in frying pan until about 1 cupful remains. Cream 3 tablespoons softened butter. Add 3 tablespoons flour. Add to the liquid and simmer until thickened. Sprinkle fish with parsley. Pour sauce over fish. Broil until browned over top.

If desired, small cooked potato balls may be placed around fish before pouring over sauce and broiling. Serves 4.

*Poached
Fillets with Almonds*

GEFILTE FISH
(Traditional Jewish Filled Fish)

3 pounds fish (see below)
2 onions
1 egg
2 tablespoons breadcrumbs or matzo
    meal
About 1 teaspoon salt
About 1/8 teaspoon pepper
Few dashes of cinnamon
About 1/2 cup water
1 carrot, sliced
1 potato, sliced (optional)
1 stalk celery, sliced

Use any firm-fleshed fish, preferably pike, carp, whitefish, buffalo, or a combination of these.

Clean and wash fish thoroughly; sprinkle with salt and place in refrigerator until ready to prepare.

Either leave fish whole or cut it into 2-inch slices. If the fish is left whole, do not remove head or tail. In either case, fillet the fish by removing flesh with bones leaving the skin intact.

Remove the flesh from bones; put the filleted parts or flesh and 1 onion through food chopper, then place in wooden chopping bowl.

Add egg, breadcrumbs, or matzo meal, seasoning, and enough water to make a soft light mixture. Chop until thoroughly blended and smooth.

Wet the hands with cold water and fill the skin with this mixture. If the fish has been sliced form the mixture into oval cakes and fit them into bands of skin.

Place the bones, 1 sliced onion, carrot, potato, and celery in a deep kettle. Season with salt, pepper, and cinnamon.

Place fish sections neatly on top; add cold water to cover. Cover kettle and bring to quick boil. Remove cover, turn down heat, and keep fish at a slow boil 1½ to 2 hours.

The liquid should be reduced by half. When cool, remove to a platter carefully to retain shape of each section.

Strain liquid over fish or into a separate bowl.

Chill thoroughly before serving, using carrot for garnish.

The jelled sauce may be cut and served separately or as an additional garnish. Serves 4 to 6.

Gefilte Fish Balls: Place bones, head, and skin removed in the process of filleting fish on bottom of deep kettle. Arrange several stalks of celery across.

Form the fish mixture into balls and place on top of celery to make removal easier when cooked.

The bones and skin add flavor to the fish sauce; discard after removing fish and straining sauce.

COD PROVENÇAL

4 thick slices cod
Salt and pepper
1 medium onion, finely chopped
1 clove garlic, crushed
2 tablespoons chopped parsley
Pinch of thyme
2 medium tomatoes, peeled and
    chopped
1 cup thinly sliced mushrooms, sau-
    téed in butter or margarine
1 cup white wine
1 tablespoon butter or margarine

Season fish with salt and pepper. Place in well greased shallow baking dish. Sprinkle with onion, garlic, parsley, and thyme. Add tomatoes, sautéed mushrooms, and wine.

Place over low heat and simmer gently until fish is tender and flakes apart 15 to 20 minutes.

Remove fish to heated platter and keep warm while sauce cooks down to about half its original volume. Add butter and pour sauce over fish. Serve at once. Serves 4.

Note: Haddock, ocean perch, or flounder fillets may be substituted for cod.

To poach or "boil" fish, whole or in slices, place on a plate and tie in cheesecloth before lowering into pan.

Butter Barbecued Fillets

BUTTER BARBECUED FILLETS

½ cup (1 stick) butter or margarine
½ cup minced onion
2 tablespoons chopped green pepper
1 tablespoon Worcestershire sauce
2 tablespoons ketchup
2 teaspoons vinegar
2 slices lemon
1 teaspoon prepared mustard
2 pounds frozen fish fillets (2 boxes)

Sauté onion and green pepper in butter in a large skillet. Add Worcestershire sauce, ketchup, vinegar, lemon slices, and prepared mustard and simmer for 5 minutes.

Cut each package of fish fillets into 4 equal pieces and place in the skillet. Cover and simmer for 10 minutes. Turn.

Simmer 10 to 15 minutes more or until the fish is done and can be flaked with a fork. Serves 4 to 6.

CREOLE BOUILLABAISSE

2 pounds fish fillets
¼ pound mushrooms
1 tablespoon margarine or butter
1 large onion, minced
1 clove garlic, mashed
1 tablespoon flour
2 cups tomato pulp
1 cup water
1½ bay leaves
¾ teaspoon curry powder
¼ cup sherry
Dash of Tabasco sauce
½ teaspoon salt
4 whole cloves

For best results, use 2 kinds of fish such as redfish and red snapper.

Poach fish in boiling water for 15 minutes.

Slice mushrooms very thin and sauté in fat with onion, garlic, and flour. When golden brown, add remaining ingredients and simmer for 30 minutes.

Add this sauce to drained fish and cook about 5 minutes. Place pieces of fish on buttered toast, cover with the sauce and serve. Serves 6 to 8.

ARROZ CON PESCADO
(South American Fish With Rice)

1½ cups water
3 cloves garlic, well ground
1 cup uncooked rice
2 pounds fish
2 tablespoons butter, margarine, or olive oil
2 chili peppers, dried and toasted

Although any kind of fish may be used in the preparation of this dish, the corvina (weakfish) is generally used.

Put water on to boil. Salt to taste, and add ground garlic. Bring to a boil.

Add rice and, when boiling is resumed, put in fish. Cover and let simmer.

As soon as water is consumed, add butter without stirring, and chili peppers.

One-half cup cooked green peas is sometimes added to the rice and fish stew. Serves 6.

OVEN POACHED FISH

2 pounds fish fillets, 1 inch thick
Salt and pepper
2 tablespoons lemon juice
1 tablespoon finely minced parsley
4 tablespoons butter or margarine

Cut fish into individual portions or leave whole. Place in an oiled baking dish.

Sprinkle with salt, pepper, lemon juice, and parsley. Dot with butter.

Bake in moderate oven (350°F.) 20 minutes.

On account of the lower temperature, the juices will flow and the fish cooks in its own juice. This gravy should be served with the fish. It may be thickened with 1 teaspoon flour, blended to a smooth paste with 2 teaspoons cold water or used to replace part of tomatoes in making tomato sauce. Serves 6.

Note: Small whole dressed fish or steaks may be cooked by this method if desired.

CURRIED FISH

1½ to 2 pounds fish
2 tablespoons fat
1 tablespoon chopped green pepper
1 small onion, chopped
¼ cup chopped celery
2 tablespoons flour
1 cup liquid from simmered fish
¼ to 1 teaspoon curry powder
Salt, to taste
2 to 3 cups cooked rice
3 tablespoons chopped parsley

Simmer fish about 10 minutes in a small quantity of water in a shallow pan. Drain and save liquid.

Melt fat. Cook green pepper, onion, and celery in fat a few minutes. Stir in flour, then add fish liquid with milk or water to bring the quantity to 1 cup. Cook until thickened, stirring constantly.

Add curry powder and salt, to taste.

Remove skin and bones from cooked fish. Arrange on a hot platter with a border of rice. Pour sauce over fish and sprinkle with chopped parsley. Serves 6.

FISH COOKED IN MILK

2 pounds fish fillets
5 cups water
1 tablespoon salt
3 cups milk

Wipe the fish with a damp cloth, and cut in serving pieces. Soak 5 minutes in 5 cups water to which 1 tablespoon salt has been added. Drain.

Place in hot milk, and simmer until fish flakes easily with a fork, allowing about 15 minutes per inch thickness of fish. Prepare a medium white sauce, using the milk in which the fish was cooked. Serves 6.

SMELTS WITH SOUR SAUCE
(German)

12 or more smelts
1 onion, sliced
1 teaspoon caraway seed
4 whole black peppers
1 teaspoon salt

Sour Sauce:

2 tablespoons butter or margarine
¼ pound pickled pork, sliced or diced
1 onion, minced
2 tablespoons flour
1 scant cup water
Vinegar, to taste
1 bay leaf
1 teaspoon sugar
Salt and pepper, to taste

Place cleaned smelts in a saucepan with cold water to cover. Add onion, caraway seed, whole black peppers, and salt. Let simmer 15 minutes.

Remove fish; let this court bouillon simmer 15 minutes. Return fish to it and cook until tender. Drain and serve with sour sauce.

Sour Sauce: Melt butter in a saucepan. Add pickled pork and cook until lightly browned. Add onion and sprinkle with flour, cooking until it is light brown. Add water and remaining ingredients. Let sauce cook uncovered until reduced one half. Serve over fish.

Roe and Milt

Roe are the eggs of fish which are removed intact. They are commonly found in fish in the spring. Roe may be bought by the pound or in cans.

Milt are the spermatic glands of the male fish. It is prepared like roe.

Canned roe may be used in place of parboiled roe. Shad roe is considered a great delicacy and it is the most expensive; however roe is commonly obtained from cod, haddock, herring, flounder, mackerel, and salmon as well as shad. Salt herring and mackerel usually contain roe or milt.

Roe should be parboiled before using in recipes. Follow the method for parboiled shad roe, but cut the time for roe from smaller fish. Five to 10 minutes is usually enough, depending upon size of roe. The roe is sufficiently done when it blanches (whitens).

A pair of roe from 1 shad will serve 2. For other roe or milt, allow about 1 pound to serve 4 to 5, depending upon how it is served.

PARBOILED SHAD ROE

Handle roe carefully in pairs with the membrane intact. Cover with boiling water and for each quart of water add 1 tablespoon vinegar or lemon juice, ½ teaspoon salt, and, if desired, ½ teaspoon pickling spice.

Lower heat and simmer until white and firm, 5 to 20 minutes, depending on size of roe. Drain, cover with cold water, cool, and drain again. Remove membrane or not as desired.

Note: Roe of very small shad do not have to be parboiled or at the most parboil for 2 minutes.

BROILED SHAD ROE

Brush dried parboiled shad roe with melted butter or margarine seasoned with salt and pepper, and a little lemon juice if desired.

Place in shallow greased baking dish or pan. Broil about 2 inches from heat source until golden brown. Turn and broil other side.

Baste several times with melted butter or margarine. It should be firm but not dry or hard. Serve with lemon wedges.

BAKED SHAD ROE

Place drained parboiled shad roe in a greased baking dish. Cover with tomato sauce.

Bake in hot oven (400°F.) about 20 minutes, basting 5 times with sauce in pan. Serve with additional tomato sauce.

FRIED OR SAUTÈED SHAD ROE

Season drained, parboiled shad roe with salt and pepper. Sprinkle with lemon juice if desired.

Dip in fine cracker crumbs, then in beaten egg, diluted with 1 tablespoon milk or water, and again in crumbs.

Sauté in butter or margarine until done throughout and lightly browned or fry in hot deep fat (390°F.).

Serve with lemon wedges or tartar sauce.

SHAD ROE MEUNIÈRE

Cook parboiled shad roe in butter or oil. Add lemon juice, salt, and pepper to taste. Sprinkle with chopped parsley. Cover with melted browned butter.

Shad Roe Amandine: Follow recipe for Shad Roe Meunière, and garnish with chopped almonds which have been browned in the oven.

SHAD ROE SCRAMBLE

1   small parboiled shad roe
4   eggs
½   teaspoon salt
⅛   teaspoon pepper
⅓   cup light cream or milk
1½ tablespoons butter or margarine

Skin roe and mash to separate.

Beat eggs and add salt, pepper, and cream or milk, and roe.

Heat fat in skillet. Add roe-egg mixture and cook, stirring constantly, until firm as desired. Serves 4.

Tuna-Spaghetti Casserole

Canned or Cooked Fish

BUYING CANNED FISH

In using canned fish, the more attractive high grades are better for salads or serving plain. For such dishes as casseroles or fish cakes, lower grades will do. They are just as nutritious and flavorful as top quality.

The oil or salty liquid from canned fish adds flavor and food value to seafood dishes. Use the oil, for instance, as fat in the white sauce in making creamed tuna fish. Brine may be part of the liquid in jellied fish salad.

TUNA-SPAGHETTI CASSEROLE

6   tablespoons butter or margarine*
6   tablespoons flour
1   teaspoon salt
Few grains pepper
1   tall can (1⅔ cups) evaporated milk
1   8-ounce can tomato sauce
⅔ cup water
¼ teaspoon thyme
¾ teaspoon Ac'cent
1   13-ounce can tuna
1   8-ounce package thin spaghetti, cooked
2   cups cooked or canned green peas
2   cups well seasoned mashed potatoes
Melted butter or margarine

Melt butter or margarine in top of double boiler; blend in flour, salt, and pepper.

Combine evaporated milk, tomato sauce, and water; add all at once. Stir over low heat until smooth and thickened. Add thyme and Ac'cent; cover; set over hot water; cook 10 minutes.

Meanwhile break tuna into fairly large pieces; combine with spaghetti and peas. Add sauce; mix well; pour into casserole. Top with ring of mashed potatoes; brush with melted butter or margarine.

Bake in hot oven (425°F.) about 15 minutes or until potatoes are golden brown. Serves 6.

*Note: Or, measure oil from tuna and add enough butter or margarine to make 6 tablespoons.

TUNA, TOMATOES AND LIMA BEANS

1   7-ounce can solid-pack tuna
1   medium-sized onion, chopped
1   clove garlic, minced
¼ cup chopped green pepper
1   cup canned tomatoes
4   drops Tabasco sauce
1   canned pimiento, chopped
2   cups cooked lima beans
Salt and pepper to taste

Drain tuna and reserve oil; break tuna into large pieces with fork.

Heat tuna oil over low heat; add onion, garlic, and green pepper and sauté until tender. Add tomatoes, Tabasco, pimiento, lima beans, and tuna; mix well.

Season to taste with salt and pepper; heat to serving temperature. Serves 4.

SALMON CASSEROLE

⅓ cup chopped onion
¼ cup chopped green pepper
¼ cup diced celery
½ cup sliced mushrooms
¼ cup butter or margarine
3 tablespoons flour
1½ teaspoons salt
¼ teaspoon pepper
1 tall can (1⅔ cups) evaporated milk
1 cup water
1 1-pound can salmon, boned and flaked
2 cups fresh, frozen, or canned peas
2 cups crushed potato chips

Sauté onion, green pepper, celery, and mushrooms in melted butter until lightly browned. Add flour, salt, and pepper and mix well.

Gradually stir in evaporated milk, then water and cook until smooth and thickened, stirring constantly.

Arrange layers of salmon, peas, white sauce, and potato chips in buttered 2-quart casserole. Top with layer of potato chips and dot with butter.

Cover and bake in moderate oven (375°F.) 25 minutes. Uncover and bake 10 minutes longer or until top is brown.

When using individual casseroles, cut cooking time in half. Serves 6.

Salmon Casserole

SCALLOPED SALMON AND LIMA BEANS

1   8-ounce can salmon
1   No. 2 can or 1 12-ounce package
       frozen lima beans
Milk
4   tablespoons butter or margarine
1/4 cup flour
1   teaspoon salt
Few grains pepper
1/2 teaspoon Ac'cent
1   cup milk
1   cup buttered soft breadcrumbs

Drain salmon liquid into measuring cup.

Cook lima beans according to directions on package; drain; pour cooking water into cup of salmon liquid. Fill cup with milk.

Melt butter or margarine; blend in flour, salt, pepper, and Ac'cent.

Add contents of measuring cup plus the milk; stir over low heat until smooth and thickened.

Flake salmon, removing bones. Combine with lima beans in 1-quart casserole.

Pour sauce over all; top with buttered crumbs.

Bake in moderate oven (375°F.) until crumbs are brown, 15 to 20 minutes. Serves 4.

SALMON CASSEROLE #2

1   1-pound can salmon
2   cups riced cooked potatoes
1   teaspoon salt
1/8 teaspoon cayenne
1/4 teaspoon white pepper
2   egg whites
1/2 cup heavy cream

Remove dark skin and bones from salmon; flake and mix lightly with riced potatoes. Add salt, cayenne, and white pepper.

Beat egg whites until stiff. Beat cream until stiff and fold into beaten egg whites.

Turn salmon mixture into a greased 2-quart baking dish.

Pile egg white-cream mixture around edge of baking dish. Bake in hot oven (400°F.) 20 to 25 minutes.

If desired, just before serving, fill center with hot cooked peas or any other cooked vegetable of your choice. Serves 4.

CREAMED SALMON AND CORN

2   tablespoons butter or margarine
4   tablespoons flour
3/4 teaspoon salt
Few grains pepper
1   teaspoon sugar
2   cups milk
3/4 cup cooked or canned salmon
1 1/2 cups cooked or canned whole kernel corn
1   tablespoon chopped pimiento
Toast slices

Melt butter or margarine; blend in flour, salt, pepper, and sugar. Gradually add milk.

Cook over hot water, stirring constantly, until thick. Add salmon, corn, and pimiento. Serve on toast. Serves 4.

Scalloped Salmon and Lima Beans

Tomato-Salmon Pie

TOMATO-SALMON PIE

Biscuit Crust:

2 cups enriched flour
3 teaspoons baking powder
1/2 teaspoon salt
1/4 cup margarine or butter
2/3 cup milk

Sift, measure flour. Resift with baking powder and salt. Cut in margarine or butter.

Add milk and toss lightly with fork. Knead lightly on floured pastry cloth until smooth on one side. Roll out 1/4 inch thick. Fit into baking dish.

Filling:

3 tablespoons chopped onion
1/4 cup chopped green pepper
1/4 cup margarine or butter
3 tablespoons enriched flour
2 1/2 cups canned tomatoes
1/4 teaspoon salt
1/8 teaspoon pepper
2 teaspoons sugar
1 1-pound can salmon
Grated cheese

Sauté onion and green pepper in margarine or butter. Blend in flour. Add tomatoes, seasonings, and sugar and cook 15 minutes.

Spread salmon on top of biscuit dough. Cover with tomato sauce.

Bake in hot oven (400°F.) 20 to 25 minutes. Sprinkle with cheese. Serves 6.

TUNA CHEESE RABBIT

1/4 cup butter or margarine
3 tablespoons enriched flour
1 1/2 cups milk
2 cups grated processed Cheddar cheese (1/2 pound)
1/2 teaspoon salt
1/4 teaspoon dry mustard
1/4 teaspoon paprika
Dash of red pepper
1 tablespoon grated onion
1 teaspoon Worcestershire sauce
1/2 cup canned tomatoes
1 7-ounce can solid-pack tuna

In a saucepan, melt butter or margarine over low heat; add flour and blend. Add milk and cook until thickened, stirring constantly.

Add cheese, salt, mustard, paprika, pepper, onion, Worcestershire sauce, and tomatoes. Stir until cheese is melted.

Add undrained tuna; mix lightly with fork, breaking tuna into large chunks.

Serve over toasted bread or rolls. Serves 6.

CHEESE SALMON RING WITH CREAMED VEGETABLES

4   tablespoons butter or margarine
1/2 cup diced onion
1/2 cup diced green pepper
4   tablespoons flour
1 1/2 teaspoons salt
1/4 teaspoon pepper
2 1/2 cups milk
2   eggs, separated
2   tablespoons lemon juice
1   cup grated American cheese
1   cup dry breadcrumbs
1   cup diced cooked celery
1   1-pound can salmon, flaked

Cook onion and green pepper in butter until tender. Add flour and seasonings and blend. Stir in milk and cook until sauce boils and thickens, stirring constantly.

Pour a little hot mixture into slightly beaten egg yolks. Return to sauce. Add remaining ingredients and stir to blend. Fold in stiffly beaten egg whites.

Turn mixture into a buttered 1 1/2-quart ring mold.

Bake in a moderate oven (350°F.) for about 40 to 45 minutes. Unmold on hot serving plate. Fill center with creamed peas. Serves 6.

FISH TURNOVERS

Piecrust made from 2 cups flour or prepared piecrust mix
3/4 cup cooked fish, flaked (or use canned tuna or salmon)
1/2 cup canned condensed mushroom soup or medium white sauce
1   slightly beaten egg
1/2 tablespoon chopped parsley
1   teaspoon lemon juice
1   hard-cooked egg, chopped
Salt and pepper to taste
1   beaten egg yolk, for brushing turnover tops

Roll out piecrust dough about 1/8 inch thick and cut into 12 equal squares.

Combine fish, mushroom soup or white sauce, beaten egg, parsley, lemon juice, and hard-cooked egg; blend well. Taste for seasoning.

Put a tablespoonful of this mixture on each square. Brush edges with water and fold over. Press edges with a floured fork to seal them.

Brush with beaten egg yolk and prick with fork. Set on greased baking sheet.

Bake in moderate oven (375°F.) 20 minutes. Serve with green salad. Serves 6.

se Salmon
g with
med Vegetables

Fish Patties with Creamed Peas

FISH PATTIES

1½ cups flaked, cooked or canned fish
½ teaspoon salt
1 egg
1½ cups mashed potatoes
1 tablespoon minced onion
⅛ teaspoon pepper
Flour and fat

Combine all ingredients except flour and fat. Shape mixture into patties and roll in flour. Brown in fat. Serve with creamed peas. Serves 4.

Fish Potato Puffs: In fish patties recipe, add 2 egg yolks instead of a whole egg to the mixture of fish and potato. Add seasonings and fold in stiffly beaten egg whites.

Put mixture into greased custard cups and bake in a moderate oven (350° F.) 30 minutes. Serves 4.

SALMON SHORTCAKE AU GRATIN

3 cups medium white sauce
1 cup freshly grated cheese
1½ cups flaked salmon
1 cup cooked peas
1 tablespoon lemon juice
Baking powder biscuit dough

Make 3 cups medium white sauce. Add cheese, salmon, peas, and lemon juice. Heat thoroughly.

Make baking powder biscuit dough and bake in a round cake pan. Split and serve hot salmon mixture as a filling and topping for biscuit shortcake. Or serve on split hot biscuits, or on toasted bread. Serves 6.

Salmon Shortcake Au Gratin

FISH CROQUETTES

3 cups cooked flaked fish
5 tablespoons butter or margarine
5 tablespoons flour
¾ teaspoon salt
⅛ teaspoon pepper
1½ cups milk
1 tablespoon minced onion
1 tablespoon minced parsley
1 teaspoon vinegar
1 cup fine dry breadcrumbs
1 slightly beaten egg
2 tablespoons cold water

Mash fish with fork. Melt butter in saucepan; blend in flour, salt, and pepper. Add milk slowly and cook until very thick, stirring constantly.

Add onion, parsley, vinegar, and fish. Mix well. Chill several hours.

Shape into croquettes (about 12). Roll in crumbs; dip in egg mixed with water. Roll again in crumbs. Chill at least 1 hour.

Fry in hot deep fat (375°F.) until golden brown, 2 to 3 minutes. Drain on absorbent paper. Serve with creamy egg sauce or Creole sauce. Serves 6.

PILCHARD TIMBALES
(Canadian)

2 cups macaroni
2 cups soft breadcrumbs
1 cup tomato juice
1 egg
1 teaspoon salt
¼ teaspoon pepper
1 tablespoon minced parsley
2 cups canned pilchards

Cook macaroni in 4 cups boiling water to which two teaspoons salt has been added. Drain and rinse in cold water.

Mix soft breadcrumbs, tomato juice, beaten egg, salt, pepper, minced parsley, and flaked canned pilchards.

Line greased timbale molds with cooked macaroni to form a cup and fill center with fish mixture.

Place in a pan of hot water, cover with waxed paper and bake in hot oven (400°F.) 20 minutes. Unmold and serve hot with a tomato sauce. Serves 6.

Note: Herring or mackerel may be used instead of pilchards.

BAKED SALMON CUTLETS

2 cups thick white sauce
2 teaspoons Worcestershire sauce
2 teaspoons lemon juice
1 tablespoon minced onion
⅛ teaspoon celery salt
2 cups cooked or canned salmon

Prepare 2 cups thick white sauce. Add Worcestershire sauce, lemon juice, minced onion, and celery salt. Mix well.

Flake salmon, removing skin but using soft bones and oil, and add fish to sauce. Chill well.

Form into cutlets and roll in finely sifted dry breadcrumbs. Place on greased pan. Bake in hot oven (400°F.) 20 minutes.

Serve with lemon sections, chili, or tartar sauce. Serves 6.

BAKED SALMON CROQUETTES

1½ cups water
⅔ cup farina
¾ teaspoon salt
1 cup flaked salmon
1 tablespoon lemon juice
1 tablespoon finely chopped parsley
Dash of Tabasco sauce
4 teaspoons grated onion
⅛ teaspoon pepper
1 beaten egg
1 cup crushed corn flakes

Bring water to boil. Add farina and salt, stir until thickened. Cook 5 minutes.

Flake salmon; add with lemon juice, parsley, Tabasco, onion, and pepper. Form into 8 cylinders.

Dip croquettes in egg; coat with corn flake crumbs.

Bake in moderate oven (350°F.) 20 minutes. Serve with sauce made by adding 2 sliced hard-cooked eggs to 1½ cups medium white sauce. Serves 4.

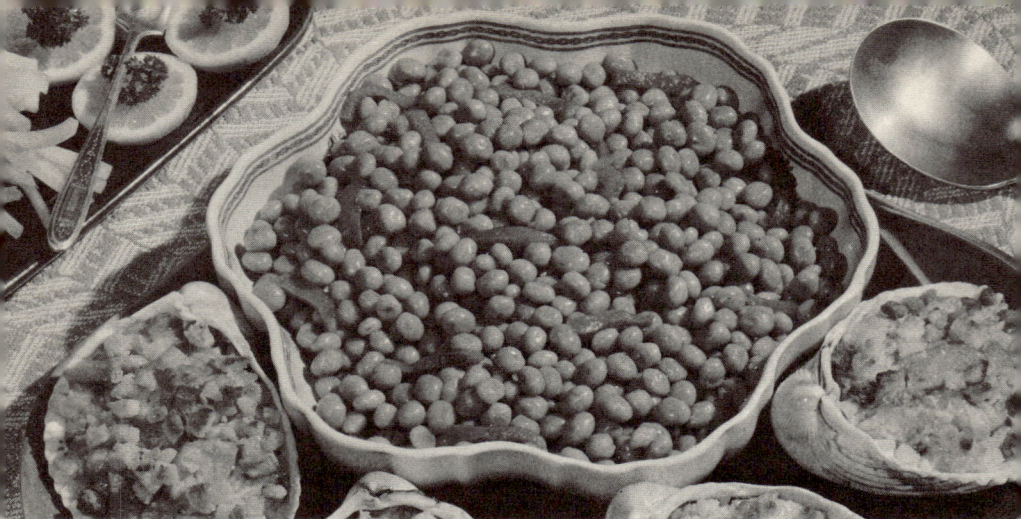

Baked Tuna in Sea Shells

BAKED TUNA IN SEA SHELLS

1   7-ounce can tuna
1/4 cup chopped green pepper
1/4 cup chopped onion
1/2 cup chopped celery
1/4 teaspoon salt
Dash of pepper
1/2 teaspoon Worcestershire sauce
1/2 cup mayonnaise
1/2 cup buttered breadcrumbs

Break tuna into chunks and combine ingredients except breadcrumbs.

Place in individual sea shells or baking dishes. Sprinkle with buttered crumbs.

Bake in a moderate oven (350°F.) about 30 minutes. Serves 4.

KEDGEREE

1   pound cooked fish (see below)
2   cups hot cooked rice
4   hard-cooked eggs
1/8 teaspoon pepper
3   tablespoons minced parsley
1/2 cup light cream
1   tablespoon butter or margarine
1   teaspoon salt

Use cod fillets, pickerel, pike, sole, flounder, or haddock. Flake fish; place in top part of double boiler with remaining ingredients. Heat thoroughly over boiling water. Pinch of curry powder may be added, if desired. Serves 4.

SALMON, RICE, AND TOMATOES

2   cups cooked or canned tomatoes
      and juice
1/4 cup diced onion
1/4 cup diced green pepper
2   tablespoons bacon fat or meat
      drippings
1 1/2 cups boiling water
Salt and pepper
1/3 cup uncooked rice
1/4 cup chopped olives, if desired
2   cups flaked canned or cooked
      salmon

Combine tomatoes, onion, green pepper, fat, water, salt, and pepper in a large saucepan. Bring to boil. (2 1/2 cups raw tomatoes, cut in pieces, may be used instead of 2 cups cooked.)

Add rice and simmer until rice is tender (20 to 25 minutes), adding more water if needed.

Add olives and fish and cook 2 or 3 minutes longer to blend flavors.

Serves 6.

Variations: Other cooked fish may be used in place of salmon.

One cup of cooked rice may be used instead of the uncooked rice. Omit boiling water. Add the rice, olives, and fish as soon as the vegetables are tender and cook 5 to 10 minutes longer.

Celery may be used instead of green pepper.

SAVORY FISH LOAF

2   cups flaked cooked fish or 14-ounce can
1½ cups soft breadcrumbs
¾   cup cooked or canned tomatoes
1   beaten egg
2   tablespoons melted fat
1   tablespoon minced onion
¼   teaspoon savory seasoning
Salt and pepper to taste

Combine all ingredients; pack into greased loaf pan.

Bake in moderate oven (350°F.) until firm, about 45 minutes. Serves 6.

Scalloped Fish in Shells

SCALLOPED FISH
(Master Recipe)

2   cups flaked, cooked fish
2   teaspoons grated onion
1   teaspoon lemon juice
1½ cups medium white sauce
1   cup buttered crumbs

Arrange fish in a greased casserole or individual ramekins. Sprinkle with onion and lemon juice. Add white sauce. Cover with buttered crumbs.

Bake in moderate oven (375°F.) until crumbs are brown, 20 to 25 minutes. Serves 6.

Scalloped Fish Variations

Scalloped Fish Mushroom Casserole: In master recipe, substitute canned cream of mushroom soup for white sauce. If necessary, dilute soup with a little milk.

Scalloped Fish with Potato Border: In master recipe, substitute mashed potatoes for buttered crumbs.

Scalloped Fish and Eggs: In master recipe, increase medium white sauce to 2 cups. Arrange fish, 3 sliced hard-cooked eggs, and sauce in alternate layers in casserole, sprinkling each layer with onion and lemon juice.

FISH SURPRISE

2½ cups cooked rice
2   cups cooked or canned fish
¼   cup breadcrumbs
1   beaten egg
2   tablespoons milk
2   tablespoons melted butter or margarine
½   teaspoon salt
⅛   teaspoon pepper
1   tablespoon minced parsley
1   tablespoon minced onion

Grease 6 individual timbale molds and line with cooked rice.

Mix fish, breadcrumbs, beaten egg, milk, melted butter, salt, pepper, minced parsley, and onion.

Fill rice cups with fish mixture and cover with rice. Place in a pan of hot water and bake in hot oven (400°F.) 30 minutes.

Unmold and serve hot with a tomato sauce, if desired. Serves 6.

JIFFY TUNA-RICE CASSEROLE

1   12-ounce can cooked converted rice
1   6½-ounce can grated tuna
1   cup grated American cheese
¼ to ½ cup minced parsley
2   tablespoons minced onion
1   cup milk
2   beaten eggs
Salt and pepper
½   teaspoon Ac'cent

Combine all ingredients, seasoning to taste. Turn into greased casserole.

Bake in moderate oven (350°F.) about 1 hour. Serves 4 to 5.

Salmon Loaf

SALMON LOAF

1   cup soft breadcrumbs
½ cup evaporated milk diluted with
     ½ cup water
1   No. 1 can salmon, drained and
     flaked
1   teaspoon salt
1   tablespoon butter or margarine
1   tablespoon minced onion
1   teaspoon lemon juice
2   beaten egg yolks
2   egg whites, stiffly beaten
4   hard-cooked eggs

Soak breadcrumbs in diluted milk for 10 minutes. Add salmon, salt, butter, onion, lemon juice, and egg yolks. Blend.

Fold in stiffly beaten egg whites.

Fill well greased loaf pan (8½ x 4½ x 2½ inches) half full; top with a row of 4 hard-cooked eggs. Pack rest of mixture firmly around and over eggs.

Bake in moderate oven (350°F.) about 45 minutes.

Unmold on platter. Serve with sweet pickle sauce. Serves 6.

CELERY SALMON LOAF

1   1-pound can (2 cups) salmon with
     juice, flaked
1½ cups dry breadcrumbs
½ cup minced green pepper
2   slightly beaten eggs
1   can (1¼ cups) condensed cream
     of celery soup

Combine ingredients as listed and mix. Pack lightly into a greased, small loaf pan.

Bake in a moderate oven (350°F.) about 1 hour or until done. Pour off extra juice and turn out on a warm platter. Serve with celery sauce. Serves 6.

FISH LOAF

2 cups cooked or canned fish, flaked
2 cups mashed potatoes
1 cup evaporated milk
1 egg
½ teaspoon salt
⅛ teaspoon pepper

Combine flaked fish and mashed potatoes.

Beat egg and milk together. Stir into fish mixture. Add seasonings and mix well. Pour into greased loaf pan.

Bake in hot oven (425°F.) until brown, about 30 minutes.

Serve plain or with tomato or egg sauce. Serves 8.

CREAMED FISH
(Master Recipe)

Combine 1½ cups flaked fish (cooked or canned) and 1½ cups medium white sauce. Heat in double boiler over hot water.

Season to taste with salt and pepper. Serve on toast, crisp crackers, or corn bread. Serves 4 to 6.

Note: Tomato or Creole sauce may be substituted for white sauce.

Creamed Fish Variations

Creamed Fish with Eggs: In master recipe use 1 cup flaked fish and 2 or 3 hard-cooked eggs, sliced.

Creamed Fish with Vegetables: In master recipe increase white sauce to 2 cups and add 1½ cups diced cooked vegetables.

Fish Au Gratin: Place creamed fish in greased baking dish and cover with ½ cup buttered crumbs mixed with ¼ cup of grated cheese.

Bake in hot oven (400°F.) until sauce is bubbly and the top is well browned, 20 to 30 minutes.

Creamed Fish in Noodle Ring: Prepare noodle ring. Place on hot serving plate. Place creamed fish in center. Garnish.

TUNA-MUSHROOM LOAF

1 2-ounce can sliced mushroom buttons
1 7-ounce can tuna
1 can condensed cream or mushroom soup
1½ cups soft breadcrumbs
1 tablespoon chopped pimiento
1 tablespoon parsley flakes
¼ teaspoon salt
2 beaten eggs

Arrange 2 rows of mushroom slices on bottom of greased loaf pan. Add remainder of mushrooms to rest of ingredients. Mix well.

Put mixture in pan. Bake in moderate oven (375°F.) 45 minutes, until firm. Serves 6.

FISH PROVINCIAL

4 tablespoons oil
3 large onions, sliced
½ clove garlic, chopped
3 or 4 large fresh tomatoes, skinned and quartered (or use canned)
2 tablespoons chopped parsley
1 tablespoon chopped ripe olives
1 tablespoon capers
Salt and pepper to taste
3 cups cooked fish (canned or leftover), drained and flaked

Cook onions and garlic in hot oil 5 minutes; add tomatoes, parsley, olives, and capers; cook over low heat 10 minutes. Taste for seasoning.

Add fish and cook 10 minutes longer, stirring occasionally.

Serve over cooked rice or on toast. Serves 6.

BAKED FISH TURBOT

Almost any type of fish may be used in this baked dish. Cod or haddock are particularly good.

To 2 cups medium white sauce add 2½ cups of cooked flaked fish.

Pour into a greased casserole. Cover with buttered crumbs.

Bake in moderate oven (375°F.) ½ hour. Grated cheese may be sprinkled over top before baking. Serves 6.

Sardine-Spaghetti Bake

MEXICAN SALMON

1 1-pound can salmon (pink), undrained
1 egg
1 green pepper, minced
1 small onion, minced
1 cup canned tomatoes
1/8 teaspoon pepper
2 teaspoons chili powder
1 teaspoon salt
1/3 cup breadcrumbs
3 sprigs parsley, minced

Bone salmon and blend with egg in skillet. Add next 7 ingredients, reserving 2 tablespoons of the crumbs. Simmer 10 minutes; add parsley.

Turn into buttered baking dish or individual casseroles. Top with balance of breadcrumbs.

Bake in hot oven (400°F.) until crumbs are brown. Serves 6.

SARDINE-SPAGHETTI BAKE

1 8-ounce package spaghetti
1 medium-sized onion, chopped
1/2 green pepper, chopped
2 tablespoons butter or margarine
1 8-ounce can tomato sauce
1 teaspoon sugar
1/2 teaspoon salt
1/4 teaspoon oregano
1 or 2 cans (3 1/4- to 4-ounce each)
   Maine sardines
1/2 cup shredded Cheddar cheese

Cook spaghetti according to label directions; keep hot.

Cook onion and green pepper in butter or margarine 2 minutes; add tomato sauce, sugar, salt, and oregano. Simmer, stirring occasionally, about 5 minutes, or until vegetables are tender.

Combine spaghetti and tomato sauce; pour into 8 x 8 x 2-inch baking dish. Arrange sardines over spaghetti; top with cheese.

Place under broiler or in heated oven until cheese is melted. Serves 4.

CREOLE TUNA

2 tablespoons butter or margarine
2 tablespoons chopped green pepper
1 small tomato, peeled and cut in
   eighths
2 tablespoons flour
1 1/2 cups milk
Salt and pepper
1 7-ounce can tuna, flaked

Melt butter in a saucepan. Add green pepper and tomato; cook 3 minutes. Blend in flour. Gradually add milk and cook, stirring until smooth.

Season with salt and pepper to taste. Add tuna and cook for about 10 minutes. Serve on toast. Serves 6.

TUNA-CELERY-NOODLE BAKE

1 6-ounce package egg noodles
1 10 1/2- or 11-ounce can condensed
   celery soup
1/2 cup milk
1 6 1/2- or 7-ounce can tuna, flaked
1/3 cup buttered crumbs
1/2 cup grated American cheese

Cook noodles in boiling, salted water until tender. Drain. Combine soup and milk.

Alternate layers of noodles and tuna in greased 1 1/2-quart casserole. Pour soup mixture over tuna and noodles. Top with buttered crumbs and grated cheese. Bake in moderate oven (350°F.) 20 minutes.

Garnish with stuffed olive slices and parsley. Serves 6.

Dried, Smoked, and Salt-Cured Fish

Codfish Cakes

CODFISH CAKES

1   cup (5 ounces) shredded salt cod-
      fish
1   cup hot mashed potatoes
20   saltine crackers, finely rolled
1   egg
1   tablespoon minced onion
Few grains pepper
Cracker meal

Place fish in cheesecloth or fine
strainer and run cold water through it
for 1 minute before using.

Blend together fish, potatoes, cracker
crumbs, egg, onion, and pepper.

Shape into 8 patties; roll in cracker
meal. Sauté until golden brown. Serve
with tomato sauce. Serves 4.

HOW TO FRESHEN DRIED SALT FISH

Shred fish, wash it several times in
fresh cold water. Cover with fresh
cold water and bring to boil.

Pour off water and repeat the operation, depending on the amount
of salt in the fish.

Do not cut dried, salt fish with a
steel knife as the fish will have a
"steely" taste.

CODFISH VEGETABLE PIE

2 cups cooked codfish
4 tablespoons butter or margarine
2 tablespoons chopped onion (optional)
6 tablespoons flour
1/4 teaspoon pepper
3 cups milk
1 cup cooked peas
1 cup cooked celery
1 cup cooked carrots
3 1/2 cups mashed potatoes

Shred cod, pulling it apart with forks, or shears. If salt cod is used, freshen by covering with cold water and heating to boiling point. Drain, cover with cold water, and repeat process until codfish tastes fresh, about 4 times.

If fresh cod is used, simmer fish in water until tender.

Melt butter in top of double boiler. Add onion and cook over direct heat 5 minutes but do not brown. Blend in flour and pepper. Add milk and cook over hot water until thick, stirring occasionally. Add diced cooked vegetables and codfish. Pour into a 1 1/2-quart casserole. Top with border of mashed potato.

Brown in a hot oven (400°F.) for 15 to 20 minutes. Serves 6.

CREAMED CODFISH

2 cups shredded codfish
4 tablespoons butter or margarine
4 tablespoons flour
2 cups milk
1/8 teaspoon pepper

Cover codfish with water. Heat slowly to boiling point. Repeat once or twice if fish is hard and very salty. Drain well.

Heat butter. Add codfish and cook over low heat about 2 minutes. Blend in flour. Slowly add milk. Cook until thickened, stirring constantly. Add pepper.

Serve on toast or baked potatoes. Serves 6.

Codfish Vegetable Pie

CODFISH BALLS
(Master Recipe)
2   cups flaked salt codfish
3½ cups diced, pared raw potatoes
2   slightly beaten eggs
2   tablespoons butter or margarine
¼   cup milk
⅛   teaspoon pepper
Dash of celery salt
Paprika

Shred fish into small flakes; place in saucepan. Cover with cold water. Heat slowly to boiling point. Drain. Repeat, using fresh water if fish is hard and salty.

Combine with potatoes and cook, covered, in about 2 cups boiling water, until potatoes are tender. Drain well and mash thoroughly. Add remaining ingredients. Beat with spoon until light and fluffy. Chill.

Shape into balls or drop by spoonfuls into hot deep fat (375°F.). Fry until browned. Drain on absorbent paper.

Serve with tomato sauce, ketchup, egg sauce, or chili sauce. Serves 6.

Variations of Codfish Balls

Codfish Hash: Spread mixture evenly in a large, hot, well greased skillet. Cook slowly until a brown crust forms on bottom. Fold like an omelet.

Codfish Patties: Shape into patties. Brown on both sides in hot fat.

Curried Codfish Balls: Add 1 teaspoon curry powder to mixture.

LUTFISK
Lutfisk is dried cod, preserved in lime and birch ashes. It is sold by stores in Scandinavian neighborhoods during the Christmas season.

To prepare, wash the fish, remove skin, and cut fish in pieces. Tie fish loosely in cheesecloth. Cook in salted water (be sure not to use an aluminum kettle) until tender, 20 to 25 minutes. Do not allow to boil rapidly.

Serve with melted butter or milk gravy seasoned with mustard.

Peas, potatoes, and lingonberries are the usual accompaniments.

KIPPERED HERRING
Cover fish with boiling water and simmer 10 minutes. Drain well, dot with butter and serve hot.

SAUTÉED KIPPERED HERRING
Soak smoked kippers in boiling water to cover 10 minutes. Drain.

Sauté in hot oil or butter in skillet about 5 minutes, turning once. Serve with butter sauce.

BROILED KIPPERED HERRING
Remove head and tail from herring; wipe with a damp cloth.

Place skin side up, on a broiler 4 inches from heat and broil 3 minutes.

Turn fish, dot with butter, broil 3 minutes longer. Serve with lemon.

BAKED KIPPERED HERRING
4   kippered herring
½   green pepper, minced
¼   cup minced onion
1   tablespoon butter or margarine
1½ cups tomato juice
¼   teaspoon pepper

Remove head and tail from herring and wipe with a damp cloth. Place in a greased baking dish.

Sauté minced green pepper and onion in butter; spread over fish. Pour tomato juice over fish; sprinkle with pepper.

Bake in hot oven (425°F.) 15 minutes. Serves 4.

CANNED KIPPERED HERRING
Place kippers in a shallow baking dish or ovenproof platter. Brush with melted butter and lemon juice. Sprinkle with pepper. Pour over juice from can.

Heat in oven. Garnish with lemon wedges and chopped parsley.

MARINATED (PICKLED) HERRING

12 milter herring
2 lemons, sliced very thin
4 large onions, sliced
12 bay leaves
2 tablespoons mustard seed
2 tablespoons whole black peppers
2 cups vinegar
1 cup water
3 tablespoons sugar

Soak herring in cold water to cover for 3 hours, changing water twice. (Or soak in cold water to cover overnight.)

Drain. Cut off heads and tails. Split the herring. Remove and reserve the milt. If desired, skin and bone the herring. Remove the skin by running a knife from head to tail. Leave fillets whole or cut into 3-inch pieces.

Place herring in a crock in alternating layers with sliced lemon, sliced onions, a few pieces of bay leaf, and a sprinkling of mustard seed and whole black peppers.

Bring the combined vinegar, water, and sugar to a boil; cool. Mash the milt with a fork; add a little of the cooled vinegar mixture to thin it. Put through a sieve, then combine with remaining vinegar mixture. Pour over herring to cover.

Cover crock and put in a cool place. The herring are ready to be served in 4 to 6 days.

Note: If desired, 1 large apple, grated, may be added with the vinegar mixture.

MARINATED HERRING WITH CREAM

6 milter herring
¼ cup vinegar
1 lemon, very thinly sliced
1 onion, thinly sliced
2½ tablespoons mixed pickling spices
1 cup sour cream

Soak, clean, and fillet herring as directed in marinated herring recipe. Cut fillets into 1½-inch pieces.

Mash ½ the milt; combine with vinegar. (Dilute the vinegar with a little water if it is very strong.)

Place remaining milt and herring in a crock in alternating layers with the lemon, onion, and a sprinkling of pickling spices.

Pour vinegar mixture over herring. Add sour cream. Keep in a cool place. Serve it after 48 hours.

WINNIPEG GOLD EYES

Brush gold eyes with softened butter. Bake in hot oven (400°F.) 10 minutes.

Broiled: Brush with melted butter and place, skin side down, on oiled broiler. Broil 10 minutes.

These fish are smoked and do not require long cooking.

BOILED SALT MACKEREL

Soak salt mackerel, skin up, well covered with cold water overnight.

Drain and place in a shallow pan. Cover with water and simmer until tender, about 12 minutes. Drain well.

Place on hot platter; pour melted butter over it, to which add chopped chives or parsley and lemon juice or Worcestershire sauce.

BAKED SALT MACKEREL

Soak salt mackerel 8 to 12 hours in cold water. Drain. Dry and dredge with flour.

Place in greased baking dish. Add ½ cup milk per 2 pounds fish. Sprinkle with paprika. Bake in moderate oven (350°F.) about 25 minutes.

BROILED SALT MACKEREL

Soak salt mackerel 8 to 12 hours in cold water. Drain and wipe dry.

Place skin side down on greased broiler rack. Brush with melted butter. Broil 10 to 12 minutes, basting frequently.

Serve with butter and lemon wedges or any fish sauce. Allow about ⅓ pound per serving.

CREAMED FINNAN HADDIE

2 pounds finnan haddie
2 tablespoons butter or margarine
1/2 cup cream or top milk

Cover fish with water and simmer 10 minutes. Drain.

Place on a hot platter; dot with butter and add hot milk or cream before serving. Garnish with parsley. Serves 6.

FINNAN HADDIE AND POTATO SCALLOP

2 cups cooked, sliced potatoes
2 cups flaked finnan haddie
1/2 teaspoon salt
1 tablespoon grated onion
1 cup thin white sauce
1/2 cup dry breadcrumbs
1 tablespoon butter or margarine

In a greased casserole arrange alternate layers of cooked sliced potatoes and flaked finnan haddie. Season with salt and grated onion.

Add sauce to casserole; sprinkle top with dry breadcrumbs and dot with butter.

Bake in moderate oven (375°F.) 20 minutes, or until top is nicely browned. Serves 6.

Note: Canned celery soup may replace sauce.

FINNAN HADDIE BAKED IN MILK

2 pounds finnan haddie
2 tablespoons butter or margarine
1 cup milk

Cover fish with boiling water; simmer 10 minutes. Drain.

Add milk and butter to fish. Bake in moderate oven (350°F.) 15 minutes. Serves 6.

STEAMED FINNAN HADDIE

Steam over boiling water until tender, 15 to 20 minutes. Each piece should be exposed to steam. Do not pile on top of each other. Serve with butter sauce.

FINNAN HADDIE RABBIT

In double boiler, heat 1/2 pound old English cheese, cut small, with 1 cup heavy cream and 1 cup flaked steamed finnan haddie. When well blended, stir in 1 beaten egg and serve on toast. Serves 6.

FORSHMAK

2 salted herring
1 chopped onion
2 well beaten eggs
1 or 2 slices white bread, soaked in milk
1 grated apple
Mashed potatoes
Breadcrumbs

Soak herring in cold water several hours. Remove skin and all bones and chop very fine. Brown onion in butter and add to herring.

Place in casserole and cover with well beaten eggs, bread, apple, and a layer of mashed potatoes. Sprinkle top with breadcrumbs. Bake in moderate oven (350°F.) 30 minutes. Serves 5 to 6.

Forshmak

Shellfish

Shellfish include any aquatic animal with a shell such as abalone, clams, crabs, crayfish (or crawfish), lobsters, mussels, oysters, scallops, shrimp (or prawns), and snails. Frog legs, terrapin, and turtle have been placed in this section although they are not in the same generic class as shellfish.

ABALONE

Abalone is an extra large mollusk found chiefly along the California shores. The edible part is the central muscle and it resembles a very large scallop. It is sold fresh or canned.

Allow one pound fresh sliced abalone to serve 2 or 3. It is best chopped and served in chowders or fish soups. Simmer abalone in water to cover until tender. Chop fine and use in recipes for chowder or fish soup.

FRIED ABALONE

Pound the raw slices with a wooden mallet. Wipe dry. Roll in seasoned crumbs, then in beaten egg diluted with water, and again in crumbs. Sauté in oil or butter 1 to 1½ minutes on each side. Take care not to overcook because it toughens.

CREAMED ABALONE

Add 1½ cups diced raw abalone to 2 cups medium white sauce. Season to taste and simmer 2 minutes. Stir in 1 slightly beaten egg yolk. Serve on hot toast. Garnish with chopped hard-cooked egg. Serves 4.

Clams

There are three varieties of clams generally used—the hard-shell or quahog as they are known in New England, the soft-shell, and the razor clam.

The hard-shell is the one that is most usually available. It has a stronger flavor than the soft-shell and is the one used in chowders. The smallest hard-shell clams are known as "little necks." The medium-sized hard-shell clams are the type generally served raw on the half-shell and are called "cherry stones." The large hard-shell, although parts of it are tender, are usually tough and have to be chopped before being eaten. Soft-shell clams have a tender meat somewhat resembling oysters.

Clams bought in the shell must be tightly closed, thereby proving that they are alive. They will usually be opened on request at the market. To prepare them at home, scrub thoroughly, rinse and steam open or force open with a special heavy knife.

For clam chowder, buy whole or chopped clams in bulk by the pint or quart. Whole or chopped canned clams are also available.

STEAMED CLAMS

Allow 10 to 15 per person. Soft-shell clams are best for steaming. Tightly closed shells indicate that the clams are fresh. Scrub thoroughly and wash in running water to remove all sand. Steam in covered kettle with ½ cup water per 4 quarts of clams, over moderate heat until shells partially open, 15 to 20 minutes. Do not overcook.

Remove clams to hot platters. Strain the clam broth left in kettle into small glasses. Serve with clams together with small individual dishes of melted butter seasoned with lemon juice, salt, and pepper.

To eat steamed clams, remove from shells by neck, and dip in clam broth, then in butter. Eat all but the hard black skin of neck.

ROASTED CLAMS

Scrub clams well with a brush and wash thoroughly. Place them in a flat layer in a pan over a layer of rock salt, if desired. Bake in hot oven (425°F.) until shells open.

Remove upper shells carefully to avoid spilling liquor. Serve with seasonings, melted butter, and lemon wedges.

BROILED CLAMS

Arrange small hard-shell clams on half-shells. Sprinkle with breadcrumbs. Dot with bits of butter. Broil 5 to 7 minutes. Serve very hot.

FRIED CLAMS

Clean and dry soft-shell clams. Roll clams in seasoned flour or roll in fine corn meal and shake off excess corn meal by placing in a strainer.

Fry in hot deep fat (375°F.) until browned. Drain on absorbent paper.

CLAMBAKE CLAMS

The traditional clambake of New England frequently calls for a deep pit and a variety of seafood. For the most simple type, make a wood fire and preheat a bed of stones. After the fire dies down, cover the hot stones with a very thin layer of sea weed.

Have the clams thoroughly scrubbed with sea water and place them on this. Cover with sea weed and a piece of sail cloth to keep in the steam. Let the clams steam until they open.

MINCED CLAM AND RICE CASSEROLE

1   cup rice
3   tablespoons butter or margarine, melted
1/2 cup chopped onions
1/4 cup chopped parsley
3   tablespoons flour
1   7-ounce can minced clams
Milk
1/2 cup mayonnaise
1/2 teaspoon salt
Pepper

Cook rice according to directions on package. Drain.

Cook onions in melted butter in saucepan over low heat 5 minutes. Add parsley and cook 5 minutes longer. Remove pan from heat and stir in flour.

Drain clams, reserving clam broth. To the broth add enough milk to make 1 1/2 cups. Stir liquid gradually into onion-parsley mixture.

Return to heat and cook until sauce is thickened, stirring constantly. Add minced clams.

Blend mayonnaise, 1/4 cup milk, salt, and pepper together and mix with rice.

Place 1/2 the rice in 1-quart casserole. Cover with half the sauce, then rest of rice and remaining sauce.

Bake in moderate oven (350°F.) 30 minutes. Serves 4.

NEW ENGLAND CLAM PIE

1   cup   hard-shell   clams,   finely chopped
3/4 cup milk
2   tablespoons clam liquor
1/2 teaspoon dry mustard
1   beaten egg
1   teaspoon chopped parsley
1   tablespoon butter or margarine
Dash of salt
Pastry made from 2 cups flour or pastry mix

Mix all ingredients except pastry, adding salt to taste.

Roll pastry for bottom crust. Fit into an 8-inch pan. Trim edges. Fill with clam mixture.

Roll pastry for top. Cut gashes to allow escape of steam. Place on pie. Seal well.

Bake in hot oven (425°F.) until crust is brown, about 25 minutes. Serves 4.

CLAM FRITTERS

Drain 1 pint clams. Chop very fine and add to fritter binding batter. Fry in hot deep fat (375°F.) 3 to 5 minutes. Drain on absorbent paper. Serve with tomato or Creole sauce.

Serves 4 to 6.

DEVILED CLAMS

2 cups clams
½ cup clam liquor
2 tablespoons minced onion
2 tablespoons each minced green pepper and celery leaves
¼ cup chopped celery
4 tablespoons butter or margarine
⅛ teaspoon pepper
½ teaspoon prepared mustard
¾ cup cracker crumbs or fine bread-crumbs

Chop clams fine and simmer in their own liquor 5 minutes.

Cook onion, green pepper, celery leaves, and celery in melted butter until tender. Mix with remaining ingredients.

Combine with clams and mix well. Fill greased scallop shells or custard cups.

Bake in moderate oven (350°F.) 20 minutes. Serves 4 to 6.

Variation: Lemon juice may be substituted for the onion or green pepper or it may be added to the clam liquor before simmering.

BAKED CLAMS AND CORN

1 7-ounce can minced clams
Milk
3 beaten eggs
1 cup cream-style corn
1 tablespoon grated onion
1 tablespoon finely chopped parsley
2 tablespoons chopped ripe olives
2 tablespoons butter or margarine, melted
½ teaspoon salt
2 drops Tabasco sauce
1 cup ready-to-eat cereal

Drain clam liquid into measuring cup; add milk to make 1 cup; put in mixing bowl. Add all remaining ingredients, except cereal. Add clams. Mix together.

Grease 1½-quart casserole; pour in clam-corn mixture. Slightly crush cereal and sprinkle over top.

Bake in moderate oven (375°F.) until "custard" is firm, about 45 minutes. Serves 5 to 6.

Deviled Clams

Crabs

Crabs should always be alive and active when purchased to be sure that they are fresh. Some markets, however, sell freshly cooked meat from the hard-shell crab. Fresh crabmeat should be used as quickly as possible. Markets will kill and clean the soft-shell crabs on request. The tough cartilage should be removed from canned or fresh crab-meat.

Allow 1 to 2 soft-shell crabs per serving, depending upon size.

HOW TO PREPARE SOFT-SHELL CRABS

Stick a knifepoint into the body between the eyes. Lift the pointed ends of the top shell and scrape off the spongy white substance between the shell and body on each side.

Place the crab on its back and, with a small sharp knife, remove the "apron" or small loose shell which comes to a point at about the middle of the under-shell. Wash the crabs and cook at once.

FRIED SOFT-SHELL CRABS

Prepare as above. Dry and sprinkle with salt and pepper. Dip in slightly beaten egg and roll in crumbs. Fry in hot deep fat (365° to 375°F.) until well browned, 3 to 5 minutes. Being very light, the crabs will rise to the top and should be turned 2 or 3 times while frying. Drain on absorbent paper.

Serve at once with tartar sauce and lemon wedges. The entire crab, including shell, is edible.

SAUTÉED SOFT-SHELLED CRABS

Sauté, cleaned prepared crabs in butter or other fat over moderate heat. Transfer to hot platter. Pour the drippings over them.

BROILED SOFT-SHELL CRABS

Sprinkle the cleaned, dried soft-shell crabs with salt, pepper, and lemon juice. Brush with melted butter.

Broil about 2 inches from heat. Cook until brown on both sides, about 5 minutes for each side or a total of 10 minutes in all.

Serve with tartar sauce and lemon wedges.

BOILED HARD-SHELL CRABS

Plunge live crabs head first into boiling salted water, using 1 teaspoon salt per quart water. Boil in covered kettle until shell is red and meat white, 20 to 25 minutes.

Fold back tapering points on each side of back shell and remove spongy material underneath. Remove apron, small pointed piece at lower part of shell.

Serve in shell or remove the meat for other dishes. The edible crabmeat is in the inner top of the back and in the claws. Crack claws with nutcracker.

Allow 1 hard-shell crab or 1/2 cup meat per serving.

CRABMEAT CASSEROLE

6   slices bread, crusts trimmed
1 1/2 cups (2 7-ounce cans) crabmeat
1/2   pound Cheddar cheese, shredded
4   eggs
2   cups milk
About 1 teaspoon salt
Dash of pepper
Dash of cayenne

Arrange slices of bread in bottom of greased casserole. Cover with flaked crabmeat. Sprinkle with cheese.

Beat eggs; add milk and season to taste. Pour over cheese.

Bake in slow oven (325°F.) until set, 45 to 50 minutes. Serves 6 to 8.

Crabmeat Coquilles

CRABMEAT COQUILLES

1   4-ounce can sliced mushrooms
3   tablespoons butter or margarine
3   tablespoons flour
Milk
1/2 teaspoon salt
Dash of pepper
2   tablespoons chopped green pepper
1   6-ounce can crabmeat
2   tablespoons breadcrumbs

Drain mushrooms and reserve liquid.

Melt butter. Add flour and blend thoroughly.

Add milk to mushroom liquid to make 2 cups and add to butter and flour mixture. Cook until thickened, stirring constantly.

Add mushrooms, salt, pepper, and green pepper.

Remove hard fiber from crabmeat. Flake, and add to cream sauce. Pour into individual shells or medium sized baking dish. Top with breadcrumbs.

Bake in moderate oven (375°F.) 20 minutes. Serves 4 or 5.

CREAMED CRABMEAT

Heat 1 cup crabmeat in 1 cup medium white sauce or cream sauce. Serve on toast or in patty shells. Serves 4.

Variations of Creamed Crabmeat

Crabmeat À La King: To above, add 1 tablespoon finely chopped red and green pepper and 1/2 cup cooked or canned sliced mushrooms. Season to taste with sherry.

Crabmeat Creamed with Mushrooms: Combine the white sauce with 1 cup crabmeat, 1/2 cup sliced mushrooms, and 1 diced pimiento.

Cook in top of double boiler over hot water for 10 minutes.

Crabmeat Au Gratin: Pour creamed crabmeat in casserole or ramekins. Top with a mixture of 1/3 cup buttered crumbs and 1/4 cup grated cheese.

Bake in moderate oven (350°F.) until crumbs are lightly browned.

CRABMEAT SUPREME

2 cups flaked crabmeat
1/2 cup grated cheese
2 well beaten eggs
2 cups milk
Cracker crumbs
2 tablespoons melted butter or margarine
Juice of 1 lemon

Combine crabmeat and cheese. Add beaten eggs and milk. Pour into buttered casserole.

Cover with cracker crumbs mixed with melted butter. Pour lemon juice over all. Cover and set casserole in a pan of warm water.

Bake in moderate oven (350°F.) about 30 minutes. Serves 6 to 8.

Salmon or Lobster Supreme: Use 2 cups canned salmon or 2 cups canned lobster instead of crabmeat.

CRABMEAT ALASKA

1 1/2 cups flaked crabmeat, canned or fresh
1/2 cup cream
1 egg yolk
1 teaspoon salt
Dash of pepper
1/4 teaspoon Worcestershire sauce
6 slices white bread
4 tablespoons butter or margarine
6 large oysters
1/4 cup buttered breadcrumbs

Combine the crabmeat, cream, egg yolk, and seasonings.

Remove crusts from bread; fry slices in butter until golden brown. Spread each slice with crab mixture; top with an oyster and sprinkle with buttered breadcrumbs.

Arrange slices on a cooky sheet; place in hot oven (400°F.) for about 10 minutes or until delicately browned. Serve hot. Serves 6.

DEVILED CRAB

2 7-ounce cans crabmeat
1 small onion, minced
3 tablespoons butter or margarine
2 tablespoons flour
1 teaspoon dry mustard
1 cup milk
1/2 teaspoon salt
1/5 teaspoon pepper
2 sprigs parsley, chopped
1/2 teaspoon nutmeg
1 egg, beaten
1 cup grated Italian cheese

Pick over crabmeat and remove any fibrous membranes. Set aside.

Sauté onion in butter until tender but not brown. Remove pan from heat and stir in flour and dry mustard until well blended.

Gradually add milk and stir until smooth. Return pan to heat and cook sauce, stirring constantly until thick, about 2 minutes. Add salt, pepper, parsley, and nutmeg.

Stir a little of the sauce into beaten egg and then add mixture to hot sauce. Stir constantly until sauce starts to boil.

Remove from heat before sauce boils and stir in grated cheese and crabmeat. Turn into 6 or 8 individual ramekins or shells.

Brown in hot oven (400°F.) about 10 minutes or until top is brown. Serves 6 to 8.

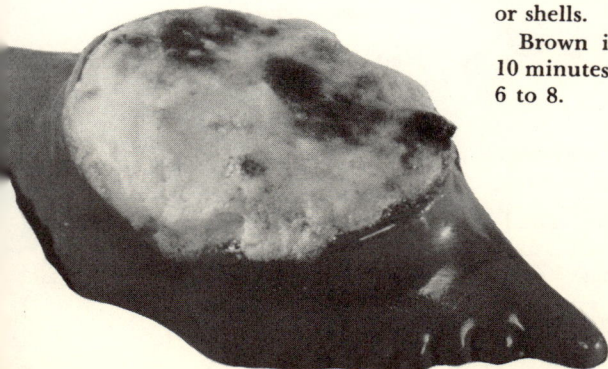

Deviled Crab

SPANISH CRABMEAT

2 tablespoons butter or margarine
1 green pepper, finely shredded
2 tablespoons flour
1/2 teaspoon salt
1/4 teaspoon mustard or 1/8 teaspoon paprika
3/4 cup scalded milk
1 beaten egg
1 cup grated cheese
1 can condensed tomato soup
1 can (7 ounces) crabmeat, flaked
Crisp crackers or thin toast

Melt butter or margarine in a saucepan over low heat. Add green pepper and sauté gently without browning.

Combine flour, salt, and mustard or paprika, and stir into the saucepan, cooking and stirring over low heat until the mixture is smooth and well blended. Gradually add scalded milk, stirring constantly until mixture has thickened.

Remove from heat and add a little of hot mixture to beaten egg. Stir well and add egg mixture to first mixture, blending well. Stir in cheese.

Heat the soup in another saucepan and, when just at the boiling point, add to the thickened mixture with the crabmeat.

Place over heat just long enough to heat through. Do not boil.

Serve at once over crackers or toast. Serves 6 to 8.

CRABMEAT OR LOBSTER CUTLETS

2 1/2 tablespoons butter or margarine
1/3 cup flour
1 cup warm milk
1 egg yolk
1/2 teaspoon salt
1/4 teaspoon pepper
1 1/2 tablespoons lemon juice
2 cups cooked or canned crabmeat or lobster

Melt butter. Blend in flour. Gradually add milk, stirring until sauce boils. Add egg yolk, seasonings, lemon juice, and seafood.

Spread on plate to cool. When cold, shape in cones or cutlets. Dip in fine, dry breadcrumbs, then in beaten egg and again in crumbs.

Fry 1 minute in deep, hot fat (375°F.). Serve with green peas.

Serves 6.

CURRIED JAPANESE CRABMEAT

3 tablespoons butter or margarine
1 1/2 teaspoons minced onion
4 tablespoons flour
3/4 teaspoon salt
1 tablespoon curry powder
1 1/2 cups chicken stock
1 1/2 cups canned crabmeat
1 tablespoon lemon juice

Heat butter in saucepan. Add onion; cook until clear and limp.

Add flour, salt, and curry powder. Stir until smooth. Blend in chicken stock.

When thickened and smooth, add crabmeat and lemon juice. Heat through and serve with hot rice. Serves 6.

CRABMEAT POTATO CHIP CASSEROLE

1/4 cup butter or margarine
1/2 cup flour
Dash of celery salt
2 cups milk
1/2 cup mayonnaise
1 can crabmeat, flaked
3 cups crushed potato chips
1/2 cup shredded Cheddar cheese
1/8 teaspoon paprika

Melt butter in saucepan over low heat. Stir in flour and celery salt.

Add milk gradually; stir until thickened and smooth. Stir in mayonnaise.

Put alternate layers of flaked crabmeat, sauce, and crushed potato chips in greased 1 1/2-quart casserole. Sprinkle cheese and paprika over top.

Bake in moderate oven (350°F.) 20 to 30 minutes. Serves 6.

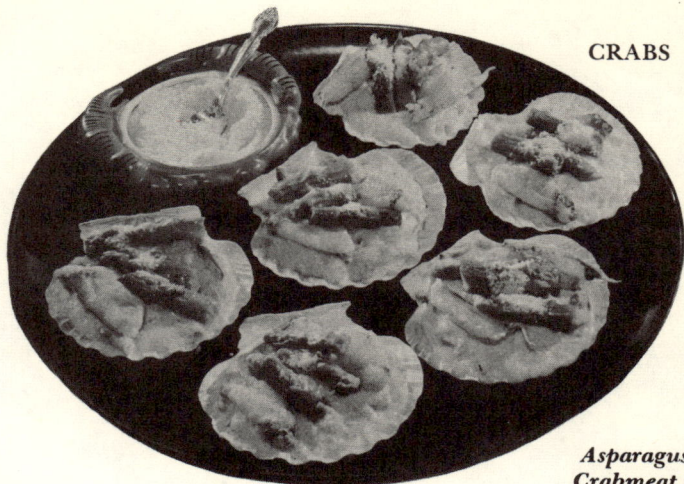

Asparagus-Topped
Crabmeat Imperial

CRABMEAT CATALAN (SPAIN)

- 2 tablespoons butter or margarine
- 2 tablespoons grated Parmesan cheese
- 6 tablespoons ketchup
- 1 teaspoon Worcestershire sauce
- 3 tablespoons heavy cream
- 1 scant cup flaked crabmeat, canned or fresh cooked
- 12 medium oysters, drained

Melt butter in a pan. Add Parmesan cheese and stir until it melts, then add ketchup and Worcestershire sauce. Mix until hot and boiling, then add cream.

Bring to a boil and add crabmeat. Bring to a boil and add oysters. Cook 2 minutes or until oysters are crinkled.

Serve hot poured over squares of hot buttered toast. Garnish with potato chips. Serves 4.

CRAB DELICIOUS

- 1 cup light cream
- 1 cup boiled rice
- Salt and paprika, to taste
- 1 cup flaked crabmeat
- 2 tablespoons melted butter or margarine
- 3 tablespoons ketchup
- Patty shells or toast

Heat cream and cooked rice together in top of double boiler over hot water. Season to taste, adding celery or parsley salt, if preferred to paprika.

When well heated and blended, stir in crabmeat and butter. Heat through and, just before serving, stir in ketchup.

Serve at once in patty shells or on crisp toast. Serves 4.

ASPARAGUS-TOPPED CRABMEAT IMPERIAL

- 2 cups lump crabmeat
- 4 tablespoons butter or margarine
- 4 tablespoons flour
- 1¾ cups milk
- 1 teaspoon salt
- ½ teaspoon Ac'cent
- ½ teaspoon dry mustard
- 2 teaspoons lemon juice
- 2 teaspoons chopped green pepper
- ½ teaspoon Worcestershire sauce
- 1 teaspoon finely chopped onion
- Dash of mace
- 2 beaten eggs
- 18 asparagus tips, canned or fresh cooked
- ¼ cup grated Parmesan cheese

Melt butter; stir in flour; cook until smooth. Add milk; cook until thick, stirring constantly.

Add remaining ingredients except eggs. Remove from heat; quickly stir in eggs. Blend carefully so as not to break up crab lumps.

Fill scallop shells or ramekins; top with asparagus tips and cheese.

Bake in hot oven (400°F.) until golden brown. Serves 6 to 8.

Baked Stuffed Lobster

Lobsters and Rock Lobster Tails

Lobsters may be bought alive or already cooked. Live lobsters should be active and mottled green in color. Cooked lobster is red. It should have been alive when it was cooked. Test cooked lobster by straightening the tail. It should spring back to its curled position. It should be heavy in proportion to its size.

Small chicken lobsters weigh ¾ to 1 pound, medium lobsters up to 1¼ pounds, and the large or select lobsters, 1½ to 2 pounds.

Cooked lobster meat may also be purchased canned or frozen.

Lobster tails which are sold under a variety of names such as South African lobster or rock lobster are actually sea crayfish. The meat may be used just like lobster in recipes calling for lobster meat.

HOW TO SPLIT A LIVE LOBSTER FOR BROILING

Place the lobster on its back. Cross the large claws and hold firmly with the left hand. Insert the point of a sharp knife into the lobster at the head and cut the shell open from head to tail.

Cut through the back shell. Remove the stomach and the intestinal vein that runs the length of the tail section close to the back.

Do not remove juices, or liver. The liver (called tomalley) is the grayish-looking meat found in the body cavity. It turns green when cooked.

To Broil: Place split lobster in preheated broiling pan. Brush with butter. Broil 15 to 20 minutes, never longer. Have the pan far enough from the heat so the lobster will not scorch. Serve with melted butter and lemon wedges.

BAKED STUFFED LOBSTER

Split the live lobsters as for broiling. Fill the cavity in the head with dressing (below).

Pour melted butter over lobster and bake in very hot oven (450°F.) 20 minutes. Serve with melted butter.

Dressing: Mix together 1½ cups cracker crumbs and ½ teaspoon salt. Moisten with 2 tablespoons Worcestershire sauce and 4 tablespoons butter. Makes enough stuffing for 4 lobsters.

BOILED LOBSTER

Pick up the lobster from behind the head and plunge it into boiling salted

Cut through the back shell

Remove the stomach and intestinal vein

water (1 tablespoon of salt to 2 quarts of water).

Boil 7 to 10 minutes, depending upon size of lobster. If lobster weighs less than 2 pounds, 7 minutes is sufficient.

When the lobster is cool, split it from end to end, starting at the head. Remove the stomach and the intestinal vein. Do not remove the tomalley (liver). Crack the claws. Extract the meat.

BROILED BOILED LOBSTER

Boil and clean as above. Flatten halves. Season with salt and pepper. Brush with melted butter.

Broil under moderate heat until lightly browned, about 5 minutes. Serve with hot melted butter.

STEAMED LOBSTER

Place live lobsters in steam cooker and cover tightly. Keep water in steamer boiling rapidly and steam 20 to 40 minutes, depending upon size of lobsters.

BUTTERED LOBSTER

Use cooked or canned lobster meat or the meat from lobster tails. Sauté in hot melted butter until heated through. Season with salt, pepper, and lemon juice.

LOBSTER STEW

1   2-pound lobster, boiled
¼   cup butter or margarine
1   quart milk
1   slice onion
1   teaspoon salt
Paprika

Cut lobster meat into small pieces. Sauté lightly without browning in melted butter.

Scald milk with onion slice. Discard onion; add lobster meat and seasonings. Heat thoroughly.

If desired, lobster coral or liver may be rubbed through a sieve and added at the last. Serves 4.

LOBSTER THERMIDOR

2 live lobsters, weighing about 2 pounds each
3 tablespoons butter or margarine
3/4 cup sliced mushrooms
1 teaspoon grated onion
3 tablespoons flour
1 1/2 cups light cream (may be part milk)
2 slightly beaten egg yolks
1 teaspoon salt
1/2 to 3/4 teaspoon mustard
Dash of cayenne
1/3 cup grated Parmesan cheese or 1 cup grated American cheese
2 to 3 tablespoons sherry (optional)
1 tablespoon lemon juice

Plunge lobster headfirst into boiling salted water to cover. Boil 8 minutes after water returns to a boil.

Remove lobsters and cool. Split lengthwise from head to tail and remove meat, discarding hard sack (lady) near head and dark intestinal vein. Twist off big claws, crack and remove the meat.

Dice meat from body and claws. Wash shells and reserve.

Heat butter, add mushrooms and onion. Cook slowly until tender but not browned.

Add flour and blend well. Add all but 2 tablespoons of cream. Cook, stirring, until mixture thickens.

Add egg yolks, while stirring briskly, and then cook, stirring, until thickened again.

Add salt, mustard, cayenne, and about 2/3 of cheese. When cheese has melted, add sherry and lemon juice. Add lobster meat.

Fill the reserved lobster shells with the lobster in the thickened sauce.

Spread the surface with remaining 2 tablespoons cream. Sprinkle with remaining cheese.

Slide the stuffed lobsters under the broiler flame. Broil until the surfaces are brown and bubbling. Good accompaniments are cucumbers and rice pilaf. Serves 4.

LOBSTER AMERICAINE

2 live lobsters, 1 1/2 to 2 pounds each
1/4 cup olive oil
1 tablespoon butter or margarine
1 bay leaf
Pinch of thyme
2 tablespoons chopped shallot or onion
Pinch of cayenne pepper
1/4 cup tomato paste or tomato sauce
1 clove garlic, crushed (optional)
About 1/2 cup dry white wine

Remove and crack claws of lobsters. Remove tail sections from the bodies and cut into 3 or 4 slices. Split lobsters in halves, lengthwise. Discard veins and sacs. Remove and save livers and corals. Season lobsters with salt.

Heat oil and butter in large heavy skillet. Add bay leaf, thyme, and shallot or onion. Add lobster. Sprinkle with cayenne. Add tomato paste. Add garlic, if desired.

Cover and cook very gently until shells are red and lobster tender, 10 to 15 minutes.

Take lobster meat from shells. Strain sauce. Add livers and corals to strained sauce. Cook, stirring constantly, 3 to 4 minutes, or until thickened. Add wine to taste. Add lobster meat and reheat, without cooking. Serves 4.

SCALLOPED LOBSTER

2 tablespoons butter or margarine
3 tablespoons flour
1/2 teaspoon celery seed
1 teaspoon salt
1/2 teaspoon paprika
2 cups milk
1 cup cooked lobster meat
1 cup cooked green peas
2 hard-cooked eggs, sliced
1/2 cup bread cubes
1 tablespoon melted butter or margarine

Melt butter or margarine. Add flour, celery seed, salt, and paprika, stirring until all ingredients are well blended.

Add milk and cook over low heat, stirring constantly, until thickened.

Golden Fish Sauce
Combine 1 cup mayonnaise with 2 tablespoons each A.1. Sauce and prepared mustard. Serve with fried, baked, or broiled fish. Makes 1¼ cups.

Planked Whitefish with Vegetables

Baked Trout with Dressing

Cut lobster into pieces about 1 inch in size, reserving about 4 fairly large pieces for garnishing. Add lobster to cream sauce.

Pour half of creamed lobster into well greased 1-quart baking dish. Cover with cooked peas and with layer of sliced eggs. Place remaining creamed lobster over ingredients in dish. Top with bread cubes and large pieces of lobster. Pour melted butter over bread cubes and large pieces of lobster.

Bake in moderate oven (350°F.) about 30 minutes. Garnish with parsley. Serves 6.

HOT LOBSTER MOUSSE

2 cups lobster meat, ground very fine
1/2 cup medium white sauce
2 beaten eggs
Salt, pepper, and paprika
2 tablespoons sherry

Use cooked or canned lobster. Combine very finely ground lobster with white sauce, eggs, seasonings, and sherry. Turn into a buttered casserole or individual molds. Set in pan of hot water. Cover with greased paper.

Bake in moderate oven (350°F.) 35 to 40 minutes for casserole, about 20 minutes for small molds.

Unmold and serve with mushroom sauce. Serves 4.

Hot Crab or Shrimp Mousse: Substitute cooked or canned shrimp or crabmeat for lobster in above recipe.

LOBSTER JAMBALAYA LOUISIANE

1 2-pound boiled lobster
1/4 cup uncooked rice
4 cups boiling water
2 tablespoons butter or margarine
1/2 onion, minced
1/2 green pepper, minced
2 tablespoons flour
1/2 teaspoon salt
Dash of paprika
2 cups tomato purée

Remove the lobster meat from the shell and cut into small pieces. Add rice to boiling water and cook in double boiler until tender.

Melt butter in a saucepan. Add onion and green pepper. Stir in flour, salt, and paprika. Add tomato purée and stir until thickened and boiling. Set over boiling water and lightly mix in rice and lobster. Heat through and serve. Serves 4 to 5.

LOBSTER NEWBURG
(Master Recipe)

1 1/2 cups diced cooked or canned lobster
2 tablespoons butter or margarine
1/2 tablespoon flour
1/2 cup light cream
2 tablespoons sherry
2 slightly beaten egg yolks
1/2 teaspoon salt
Few grains cayenne

Cook lobster (3 pounds of lobster in shell gives 1 1/2 cups of meat) in melted butter over low heat 5 minutes.

Sprinkle in flour. Add cream slowly, stirring constantly, until sauce boils.

Stir in sherry and egg yolks. Cook 1 minute. Remove from heat.

Overcooking will curdle sauce. Season with salt and cayenne. Serve on crisp toast or in patty shells. Serves 4 to 5.

Variations of Lobster Newburg

Clam Newburg: Drain liquid from 1 pint clams.

Chop hard parts fine. Leave soft parts whole. Use in place of lobster. Canned clams may also be used.

Crab Newburg: Use 1 1/2 cups flaked crabmeat instead of lobster.

Scallops Newburg: Cook 1 pint of scallops in their own liquid for 3 minutes. Drain and substitute for lobster.

Shrimp Newburg: Use 1 1/2 cups cooked or canned shrimp instead of lobster.

LOBSTER AND MUSHROOM CASSEROLE

6   tablespoons butter or margarine
½ pound mushrooms, sliced
3   stalks celery, diced
½ small onion, grated
½ green pepper, minced
⅛ teaspoon basil
1   pound lobster meat
2   cups medium white sauce
½ cup cracker crumbs
¼ cup grated Cheddar cheese

Melt 4 tablespoons butter in a large saucepan over moderate heat. Add mushrooms, celery, onion, green pepper, and basil; simmer gently until mushrooms and celery are tender, but not soft, about 10 minutes.

Add lobster to mushroom mixture. Mix well and heat 5 minutes. Add white sauce and mix thoroughly.

Turn into casserole. Cover with layer of cracker crumbs, then with layer of grated cheese. Dot with remaining butter.

Bake in moderate oven (350°F.) until golden brown, about 25 minutes.

Serve very hot from casserole.

Serves 4.

Variations: Raw oysters, clams, or scallops may be substituted for lobster. Clams or oysters are heated only 2 minutes and baking time is reduced to 15 to 20 minutes.

LOBSTER FARCI

2   hard-cooked egg yolks
1   cup cooked lobster meat
1   tablespoon minced parsley
1   cup medium white sauce
3   tablespoons sherry
Salt to taste
Few grains white pepper
½ cup buttered crumbs

Rub egg yolks through a fine sieve. Combine with lobster, parsley, sauce, sherry, and salt and pepper to taste.

Mix well and use to fill split lobster shells or place in buttered casserole. Top with crumbs.

Bake in moderate oven (375°F.) until brown, about 15 minutes. Serves 2.

Note: Canned lobster meat may be used and the mixture may be baked in scallop shells or individual ramekins.

LOBSTER AND CRABMEAT SOUR CREAM RAMEKINS

½ pound lobster meat
½ pound crabmeat
1   cup sour cream
⅛ teaspoon salt
Dash of cayenne
4   sprigs tarragon, chopped

Use freshly cooked lobster and crabmeat. Remove bony particles from crabmeat.

Mix the seafood and place in 4 individual ramekins. Mix sour cream with salt, cayenne, and tarragon. Pour over seafood.

Bake in moderate oven (350°F.) until thoroughly heated and bubbly. Serve at once. Serves 4.

Variations: If desired, substitute cooked cleaned shrimp for lobster.

LOBSTER TAILS A LA POPUCH

6   lobster tails
4   tablespoons butter or margarine
1   teaspoon salt
Dash of cayenne
¼ cup lemon juice
¼ cup sherry

Drop lobster tails into boiling, salted water. Bring to boiling point. Reduce heat and simmer 15 minutes. Remove from water and cut shells down back. Lift meat from shells and cut into ½-inch cubes.

Make sauce by melting butter and adding salt, cayenne, lemon juice, and wine.

Pour sauce over meat and mix lightly. Refill shells. Use any remaining sauce for basting.

Broil in moderate oven (350°F.) until lightly browned, 10 minutes. Serve immediately. Serves 4.

Lobster Tails
with Drawn Butter

LOBSTER TAILS

(Sea Crayfish or Rock Lobster)

Lobster tails are not from the true lobster. They come from the large sea crayfish.

Boiled Lobster Tails: Cook lobster tails weighing about ½ pound each in boiling salted water for 5 minutes. Lower heat and simmer about 15 minutes longer, depending upon size of tails.

Let cool in water. Drain thoroughly. Remove meat and use in other recipes. See Index for recipes using cooked lobster meat.

Broiled Lobster Tails: Steam or simmer tails for 5 minutes.

When cool enough to handle, split down the back and open out.

Brush with butter and broil until lightly browned. Avoid overcooking.

LOBSTER TAILS WITH DRAWN BUTTER

Cook 6 lobster tails in boiling salted water (as above) or in accordance with package directions.

Drain, cut along each edge, and remove thin top covering. Flatten with hand and insert a skewer into tail to keep tail flat.

Drawn Butter Sauce: Melt ½ pound butter over low heat and let stand 15 minutes.

Carefully pour off the liquid fat, leaving the solids. Add lemon juice to taste, 1 teaspoon salt, and ¼ teaspoon white pepper. Reheat and serve hot. If any sauce remains, it may be refrigerated and used later.

Brush lobster meat with drawn butter; sprinkle lightly with salt and pepper. Broil 3 inches from heat about 5 minutes or until sufficiently brown. Serve remaining sauce with lobster. Serves 6.

Curried Lobster Tails

LOBSTER TAILS BAKED IN ALUMINUM FOIL

Thaw and cut undershell around edge and remove. Fold each tail securely into a piece of foil cut 4 inches longer than length of tail.

Place on baking pan. Bake in very hot oven (450°F.) 25 minutes for tails weighing 4 to 8 ounces, 30 minutes for tails weighing 9 to 12 ounces, and 35 minutes for tails weighing 13 to 16 ounces.

DEVILED LOBSTER TAILS

4 lobster tails (1/2 pound each)
1/4 cup butter or margarine
1/2 teaspoon dry mustard
1 small onion, minced
1 teaspoon Worcestershire Sauce
2 cups medium white sauce
Salt and pepper
Grated Parmesan cheese
Butter or margarine

Steam or simmer lobster tails 8 to 10 minutes. Cool and split. Remove and dice meat.

Melt 1/4 cup butter; add mustard, onion, and Worcestershire sauce. Simmer 5 minutes.

Add white sauce and lobster meat. Season with salt and pepper.

Fill shells. Sprinkle with Parmesan cheese and dot with butter. Broil until browned. Serves 4.

CREAMED SEAFOOD IN SHELLS

2 tablespoons flour
1 cup water
1 cup evaporated milk
1/2 teaspoon salt
Dash of pepper
1 cup boned lobster or crabmeat, cooked or canned
1 cup shrimp, cooked or canned
About 2 cups mashed potatoes
Cheese, if desired

Stir water slowly into flour to keep smooth. Bring mixture to a boil, stirring constantly to prevent lumping.

Add milk and seasonings and continue cooking over hot water until thickened, about 10 minutes. Add lobster or crabmeat and shrimp, and pour into individual baking dishes.

Garnish with mashed potatoes. Sprinkle with grated cheese, if desired.

Brown in very hot oven (450°F.). Serves 6.

CURRIED LOBSTER TAILS

3 quarts boiling water
3 teaspoons salt
6 frozen rock lobster tails
1 teaspoon Ac'cent
4 tablespoons butter or margarine
4 tablespoons flour
1 teaspoon salt
1/2 teaspoon paprika
1/2 teaspoon Ac'cent
1/8 teaspoon nutmeg
1 1/2 teaspoons curry powder
2 cups milk
2 1/2 tablespoons lemon juice

Bring water to boil in large kettle. Add salt, lobster tails and 1 teaspoon Ac'cent.

When water returns to a boil, lower heat and cook length of time indicated in package directions.

Drain; flush with cold water; remove meat from shells; chill, then dice.

Melt butter or margarine; blend in flour, salt, paprika, 1/2 teaspoon Ac'cent, nutmeg, and curry powder. Add milk; stir over low heat until smooth and thickened.

Add lemon juice and diced lobster meat. Heat thoroughly; refill shells. Serves 6.

THERMIDOR AFRIKAANS

4   6-ounce lobster tails, boiled
4   tablespoons melted butter or mar-
        garine
4   tablespoons flour
1   teaspoon salt
1   teaspoon paprika
½   teaspoon dry mustard
¼   teaspoon nutmeg
1½ cups hot milk and drained,
        canned mushroom liquid
½   cup cream
½   cup drained canned mushrooms
2   tablespoons sherry
1   cup soft breadcrumbs
2   tablespoons melted butter or mar-
        garine
Lemon wedges

Remove and dice meat from cooked lobster tails.

Make cream sauce of 4 tablespoons melted butter, flour, salt, paprika, mustard, nutmeg, hot milk and drained mushroom liquor, and cream.

Mix in lobster meat, mushrooms, and sherry. Refill lobster shells. Combine breadcrumbs with 2 tablespoons butter. Sprinkle over filled shells. Brown lightly under broiler. Garnish with lemon wedges. Serves 4.

Mussels

Mussels are somewhat similar to clams in flavor. Buy them in the shell, tightly closed, or canned. Allow 8 to 10 per serving.

HOW TO PREPARE MUSSELS

Scrub and rinse mussels. Open by steaming as for steamed clams or with a knife. Remove and discard hairy beard. To serve fried or creamed, follow recipes for fried or creamed oysters.

ROASTED MUSSELS

Scrub and rinse mussels. Spread in flat layer in a pan. Bake in very hot oven (450°F.) until shells open.

Remove upper shells and bearded parts carefully to avoid spilling juice. Serve with seasonings, melted butter and cups of hot broth.

MUSSELS MARINIERE

4   to 5 dozen mussels
1   cup dry white wine
1   tablespoon minced shallots or
        minced onion
1   tablespoon minced parsley
Few grains cayenne
½   bay leaf
2   tablespoons butter or margarine
About 1 tablespoon extra parsley

Scrub mussels thoroughly, scraping shells with a knife and changing the water several times.

Place in a saucepan with the wine, shallots, 1 tablespoon parsley, cayenne, bay leaf, and butter. Cover tightly and cook over low heat until shells open, 5 to 10 minutes, shaking the pan from time to time.

Remove the mussels. Drain and reserve the liquid. Cut off the beards. Loosen from shells and place in half shells on hot serving dishes.

Pour reserved liquid into saucepan, being careful not to mix in any sediment. Boil down to ¾ cup.

Add additional butter and seasonings if necessary. Pour over mussels. Sprinkle with extra parsley. Serve very hot. Serves about 6.

BAKED MUSSEL CASSEROLE

Scrub and wash 4 to 5 dozen mussels. Steam as for steamed clams.

Remove from shells and trim off bearded parts. Place in buttered baking dish. Season with salt, pepper, and 1 teaspoon minced onion. Cover with thin slices of bacon. Sprinkle with grated Parmesan cheese. Bake in moderate oven (350°F.) 15 minutes. Serves 4 to 5.

Oysters

Oysters in the Shell

Oysters may be bought in 3 forms: live in the shell, fresh or frozen shelled, and canned.

Oysters in the shell are generally sold by the dozen and must be alive when purchased. The shells must be tightly closed.

Shelled oysters are sold by the pint or quart. They should be plump and have a natural creamy color, with clear liquid and free from particles.

Canned oysters are sold in a variety of can sizes.

The quantity to buy depends to a large extent on how the oysters are to be served. In general, for 6 servings allow 3 dozen shell oysters, 1 quart shucked oysters, 2 No. 1 cans, or 2 packages frozen oysters.

SHUCKING (OPENING) OYSTERS

Wash and rinse the oysters thoroughly in cold water. Open or shuck an oyster by placing it on a table flat shell up and holding it with the left hand. With the right hand, force an oyster knife between the shells at or near the thin end.

To make it easier to insert the knife, the thin end or "bill" may be broken off with a hammer—a method preferred by some cooks.

Now cut the large adductor muscle close to the flat upper shell in which it is attached and remove the shell.

Cut the lower end of the same muscle, which is attached to the deep half of the shell, and leave the oyster loose in the shell if it is to be served on the half shell, or drop it into a container.

After shucking, examine the oysters for bits of shell, paying particular attention to the muscle to which pieces of shell sometimes adhere.

"Billing" Oyster

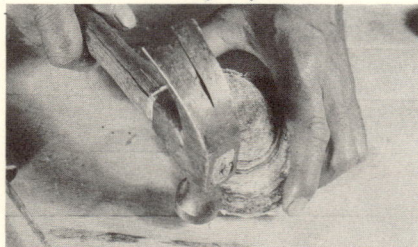

Cutting Muscle

Inserting Knife

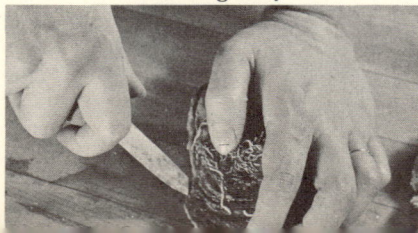

Cutting Oyster from Shell

*Oysters on
the Half Shell*

OYSTERS ON THE HALF SHELL

Open oysters. Loosen oysters from the deeper half shells but let them remain in the shells. Discard the other half shells.

Serve on a bed of crushed ice in shallow bowls or soup plates. Place 6 half-shell oysters on the ice, with a small container of cocktail sauce in the center. Garnish with lemon wedges.

FRIED OYSTERS #1

Drain oysters. Dry carefully between towels. Roll in flour, seasoned with salt and pepper, then in beaten egg diluted with 1 tablespoon water. Roll in dry bread or cracker crumbs.

Fry in deep fat (365°–375°F.) until golden brown. Drain on absorbent paper. Serve with tartar sauce.

Fried Oysters #2: Dip dried oysters in fritter cover batter and fry as above.

Fried Oysters #3: Dip dried oysters in fine dry crumbs, then in mayonnaise, and again in crumbs. Fry as above.

Sautéed Oysters: Prepare as in #1 or #2 and sauté in a single layer in butter.

OVEN-FRIED OYSTERS

Prepare oysters as in Fried Oysters #1. After coating with crumbs, dip in olive oil. Arrange in shallow baking pan.

Bake in hot oven (400°F.) until browned, about 15 minutes.

BROILED OYSTERS

Roll fresh oysters in mixture of half bread and half cracker crumbs. Press flat with hands. Broil 2 minutes on each side.

Salt lightly and brush with melted butter. Serve on buttered hot toast.

OYSTERS AU GRATIN

6 slices buttered toast
2 beaten eggs
1 teaspoon salt
1 teaspoon prepared mustard
½ teaspoon paprika
½ cup milk
1 pint oysters
1 cup grated cheese

Trim crusts from bread. Cut each slice into quarters.

Combine beaten eggs, seasonings, and milk.

Arrange layer of bread in buttered casserole. Cover with layer of oysters. Sprinkle with grated cheese. Repeat layer.

Pour milk mixture over contents of dish. Cover with grated cheese.

Place casserole in pan of hot water and bake in moderate oven (350°F.) until brown, 30 minutes. Serves 6.

Oysters
Au Gratin

DEVILED OYSTERS

1½ pints oysters
2   tablespoons minced onion
2   tablespoons butter or margarine
4   tablespoons flour
1½ cups milk

Oyster Stew

1   teaspoon salt
¼   teaspoon nutmeg
Few grains cayenne
1   teaspoon prepared mustard
1   tablespoon Worcestershire sauce
1   teaspoon chopped parsley
1   beaten egg
½   cup breadcrumbs
2   tablespoons butter or margarine

Chop oysters. Cook onion in butter until tender. Blend in flour. Add milk and cook until thick, stirring constantly.

Add seasonings, beaten egg, and oysters, and heat.

Turn mixture in buttered ramekins. Cover with crumbs tossed with 2 tablespoons butter.

Bake in hot oven (400°F.) 10 minutes, or until brown. Serves 6.

OYSTER STEW

4   tablespoons butter or margarine
1   pint oysters
1   quart milk
1½ teaspoons salt
⅛   teaspoon pepper
Paprika

Melt butter, add drained oysters, and cook 3 minutes or until edges curl.

Add milk, salt, and pepper, and bring almost to boiling point.

Serve at once. Garnish with paprika. Serves 6.

BAKED OYSTERS ON THE HALF SHELL

36 oysters in shell
1/2 teaspoon salt
1/8 teaspoon pepper
2 tablespoons minced onion
4 tablespoons butter or margarine

Remove shells and drain oysters. Place on deep half of shells.

Sprinkle with salt, pepper, and onion. Dot with butter.

Place oysters in baking pan. Bake in hot oven (400°F.) until edges begin to curl, about 10 minutes. Serves 6.

PANNED OYSTERS

1 pint oysters
4 tablespoons butter or margarine
2 tablespoons lemon juice
Salt and pepper
Lemon slices

Drain oysters. Place in frying pan and cook over low heat until edges curl.

Add butter, lemon juice, and pepper and salt, to taste. Bring to boil. Add a dash of Worcestershire sauce, if desired.

Serve on hot toast and garnish with lemon slices. Serves 4 to 6.

Oyster Luncheon Loaf

OYSTER FRITTERS

Prepare fritter binding batter (see Index). Add 1 pint drained and chopped oysters. Fry in hot deep fat (365°-375°F.). Drain on absorbent paper. Serves 4 to 6.

OYSTER LUNCHEON LOAF

1 large loaf unsliced bread
Melted butter or margarine
12 oysters
Evaporated milk
1 8-ounce can tomato sauce
6 tablespoons butter or margarine
1 green pepper, diced
4 tablespoons flour
1 teaspoon salt
Few grains pepper
1/2 teaspoon Ac'cent
1/4 teaspoon rosemary
1/4 teaspoon savory
6 hard-cooked eggs

Remove top of loaf of bread in one thin slice; do not remove crusts on sides and ends. With a sharp knife, remove center of loaf in one piece, leaving a shell about 3/4-inch thick.

Cut center into cubes and toast golden brown in moderate oven. With a star-cookie cutter, cut 4 stars from top slice. Brush shell and stars with melted butter or margarine and toast in moderate oven.

Measure oyster liquid; add enough evaporated milk to make 2 cups; add tomato sauce.

Melt 6 tablespoons butter or margarine; cook green pepper in this until soft; blend in flour, salt, pepper, and Ac'cent. Add evaporated milk mixture; stir over low heat until smooth and thickened.

Add oysters, rosemary, and savory; cover and cook over hot water 15 minutes. Add toasted bread cubes.

Place toasted bread shell on platter; surround with halves of hard-cooked eggs. Fill case with oyster mixture; cover eggs with remaining oyster mixture. Place stars on top. Serve at once. Serves 6.

OYSTERS ROCKEFELLER

36 oysters in shell
2 cups cooked spinach
4 tablespoons onion
2 bay leaves
1 tablespoon parsley
1/2 teaspoon celery salt
1/2 teaspoon salt
6 drops Tabasco sauce
6 tablespoons butter or margarine
1/2 cup breadcrumbs

Open shells and drain oysters; place on deep half of shells.

Put spinach, onion, bay leaves, and parsley through food chopper. Add seasonings to mixture, and cook in butter for 5 minutes. Add breadcrumbs and mix well. Spread mixture over oysters.

Bake in hot oven (400°F.) about 10 minutes. Garnish with lemon slices. Serves 6.

Note: If shell oysters are not available, 1½ pints select oysters may be used. Drain oysters and arrange on shallow buttered baking dish. Spread with seasonings and cook as above.

OYSTERS ON TOAST
CATALAN (SPAIN)

2 teaspoons grated Edam cheese
1 tablespoon butter or margarine
2 tablespoons ketchup
1/2 teaspoon Worcestershire sauce
2 tablespoons heavy cream
1 large cooked California crab or 3/4 to 1 cup cooked or canned crabmeat
24 medium oysters
6 rounds of hot toast

Combine in a double boiler over hot water the Edam cheese and butter. Stir and cook until melted.

Add ketchup, Worcestershire sauce, and cream. Now add finely shredded crabmeat. Cook and stir until boiling and creamy. Add drained oysters. Cook until edges curl.

Serve at once on the rounds of hot toast, plain or buttered. Serves 6.

SCALLOPED OYSTERS

1 pint oysters
2 cups cracker crumbs
1/2 teaspoon salt
1/8 teaspoon pepper
1/2 cup butter or margarine, melted
1/4 teaspoon Worcestershire sauce
1 cup milk

Drain oysters. Combine cracker crumbs, salt, pepper, and butter; sprinkle 1/3 in a buttered casserole. Cover with a layer of oysters. Repeat layer.

Add Worcestershire sauce to milk, and pour over contents of casserole. Sprinkle remaining crumbs on top.

Bake in moderate oven (350°F.) until brown, 30 minutes. Serves 6.

QUICK SCALLOPED OYSTERS

1 pint oysters
1 can (10½ ounces) condensed asparagus, celery, or mushroom soup
1 cup dry breadcrumbs
3 tablespoons melted butter or margarine
1 tablespoon finely chopped parsley
About 1/4 teaspoon salt

Drain oysters, reserving liquid. Combine soup and oyster liquid and heat to boiling point. Add oysters and cook until edges curl.

Toss crumbs with melted butter, parsley, and salt.

Line bottom of heated casserole with half the crumb mixture. Add oyster-soup mixture and top with remaining crumbs.

Brown under a moderate broiler. Serves 6.

PIGS IN BLANKETS

24 oysters or scallops
1/2 teaspoon salt
12 bacon strips

Sprinkle oysters or scallops with salt.

Cut bacon strips in half and roll oysters or scallops in bacon. Skewer with toothpicks.

Bake in very hot oven (450°F.) for 5 minutes, and baste with melted fat. Serves 6.

OYSTER PIE

1 pint oysters
½ cup diced celery
½ cup diced green pepper
4 tablespoons butter or margarine
5 tablespoons flour
2 cups milk
1 teaspoon salt
⅛ teaspoon pepper
2 tablespoons pimiento, chopped
Plain pastry

Cook oysters in their liquid about 5 minutes or until edges begin to curl. Drain.

Cook celery and green pepper in butter until tender. Blend in flour. Add milk and cook until thickened, stirring constantly. Add oysters and seasonings. Heat thoroughly. Pour in casserole. Top with pastry.

Bake in hot oven (425°F.) 15 minutes or until crust is brown. Serves 6.

CREAMED OYSTERS

1 pint oysters
2 tablespoons butter or margarine
2 tablespoons flour
Milk, cream, or stock
About ¾ teaspoon salt
About ⅛ teaspoon pepper
½ teaspoon Worcestershire sauce or
   1 teaspoon sherry

Drain oysters, reserving liquid.

Melt butter in saucepan. Slowly blend in flour. Gradually add oyster liquid with enough milk, cream, or stock to make 1 cup.

Cook over low heat, stirring constantly, until smooth. When boiling, add drained oysters. Heat thoroughly but do not boil.

Season with salt, pepper, and Worcestershire sauce or sherry. Serve on toast or in patty shells. Serves 4.

Variation: For a richer dish, blend a little of the creamed mixture with 2 egg yolks, beating constantly. Return to remaining mixture and cook, stirring constantly, for 1 minute to thicken slightly. Season to taste.

OYSTERS A LA CREOLE

1 small onion, minced
2 tablespoons butter or margarine,
   melted
1½ tablespoons flour
1 cup canned tomato juice
2 dozen raw oysters, drained
2 tablespoons minced parsley
½ teaspoon Tabasco sauce
¾ teaspoon salt
Buttered toast

Sauté onion in butter in saucepan until tender. Blend in flour; then add tomato juice, and cook, stirring, until thickened.

Add oysters, parsley, Tabasco sauce, and salt, and heat until edges of oysters curl. Serve on toast. Serves 4 to 6.

PAN ROAST OYSTERS

1 pint oysters
2 tablespoons butter or margarine
½ teaspoon salt
⅛ teaspoon pepper
Buttered toast

Drain oysters and place in shallow buttered baking dish.

Melt butter; add seasonings and pour over oysters.

Bake in hot oven (400°F.) until edges begin to curl, about 10 minutes.

Serve immediately on buttered toast. Serves 6.

BROILED OYSTERS ON HALF SHELL

36 oysters in shell
½ teaspoon salt
⅛ teaspoon pepper
½ cup breadcrumbs
2 tablespoons butter or margarine

Open shells and drain oysters. Place on deep half of shells.

Sprinkle with salt, pepper, and buttered breadcrumbs.

Place on preheated broiler pan about 3 inches from heat. Broil until brown, 5 minutes. Serves 6.

OYSTER NOODLE CASSEROLE

1 pint oysters
3 tablespoons butter or margarine
3 tablespoons flour
1½ cups milk
1½ cups cooked noodles
2 tablespoons minced green pepper
½ teaspoon salt
⅛ teaspoon pepper
½ cup breadcrumbs
2 tablespoons butter or margarine

Drain oysters. Melt butter in top of double boiler. Blend in flour. Add milk and cook until thickened, stirring constantly.

Place layer of noodles in buttered casserole. Cover with layer of oysters. Sprinkle with green pepper, salt, and pepper. Repeat with alternate layers. Pour sauce over all. Cover with buttered crumbs. Bake in moderate oven (350° F.) 30 minutes or until brown. Serves 6.

OYSTERS LOUISIANA

Coarse rock salt
Large oysters on half shell
Salt, black pepper, paprika
1½ teaspoons minced green pepper
½ teaspoon minced pimiento
Chopped bacon

Fill shallow pans with coarse rock salt and heat to smoking hot in oven. Remove from oven.

Lay on the hot salt large oysters on half shell. Season them with salt, black pepper, paprika, green pepper, and pimiento. Sprinkle with chopped bacon.

Put under broiler flame; cook at high heat 5 to 6 minutes. When bacon is crisp and oysters done, serve at once in shells, placing the pans of hot salt on platters. These are extremely popular in New Orleans.

OYSTERS MEUNIÈRE

Dip drained oysters in flour. Brown quickly but gently in butter. Serve on toast, with melted butter and lemon juice poured over each serving.

CREAMED OYSTERS AND MUSHROOMS

3 tablespoons fat
5 tablespoons flour
1 teaspoon salt
¼ teaspoon pepper
1½ cups milk
½ cup chopped mushrooms
1 pint oysters

Heat fat in top of double boiler. Add flour, salt, and pepper. Mix until smooth. Add milk gradually, stirring constantly. Cook over hot water 8 minutes.

Fry mushrooms in a little fat until tender.

Drain oysters, clean and pick over. Heat in oyster liquid until edges curl. Add to white sauce with mushrooms.

Serve over hot biscuits or toast or in patty shells. Serves 6.

OYSTER LOAF

Use 1 loaf of day-old bread. Cut out top crust about ½ inch from edge, all around, and save for a lid. Scoop out most of the crumb, leaving about ¾-inch wall on sides and bottom.

Place the loaf in a baking pan. Fill it with alternate layers of oysters seasoned with salt and pepper and breadcrumbs moistened with a little milk or oyster liquor.

When filled, replace the top crust lid. Bake in moderate oven (350°F.) about 15 minutes. Serve in slices.

Serves 6 to 8.

OYSTERS CASINO

1 pint oysters
½ cup finely minced green pepper
½ cup finely minced bacon
1 tablespoon lemon juice
Pepper to taste

Drain oysters and arrange on a greased oven-proof platter. Sprinkle with green pepper, minced bacon, lemon juice, and pepper.

Bake in very hot oven (450°F.) about 10 minutes. Serves 6.

*Scallops
in Shells*

Scallops

The only part of the scallop that is sold in the stores is the cube-shaped large muscle which opens and closes the scallop shells and it is the only part of the scallop that is used. The rest is discarded.

Two types of scallops are available, the small bay or cape scallops and the considerably larger sea scallops. The bay scallops are slightly more delicate than the larger sea scallops. Scallops should be cream colored, not white, and odorless.

Allow about 1½ to 2 pounds or 1½ to 2 pints for serving 6 to 8, or 2 packages frozen scallops. Buy the smaller quantities if the scallops are to be served in a scalloped dish or in a sauce, the larger quantities if they are to be served sautéed or fried.

SCALLOPS IN SHELLS

¼ cup butter or margarine
1 teaspoon Worcestershire sauce
¼ cup minced onion
1 pint bay scallops
¼ cup white wine

Melt butter in small frying pan with Worcestershire sauce. Add onion and cook until golden.

Pick over and rinse scallops. Divide into 4 large scallop shells or individual bakers.

Divide butter-onion mixture evenly over scallops. Add 1 tablespoon wine to each.

Bake in very hot oven (500°F.) 10 minutes. Serve at once. Serves 4.

BROILED SCALLOPS

Drain and wash scallops. Dip in milk and roll in breadcrumbs. Place in single layer in greased shallow pan. Dot with butter.

Broil, turning frequently, until browned on all sides, about 3 minutes. Serve with melted butter and lemon juice.

SAUTÉED SCALLOPS

Prepared as for broiled scallops. Fry in a well greased frying pan, turning frequently, until brown on all sides, about 3 minutes.

SAUTÉED SCALLOPS #2

Drain scallops and dry between 2 towels. Roll in flour seasoned with salt and pepper. Sauté in butter or margarine, turning constantly to brown evenly.

If large sea scallops are used, cut into small pieces before preparing.

Breading scallops

SCALLOPED SCALLOPS

1½ pounds scallops
¼ cup butter or margarine
4 cups soft breadcrumbs
1¼ teaspoons salt
1 teaspoon grated onion
1 teaspoon minced parsley
1 teaspoon minced chives
1 tablespoon lemon juice

If large sea scallops are used, quarter or slice them.

Melt butter and add all the ingredients except scallops; toss together until well mixed.

Place in alternate layers with scallops in a well greased baking dish, with crumb mixture for top layer.

Bake in hot oven (400°F.) until crumbs are brown, about 20 minutes. Serves 6.

SCALLOP STEW

1 quart milk
½ pint light cream
⅓ cup butter or margarine
1 tablespoon sugar
½ teaspoon Worcestershire sauce
1 pound scallops

Heat milk and cream in double boiler.

Melt butter in skillet, and add sugar and Worcestershire sauce.

Crush scallops, cut off the hard pieces and dice. Add to mixture in skillet. Simmer until tender.

Pour heated milk and cream over cooked scallops. Season to taste with salt and pepper. Serves 6.

FRENCH FRIED SCALLOPS

Method #1: Wipe scallops with damp cloth. Dip in batter and fry in hot deep fat (375°F.) 3 to 4 minutes, or until golden brown. Serve with a tartar sauce.

Method #2: Wipe scallops with damp cloth. Roll in flour, dip in beaten egg, and roll in dry breadcrumbs. Fry in hot deep fat (375°F.) 3 to 4 minutes, or until golden brown. Serve with tartar, chili, or tomato sauce.

SCALLOPS ON SKEWERS

Drop scallops into boiling salted water and simmer 2 minutes. Drain and dry.

Dip in melted butter. Place on skewers alternately with half slices of bacon and parboiled onions, if desired.

Broil under moderate heat until bacon is done.

Remove from skewers and place on toast rounds. Sprinkle with minced parsley. Serve with tartar sauce.

SCALLOPS AU GRATIN

3 tablespoons butter or margarine
3 tablespoons flour
1½ cups milk
½ cup grated Cheddar cheese
1 pound sea scallops, sliced
Celery salt to taste
Juice of ½ lemon
Cracker crumbs

Melt butter or margarine. Add flour and mix to a smooth paste. Add milk gradually, stirring over low heat until mixture is smooth and thick.

Add cheese and continue stirring until cheese is melted.

Place a layer of scallop slices in the bottom of greased casserole.

Add celery salt, lemon juice, and a layer of cheese sauce. Repeat until all ingredients are used up. Sprinkle with cracker crumbs.

Bake in moderate oven (375°F.) until crumbs are browned and scallops tender, about 30 minutes. Serves 4 to 6.

Shrimp

Fresh shrimp may be purchased in the shell, raw, cooked, or frozen. Or, peeled shrimp may be bought cooked, canned, or frozen.

Allow 1 pound raw in the shell to serve 4, or ½ pound cooked and peeled.

BOILED SHRIMP

Add 1 tablespoon salt to 1 quart water. Bring to boil.

Add 1 pound shrimp and bring to boil again. Turn heat down so that water just simmers. Cover saucepan and cook 2 to 5 minutes, never longer. Drain shrimp.

SHRIMP COOKED IN COURT BOUILLON

1 quart water
½ stalk celery
1 carrot, sliced
1 small white onion, sliced
Juice of ½ lemon
1 teaspoon salt
½ teaspoon pepper
1 pound raw shrimp, fresh or frozen

Put water in saucepan. Add all ingredients except shrimp. Bring water to boil.

Add shrimp and let water come to boil again. Turn heat down so water just simmers. Cover saucepan and let shrimp cook 2 to 5 minutes, never longer. Drain shrimp.

TO SHELL SHRIMP

Raw shrimp (fresh or quick frozen) may be shelled either before or after boiling. Some people think it is easier to remove the small sand vein when the shrimp is raw, while others prefer to cook the shrimp before shelling. The odor of cooking shrimp will not be as strong if they are shelled before cooking.

Wash the shrimp. Let frozen shrimp stand in cold water about 15 minutes.

To clean shrimp, hold tail end in left hand, slip thumb under shell, between feelers, and lift off 2 or 3 segments in one motion. Then still holding firmly to tail, pull out shrimp from remaining shell section and tail.

With a knife, cut along outside curvature and lift out black sand vein, if desired. Vein is harmless, but some people object to the appearance of the black line. Then, rinse with cold water.

Removing shell from raw shrimp

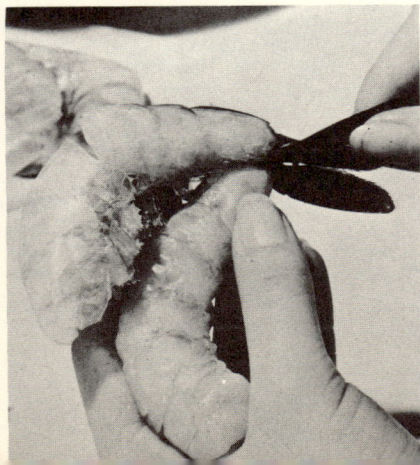

Removing black sand vein

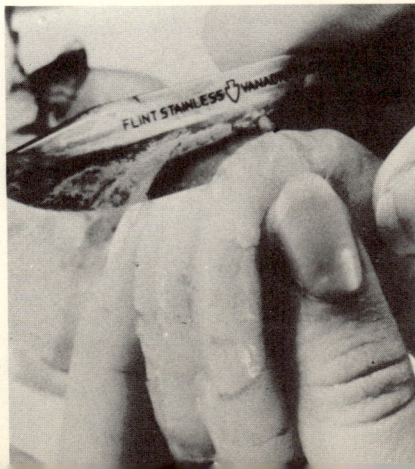

SHRIMP COCKTAIL PICTURE HINTS

SHRIMP COCKTAIL SAUCE

2   tablespoons prepared horseradish
¾ cup tomato ketchup
3   tablespoons chili sauce
2   tablespoons lemon juice
Dash of Tabasco sauce
Salt to taste

Mix together all ingredients. Serve in separate bowl or pour over individual cocktails. Makes enough sauce for 4 cocktails.

SHRIMP ARNAUD—APPETIZER

2 tablespoons tarragon or cider vinegar
1/3 cup olive oil
1 tablespoon paprika
1/4 cup strong prepared mustard (Creole mustard preferred)
About 1 teaspoon salt (more or less to suit taste)
1 cup very finely chopped celery
1/2 cup very finely chopped green onions and tops
1/4 cup very finely chopped parsley
2 pounds shrimp, cooked, peeled, and cleaned

Combine all ingredients except shrimp in a bowl and blend thoroughly.

Pour enough sauce over shrimp to moisten them and mix well. Cover and set in refrigerator 30 minutes to 2 hours before using so the sauce flavor permeates the shrimp.

Pour remaining sauce over shrimp just before serving.

STEAMED SHRIMP

Wash fresh shrimp in the shell and place in a covered steamer over boiling water. Let cook 2 minutes.

Remove steamer from heat. Keep covered and let shrimp remain over hot water 3 minutes longer. Shell, remove black vein and use in other recipes.

SHRIMP DE JONGHE

1 clove garlic
3/4 cup butter or margarine
1 teaspoon salt
1 cup fine dry breadcrumbs
1/2 cup dry sherry
2 1/2 to 3 pounds cooked shrimp
Chopped parsley

Mash garlic clove until it is almost paste.

Cream together the garlic, butter, and salt until well blended. Add crumbs and sherry. Blend well.

Place alternate layers of cooked cleaned shrimp and crumb mixture in 6 individual casseroles, ending with crumbs. Sprinkle chopped parsley over top of each.

Bake in hot oven (400°F.) 20 to 25 minutes. Serve at once. Serves 6.

BROILED FRESH SHRIMP

Remove shells, leaving on last segment and tail. Remove black veins. Dip raw shrimp in melted butter or salad oil.

Broil under moderate heat 4 to 6 minutes, depending upon size of shrimp. Season to taste with salt and pepper. Serve with a butter sauce.

CREAMED SHRIMP

Heat cleaned, cooked or canned shrimp in medium white sauce or cream sauce. Season to taste with salt and pepper.

If desired, additional seasonings may be added as given in variations of white sauce (see Index).

For color, add chopped pimiento or chopped parsley. Serve on toast. Sprinkle with paprika.

SHRIMP TEMPURA

1 pound shrimp
Oil for frying
1 cup sifted flour
1/2 teaspoon salt
1 beaten egg
3/4 cup milk

Shell shrimp, leaving tail shell on. Slash back. Heat oil for deep frying.

Combine flour and salt. Add egg and milk; beat together.

Dip shrimp in batter; add to hot oil (375°F.). Fry 2 to 3 minutes, until golden, turning once. Drain.

Serves 6 to 8 as appetizer or 4 as entrée, with tangy dip.

Sauce: Combine 1/3 cup sherry, 2 tablespoons soy sauce, 1 teaspoon sugar, and pinch of ginger.

FRIED FRESH SHRIMP

1½ pounds raw shrimp
1   cup milk
⅛   teaspoon paprika
¼   teaspoon salt
Corn meal

Shell and remove black vein from shrimp.

Combine milk, paprika, and salt.

Soak shrimp in seasoned milk 30 minutes. Season with additional salt and roll in corn meal.

Fry in deep fat (375°F.) until golden brown. Drain on absorbent paper. Serve with tartar sauce. Serves 4 to 5.

Fried Cooked or Canned Shrimp:
Season cleaned shrimp with salt and pepper. Dip in milk and roll in corn meal. Fry as above.

BUTTERFLY SHRIMP

1½ pounds very large shrimp
2   eggs
3   tablespoons flour
½   teaspoon salt
Dash of pepper

Remove shells from shrimp but leave tail on. Split along the back and remove black vein but do not cut all the way through. Wash and dry with towel.

Combine eggs, flour, salt, and pepper in bowl; mix to smooth batter.

Drop in shrimp and coat thoroughly. Lift out shrimp one at a time with a fork and drop into deep hot fat (375°F.) and fry until golden brown, 2 to 5 minutes. Serve hot. Serves 4 to 5.

SAUTÉED SHRIMP

Sauté cooked or canned cleaned shrimp in melted butter lightly. Place on hot serving dish. Pour butter over the shrimp. Sprinkle with chopped parsley.

Serve on picks as an hors d'oeuvre. Serve with melted butter flavored with lemon juice and freshly ground pepper.

FRIED SHRIMP WITH BACON

1½ pounds fresh shrimp
6   slices bacon
1   egg
1   tablespoon water
6   tablespoons fat
⅔   cup chopped onion
1½   teaspoons cornstarch
1   teaspoon soy sauce
¾   cup beef bouillon

Wash shrimp in cold water, drain; remove shells and legs and sand vein.

Cut bacon in 1½-inch pieces. Fold a bacon strip around each shrimp and secure with a pick.

Beat egg and water together. Dip shrimp into egg mixture.

Melt fat in hot frying pan. Cook shrimp in pan over moderate heat until browned on both sides. Keep in warm place.

Pour off all but 2 tablespoons fat from frying pan. Sauté onion.

Mix cornstarch, soy sauce, and beef bouillon. Add slowly to onion and cook until thick. Serve over shrimp. Serves 4.

SHRIMP SOUFFLÉ CASSEROLE

6   slices buttered bread
Dry mustard
2   8-ounce cans shrimp, cleaned
½   pound American cheese, grated
     (about 2 cups)
3   eggs
2   cups milk
Salt and pepper

Spread bread lightly with dry mustard. Remove crusts and cut into ½-inch cubes.

Put alternate layers of bread cubes, shrimp, and cheese in a greased casserole.

Beat eggs and combine with milk. Season with salt and pepper. Pour over other ingredients.

Place in pan of hot water and bake in moderate oven (350°F.) 1¼ hours, or until silver knife inserted in center comes out clean. Serves 6 to 8.

SCAMPI
(Shrimp in Garlic Butter)

2 pounds shrimp, fresh or frozen
1/4 pound butter or margarine
1 clove garlic, minced fine
Salt to taste
Pepper to taste

Remove shells from shrimp, except portion which covers tail. Cut down center of back and remove sand vein.

Melt butter and add garlic. Simmer 3 minutes.

Place shrimp on individual flame-proof platters, or large broiling pan. Pour garlic butter over them. Sprinkle with salt and pepper.

Place in preheated broiler 3 inches from heat and broil 5 to 7 minutes or until browned and tender.

Serves 4 to 5.

SHRIMP CURRY—HAWAIIAN

4 large onions, chopped
3 large cloves garlic, chopped
4 tablespoons butter or margarine
3 cups water or coconut milk
3 large tomatoes, peeled and chopped
2 large apples, chopped
1 cup chopped celery
1 tablespoon shredded coconut
1 piece fresh ginger root or 3/4 teaspoon powdered ginger
1 tablespoon sugar
1 1/2 tablespoons curry powder
1 1/2 tablespoons flour
1 1/2 teaspoons salt
1/4 teaspoon pepper

Scampi

1 1/2 pounds cleaned raw shrimp

Sauté onions and garlic in butter until lightly browned. Add water, bring to a boil.

Add tomatoes, apples, celery, coconut, and fresh ginger root if available.

If powdered ginger is used, blend it with sugar, curry powder, flour, salt, and pepper. Add cold water to moisten to a paste and add, stirring, to boiling mixture. Simmer, stirring occasionally, until vegetables are very tender, or about 40 minutes.

Add shrimp and cook 5 minutes. Serve on rice. Makes about 2 quarts, or 12 or more servings.

CREAMED SHRIMP WITH WALNUTS

4 tablespoons butter or margarine
5 tablespoons flour
1/2 teaspoon salt
1/4 teaspoon dry mustard
Dash of cayenne
2 cups milk
1/4 teaspoon Worcestershire sauce
2 cups cleaned cooked shrimp
1/2 cup coarsely chopped walnuts
Baking powder biscuits
6 walnut halves for garnish

Melt butter; blend in flour, salt, mustard, and cayenne. Blend in milk, and cook and stir until mixture boils and is thickened.

Stir in Worcestershire sauce. Add shrimp and walnuts, and heat.

Serve over hot baking powder biscuits. Top each serving with a walnut half. Serves 6.

Creamed Shrimp with Walnuts

Shrimp Creole

SHRIMP CREOLE

4   tablespoons butter or margarine
1   large onion, chopped
½   cup minced green pepper
1   clove garlic, minced
1   teaspoon salt
Dash of pepper
⅛   teaspoon paprika
⅛   teaspoon rosemary (optional)
2   cups canned tomatoes
1   pound cooked shrimp
2   to 3 cups cooked rice

Melt butter in saucepan; add onion, green pepper, and garlic. Sauté 10 minutes or until tender.

Add salt, pepper, paprika, rosemary, and tomatoes. Bring to boiling point; cover, reduce heat. Simmer 15 minutes.

Add shrimp, heat thoroughly. Serve on rice. Serves 4.

BATTER-FRIED FRESH SHRIMP

½   cup sifted enriched flour
½   teaspoon baking powder
½   teaspoon salt
¼   teaspoon black pepper
1   slightly beaten egg
⅓   cup milk
2   or 3 drops Tabasco sauce
2   pounds cleaned shrimp

Mix and sift flour, baking powder, salt, and pepper.

Mix egg and milk and add to dry ingredients. Beat smooth. Add Tabasco sauce.

Dip shrimp in batter and fry in deep fat (375°F.) until golden brown. Drain on absorbent paper. Serve hot. Serves 6.

SHRIMP JAMBALAYA

1   tablespoon fat
1   tablespoon flour
1   cup cleaned cooked or raw shrimp
1   pound chopped cooked ham
1½   cups canned or fresh tomatoes
1   onion, sliced
1   red pepper, chopped
1   green pepper, chopped
1   clove garlic, crushed
Sprig of thyme (optional)
1   tablespoon minced parsley
1   teaspoon Worcestershire sauce
1   teaspoon salt
Dash of pepper
Paprika
4   cups water
1   cup raw rice

Melt fat; blend in flour, stirring constantly, until smooth and slightly brown.

Add shrimp, ham, and tomatoes; cook 3 minutes. Add onion, red and green pepper, garlic, thyme, parsley, Worcestershire sauce, about 1 teaspoon salt, dash of pepper, a sprinkling of paprika, and water. Bring to boiling point and simmer about 12 minutes.

Add rice, cover and cook until tender, about 30 minutes.

Do not stir the mixture but lift occasionally with a fork from bottom of pot to keep rice from burning. Serves 6 or more.

SHRIMP WIGGLE WITH TOMATO SAUCE

1 pound shrimp
1 cup water
2 whole black peppers
1 teaspoon salt
1 small bay leaf
½ stalk celery
½ teaspoon Ac'cent
1 cup sliced onions
3 tablespoons butter or margarine
2 8-ounce cans tomato sauce
2 tablespoons cornstarch
2 tablespoons cold water
½ teaspoon Ac'cent
Salt and pepper
Toast points

Wash shrimp under cold running water. Bring water to boil; add whole black peppers, salt, bay leaf, celery, and the ½ teaspoon Ac'cent.

Add shrimp, cover; simmer 5 minutes; drain; shell; remove black sand veins.

Sauté onions in butter or margarine until golden brown. Add tomato sauce. Simmer 5 minutes.

Blend cornstarch and cold water; add; stir until thickened. Add remaining Ac'cent and shrimp; heat thoroughly. Season to taste. Garnish with toast points. Serves 4.

QUICK SHRIMP CASSEROLE

3 ounces thin noodles
1 No. 1 can shrimp
1 12-ounce can whole kernel corn
1 4-ounce can mushrooms
2 tablespoons butter or margarine
2½ tablespoons flour
1 cup milk
¼ pound sharp American cheese, shredded
Salt and pepper

Cook noodles until tender in boiling salted water. Drain and place in casserole.

Clean black veins from shrimp. Arrange corn, shrimp, and sliced mushrooms over noodles. (Save liquid from mushrooms and shrimp.)

Melt butter in saucepan. Blend in flour. Add mixture of milk and liquid from shrimp and mushrooms gradually; cook over low heat, stirring constantly, until thickened and smooth.

Add half the cheese, salt and pepper to taste; stir over low heat until cheese is melted. Pour sauce over other ingredients. Mix gently. Sprinkle with remaining cheese.

Bake in hot oven (400°F.) until heated through, about 30 minutes. Serves 6.

Variations: Substitute peas for corn. Substitute clams or oysters for shrimp.

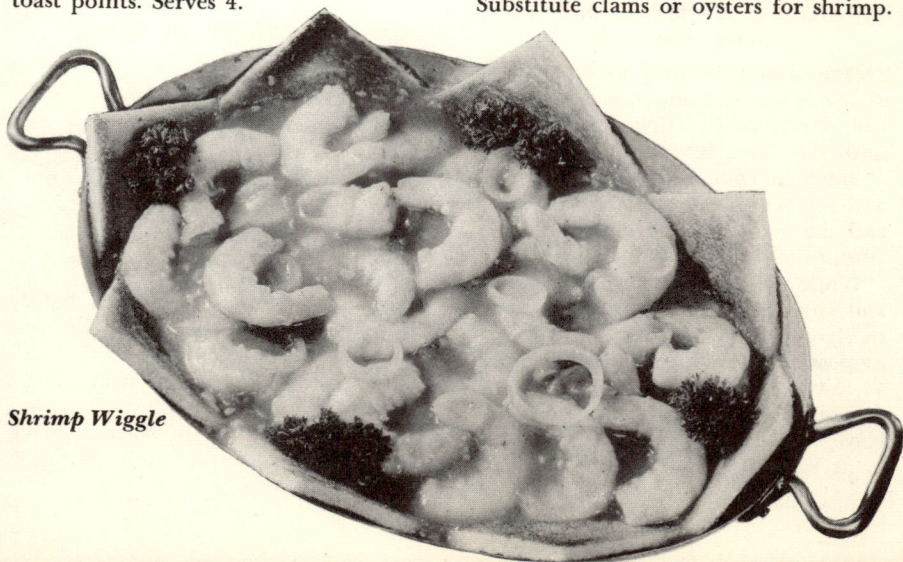

Shrimp Wiggle

Curried Shrimp
À La Ceylon

CURRIED SHRIMP A LA CEYLON

2 tablespoons butter or margarine
1 cup chopped onion
½ cup chopped green pepper
½ cup chopped celery
2 tablespoons flour
2 teaspoons curry powder (more if desired)
3 teaspoons soy sauce
1 cup water
1 No. 303 can tomatoes
1 cup uncooked white rice
1 teaspoon salt
2 cups water
1 pound frozen thawed shrimp or 2 5-ounce cans shrimp

Melt butter or margarine in skillet or saucepan. Add onion, green pepper, and celery. Cook, stirring occasionally, until the onion is yellow.

Blend in flour. Stir in curry powder and soy sauce. Stir in 1 cup of water and the tomatoes. Cover and simmer 20 minutes.

While the sauce cooks, put rice, salt, and water in a 2-quart saucepan. Bring to vigorous boil. Turn the heat as low as possible. Leave over this low heat 14 minutes.

Remove saucepan from heat but leave lid on until ready to serve rice or at least 10 minutes.

While rice cooks, peel frozen thawed shrimp. Remove sand vein easily by running knife along back of shrimp from head to tail. This pulls out vein.

Wash in water. Place shrimp in boiling salted water. Cover and return to boiling point. Turn heat down and simmer 5 minutes. Drain.

After sauce cooks, stir in cooked frozen thawed or canned shrimp. Heat 5 minutes.

Arrange cooked rice on a hot platter. Pour shrimp and sauce over rice. Serves 6.

MEXICAN SHRIMP IN SAUCE

1 onion, minced
¼ cup butter or margarine
1 teaspoon chili powder
¼ cup flour
1 cup milk
2 tablespoons minced parsley
¼ cup ketchup
2 cups cooked or canned shrimp

Sauté onion in butter until lightly browned. Stir in chili powder and flour. Slowly add milk.

Cook, stirring over low heat, for 10 minutes.

Add parsley, ketchup, shrimp; bring to a boil. Serve immediately. Serves 4.

CURRIED SHRIMP—SOUTHERN STYLE

¼ cup margarine
¼ cup flour
3 to 4 teaspoons curry powder
2 cups milk
½ teaspoon salt
¼ teaspoon ground black pepper
¼ teaspoon ground ginger
½ pound shrimp (canned or cooked fresh)
5 cups hot cooked rice
3 tablespoons margarine

Melt ¼ cup margarine in saucepan. Blend in flour and curry powder. Remove from heat.

Add milk gradually, stirring until smooth after each addition. Cook until medium thickness, stirring constantly. Stir in salt, pepper, ginger, and shrimp. Heat thoroughly.

Combine hot cooked rice and 3 tablespoons margarine, and arrange in ring around a hot serving plate or platter. Fill center with curried shrimp mixture. Serves 4 to 5.

SHRIMP AND LOBSTER IN RICE RING

1½ cups raw rice
3 tablespoons butter or margarine
3 tablespoons flour
1½ cup liquid (juice from canned lobster and shrimp, milk to make up difference)
1 teaspoon salt
½ teaspoon paprika
1 9-ounce can lobster, flaked
1 7-ounce can shrimp

Cook rice in boiling salted water until tender, about 30 minutes. Drain and rinse with hot water. Place over hot water or in oven to dry out.

Pack in buttered ring mold. Keep hot while making lobster and shrimp mixture.

Melt butter in saucepan over low heat. Remove from heat and blend in flour until smooth. Gradually add liquid. Return to heat, cook, stirring constantly until thick.

Add seasonings, flaked lobster, and shrimp. Heat thoroughly.

For serving, turn rice ring onto a hot serving platter and fill center with lobster and shrimp mixture. Serves 6.

NEAPOLITAN SHRIMP

1 pound shrimp, fresh or frozen
1 clove garlic, finely minced
¼ cup olive or other salad oil
3 anchovy fillets (optional)
1 No. 2 can Italian tomatoes
¼ teaspoon oregano
Pinch crushed red pepper
1 tablespoon chopped parsley

Remove shells from shrimp. Make a slash along back of shrimp, cutting deeply but not all the way through. Wash away sand vein. Drain shrimp on paper toweling.

Heat olive oil in large frying pan. Add garlic and shrimp, placing shrimp in the pan with backs down. Fry shrimp about 5 minutes, turning to sides to finish cooking. Remove shrimp and place on backs in a chafing dish.

Add remaining ingredients to pan. Mix thoroughly, breaking up tomatoes. Cook slowly at least 15 minutes.

Pour sauce around shrimp in chafing dish. Serve with slices of fried French bread. Serves 3 to 4.

Neapolitan Shrimp

Snails, Frogs' Legs, Turtle and Terrapin

SNAILS

While snails are becoming increasingly popular in this country, nevertheless the preparation is a laborious and wearisome task.

To serve 5 to 6, use 1 pound fresh snails (2 to 2½ dozen). Soak in heavily salted water 3 to 4 hours, then wash in several waters and simmer 30 minutes.

Remove snails from shells and cook in court bouillon (see Index) about 3 to 4 hours.

Meanwhile wash shells and dry thoroughly. Replace cooked snails in shells and pack with butter mixture (below). (It may be desirable to use 2 cooked snails in each shell.)

Place in shallow baking pan and, if desired, sprinkle with fine breadcrumbs. Bake in hot oven (400°F.) until heated through, about 20 minutes. Serve with a tiny fork or pick.

CANNED SNAILS

Canned snails are sold in special containers, with the prepared snails in one container and the cleaned shells in another.

To serve, place snails in shells, pack with butter mixture and serve as for fresh snails.

If desired, canned snails may be heated in a little white wine seasoned with chopped onion or shallot before placing in shells.

Another favorite stuffing frequently used instead of the butter mixture is a mixture of equal parts butter and ground filberts which have been creamed together in a bowl which was rubbed slightly with a cut clove of garlic.

BUTTER MIXTURE FOR SNAILS

½ cup butter or margarine
¼ cup finely chopped parsley
1 teaspoon chopped onion or shallot
1 clove crushed garlic
About ½ teaspoon salt
Dash of freshly ground pepper

Cream butter until soft and work in remaining ingredients.

Leftover butter mixture may be used as sauce for fish or vegetables.

FROGS' LEGS

The hind legs of the frog are the only ones used. If bought in the market they will come skinned, cleaned, and ready for use.

If you catch your own, cut them close to the body. The skin is thin and loose and may be turned down so that it pulls off like a glove.

Allow 4 to 6 large legs or ½ pound (8 to 10) small legs per serving.

FRIED FROGS' LEGS

Season legs with salt, pepper, and lemon juice. Dip in sifted breadcrumbs, then in egg diluted with 2 tablespoons water, and again in crumbs. Chill 1 hour.

Fry in hot deep fat (375°F.) 3 minutes, or sauté in butter until brown. Serve with tartar sauce.

FRICASSEE OF FROGS' LEGS

12 pair large frogs' legs
2 cups milk
6 tablespoons flour
1 teaspoon salt
Dash of pepper
½ cup butter or margarine
¾ cup heavy cream
2 tablespoons chopped parsley

Skin frogs' legs; cover with milk and soak 15 minutes; drain.

Mix 2 tablespoons flour with salt and pepper; roll frogs' legs in mixture. Cook in butter until browned, turning frequently (about 3 minutes).

Remove from pan. Stir in remaining flour. Add cream gradually and cook over low heat, stirring constantly, until sauce is smooth and slightly thickened (about 5 minutes).

Add frogs' legs and cook gently 3 minutes longer. Add parsley.

Serves 4 to 6.

FROGS' LEGS PROVENÇAL

12   frogs' legs
Flour
6   tablespoons butter or margarine
3   cloves garlic, crushed
1   tablespoon lemon juice
3   tablespoons chopped chives
2   tablespoons chopped tarragon
1½ tablespoons chopped parsley
Salt and pepper
1½ ounces brandy
¼   cup dry white wine

Dry cleaned frogs' legs and roll in flour.

Melt butter in skillet; add garlic and lemon juice. Blend well.

Add frogs' legs and shake skillet gently occasionally to prevent sticking.

Slowly brown well on all sides, 6 to 8 minutes.

Add chives, tarragon, parsley, and salt and pepper to taste. Cook 1 to 2 minutes, then add ignited brandy and the wine. Cook 1 minute longer. Serve at once. Serves 2 or 3.

TURTLE AND TERRAPIN

A considerable variety of turtles and tortoises are used for food in various localities; however, the diamond back terrapin is the one most favored as a table delicacy. They should be alive when purchased. The meat from a 6- to 7-inch terrapin should serve 2. Canned terrapin meat is also available.

TO PREPARE AND COOK TERRAPIN

Wash and scrub the terrapin thoroughly. Plunge the live terrapin into freshly boiling unsalted water and boil 5 to 10 minutes.

Remove from kettle and place in cold water until cool enough to handle.

Rub off the skin from the legs and tail with a towel. Pull out the head with a skewer or other sharp pointed instrument and rub off the skin.

Rinse and cover with boiling salted water. Cook until meat is tender. The time will vary but rarely will it be more than 45 minutes for the average terrapin. It is done when the meat of the legs is soft when pinched by the fingers.

If desired, add a stalk of celery, and 2 or 3 slices each of carrot and onion to the boiling water.

When done, remove from the stock, lay the terrapin on its back and let it cool enough to handle. Pull out the nails from the feet. Cut the undershell loose from the upper shell. Carefully remove the meat. Separate the legs from the body, cut in small pieces and set aside.

Empty the upper shell and discard the gall bladder, being careful not to let any particle of the gall bladder remain in the meat or it will give the dish a bitter flavor.

Remove and discard the sandbag, heart, tail, and the thick heavy part of the intestines as well as the white inside muscles.

The small intestines are usually cut small and added to the meat. The liver and eggs are also added to the meat. Cut the meat into small pieces, 1 to 2 inches. Most terrapin experts leave the bones in the meat.

Combine the meat, liver, eggs, and small intestines, if desired, in a kettle. Barely cover with cold salted water. Add a few slices each of carrot and onion, 1 bay leaf, and 2 cloves.

Cover, bring to boiling point, and simmer 30 to 40 minutes. (Some experts prefer to use the seasoned stock from the previous cooking instead of fresh water.)

When done, if the meat isn't going to be used at once, pack into a bowl, cover tightly and keep in refrigerator until wanted.

TERRAPIN BALTIMORE

Combine ¾ cup chicken stock and terrapin meat. Simmer very gently until stock is reduced by half its original volume.

Add the liver, cut into small pieces, 2 tablespoons butter, salt and black pepper to taste, and 2 well beaten egg yolks, stirring constantly while adding. (If desired, omit the egg yolks and increase the butter to ½ cup, adding the butter bit by bit.)

Before serving, season with 1½ to 2 tablespoons sherry.

TERRAPIN WASHINGTON

Melt 1½ tablespoons butter. Blend in 1½ tablespoons flour until smooth. Add 1 cup cream and bring to boiling point, stirring constantly.

Add the cooked terrapin meat with the liver cut into small pieces, chopped small intestines, terrapin eggs, ½ cup sautéed sliced mushrooms, and 1 hard-cooked egg, coarsely chopped. Simmer gently 3 to 5 minutes.

Just before serving, stir in 2 slightly beaten egg yolks. Season to taste with salt and pepper. If desired, add 1½ to 2 tablespoons sherry. Serve very hot.

TURTLE OR TERRAPIN STEW

1 cup sliced fresh or canned mushrooms
2 tablespoons butter or margarine
1 can condensed cream of mushroom soup
1 cup milk
About ½ teaspoon salt
2 cups chopped, cooked turtle or terrapin meat
¼ cup dry white wine

Pan fry the mushrooms in butter 5 minutes.

Add soup and milk; taste and add more salt if necessary. Then add cooked meat and heat 1 or 2 minutes.

Add wine and heat through, about 1 minute.

Serve hot on buttered toast or corn sticks. Serves 4 to 6.

TURTLE Ã LA KING

6 hard-cooked eggs, shelled
2 tablespoons butter or margarine
2 cups light cream
About ½ teaspoon salt
⅛ teaspoon freshly ground pepper
Dash of allspice
2 cups chopped, cooked turtle meat
1 tablespoon chopped pimiento

Mash egg yolks and cream with the butter.

Scald cream in top of double boiler over hot water. Add salt, pepper, and allspice.

Beat in creamed egg yolks. Add turtle meat and cook until thoroughly heated, about 10 minutes.

Serve very hot in individual heated ramekins. Garnish each portion with chopped egg white and pimiento. Serves 5 to 6.

CRAWFISH—BOILED

Fresh water crawfish are delicately tasting shellfish that look like infant lobsters.

Wash live crawfish thoroughly under running water. Drop into salted boiling water and boil 5 minutes. Let cool in the water. If desired, vegetables and seasonings may be added to the water as in boiled shrimp. Swedish-Americans frequently add fresh dill to the salted water.

To serve, pull out tail fin and intestinal vein with it. Crawfish are usually served in their bright red shells.

OYSTER OR PEA CRABS

These little crabs are frequently found in the oyster shell where they live. They are considered a delicious and delicate morsel and are eaten whole, shells and all. They may be bought by the pound.

To prepare them, wash and drain thoroughly. Drop into a paper bag containing flour and shake to thoroughly coat. Transfer to a sieve and shake to remove excess flour. Fry in basket in hot deep fat (390°F.) or sauté in sweet butter.

FREEZING GUIDE AND FROZEN FOOD COOKERY

Food freezing know-how, plus creative thinking, is opening bright new vistas to carefree living for today's homemakers.

Freezing foods in the home can be fun as well as constructive if the homemaker will follow a few simple fundamental rules.

The wide variety of foods that can be frozen and stored in the food freezer will not only provide a more healthful diet for the entire family, but provide the food when it is needed throughout the year at a saving if the shopping is done wisely.

Freezing is not only quick and easy; it has the advantage of more nearly retaining color, flavor, texture, and nutritional values of fresh foods than any other preserving method. It does not, however, improve upon the original quality of the food product, so that foods to be frozen should be of the highest quality and proper methods of freezing must be carefully followed.

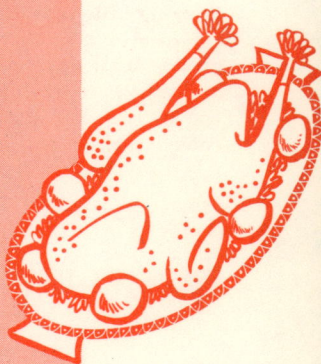

How to Freeze Ready-Cooked Foods

Freezing ready-cooked foods in advance of their need saves times. Cook more than is needed at one meal, for instance, and freeze what is left to use at some future date. Much of the food for holiday meals or dinner parties can be prepared, cooked, and frozen a week, a month or even more in advance, thus eliminating last-minute confusion and clutter in the kitchen. Frozen food needs only to be reheated or refreshed when wanted.

Practically every cooked food that is commonly used has been tested for freezing. Some frozen cooked foods are far more satisfactory than others. In this book, we are giving directions for freezing only those cooked foods which retain a high quality of flavor, texture, and general appearance after freezing and which represent a substantial saving in time for the homemaker when cooked and frozen in advance.

Three Important Things to Remember

1. The quality of food to be frozen should be top notch. Freezing may slightly improve the flavor of some foods, but it never makes a high-quality product out of inferior food. Don't waste valuable freezer space on ready-cooked foods that do not freeze well or are below standard quality.

2. Ready-cooked foods must be packaged properly. Like all other foods to be frozen, ready-cooked foods must be stored in moisture-vapor-proof containers or wrapping materials. Particular care must be taken so moisture will not evaporate, causing the foods to lose flavor and texture.

3. Follow reheating or refreshing procedures given on chart. This is most important in retaining original flavor and texture of food.

How to Freeze Breads
. . . Yeast and Baking Powder

Breads which are most satisfactory for freezing are:
Yeast Breads—white and whole wheat
Yeast Rolls—clover leaf, Parker
    House, cinnamon, tea rolls
Baking Powder Nut Bread
Steamed Brown Bread
Swedish Tea Ring

All these are baked before freezing, except brown bread which is steamed. All bread must be cooled to room temperature before freezing.

Swedish tea ring, pancakes, and waffles are particularly nice for Sunday morning breakfast, or any morning for that matter, and will reheat while the rest of the breakfast is being prepared.

If the family is small, yet enjoys homemade bread, a four-loaf recipe may be made and two or three loaves frozen. When reheated, it tastes exactly like freshly baked bread.

Frozen rolls always make a hit with the family or guests because two or three kinds may be frozen in a single bag or carton, which provides a nice variety for the meal. It is impossible to tell them from freshly baked rolls.

Use your favorite recipe for any of these breads. Nut bread is excellent for sandwiches or slicing for any occasion.

The chart will guide you as to packaging, freezing, and reheating.

Breads are packaged in a variety of ways.
Many types of breads are easily frozen.

PACKAGING, STORING AND REHEATING BREADS AND ROLLS

FOOD	SIZE OF PACKAGE	HOW PACKAGED	STORAGE TIME	HOW TO REHEAT
Yeast Bread	One loaf		Not to exceed six months	Thaw at room temperature for 1 hour, then warm in preheated 300°F. oven 10 to 15 minutes. OR, remove from wrappings, reheat unthawed bread in preheated 300°F. oven 25 to 30 minutes.
Steamed Brown Bread	According to size of family		Not to exceed six months	Thaw at room temperature for 1 hour or longer, then reheat in oven in wrappings for 15 to 20 minutes at 300° F.
Baking Powder Biscuits	As desired	Freezer-weight aluminum foil is ideal for packaging all breads and rolls. Can be placed directly in oven for heating without removing wrapping.	Not over six months	In foil for 30 to 40 minutes in 375°F. oven.
Swedish Tea Ring	One, usually. If two are wrapped together, separate with sheet of polyethylene or waxed paper		Not to exceed four months	Unwrap. One half hour on baking sheet in 350°F. oven.
Yeast Rolls	One or two dozen, assorted		Not to exceed six months	In foil for 30 to 40 minutes in 375°F. oven.
Nut Bread	One loaf		Not to exceed four months	Thaw at room temperature for 3 hours.
Pancakes Waffles	According to size of family	Separate by waxed paper	Not over two months	Remove wrapping. Reheat in automatic toaster set on "light" degree. Put through toasting twice to heat thoroughly.

If polyethylene laminated to aluminum foil is used for packaging, transfer bread or rolls to household foil or paper bag for reheating.

How to Freeze Canapés and Sandwiches

Canapés may be made a couple of weeks in advance and frozen . . . a great last-minute timesaver. Not all canapés freeze successfully, but those that do are delicious.

Freeze a quantity of sandwiches, weeks in advance, when the filling is fresh.

To prepare: Butter the bread and spread with filling or slices of meat or poultry. Wrap individual sandwiches in polyethylene or aluminum foil and freeze.

To serve: Thaw at room temperature or you can place the sandwiches still frozen in the lunch boxes. They will be thawed and deliciously fresh by lunchtime.

How to Serve Canapés

Remove canapés from freezer half an hour before needed, place on serving tray and allow to thaw at room temperature. Toasted canapés are particularly satisfactory both in flavor and texture. They remain crisp for two hours or longer after opening.

HOW TO MAKE CANAPÉS FOR FREEZING

Before starting to make canapés, remove the butter from the refrigerator and work it to a creamy consistency. This saves time and butter.

The bread must be cut very thin. Use a claw slicer, especially made for cutting ready-cut bread into two slices. Or, hold left hand gently over slice of bread placed flat on breadboard, and cut through with sharp knife. Bread used should be at least 24 hours old, 48 hours is better, as older bread cuts and toasts better than fresh. After bread is sliced, remove crusts which can be used for breadcrumbs.

Butter bread lightly on one side. Cut in strips 1 inch wide by 1½ inches in length. Place buttered rectangles on cooky sheet, turn oven to 250°F. and toast until golden brown. Watch toasting process with great care or bread will become too brown. If you prefer, bread may be toasted by using the broiler. Watch it carefully.

Add filling—recipes given. Place canapés on tray or cooky sheet and freeze. Place an assorted variety in a box— about 2 dozen is a satisfactory number. Seal and mark box.

CANAPÉ RECIPES for FREEZING

CHEESE CUP CANAPÉS

1 large package cream cheese
1 tablespoon onion juice
1 teaspoon Worcestershire sauce
2 egg yolks
Salt and pepper
½ teaspoon horseradish (optional)

To Prepare Filling: Allow cream cheese to remain at room temperature until it is easy to handle. Mix all ingredients together until well blended. Place in hollow bread cups.

To Prepare Bread Cups: Use unsliced bread. Cut in slices ¾- to 1-inch thick. Cut each slice into 4 equal parts and remove crusts.

Trim corners to make each piece round (this is easier than cutting each piece with a round cutter). Scoop out center of bread with a sharp knife . . . being careful not to cut through bottom of bread.

Brush entire surface, lightly, with melted butter. Fill bread cup with cheese filling.

Wrap carefully in aluminum foil and freeze.

Or, you may prefer to freeze cheese cups unwrapped on a pastry rack. Be sure, however, to wrap them as soon as they are frozen. Do not keep over two months.

To serve: Remove wrapping and place cheese cups on a baking sheet.

Let stand at room temperature 20 to 30 minutes.

Place in preheated hot oven (425°F.) and bake for 5 to 6 minutes. Serve piping hot.

HAM CANAPÉS

¼ pound processed cheese, grated
¼ cup deviled ham spread
2 tablespoons cornstarch
¼ teaspoon Ac'cent
6 tablespoons enriched flour
½ teaspoon Worcestershire sauce

Mix all ingredients thoroughly. Pinch off bits and shape into balls about ½ inch in diameter. Place on pastry rack and freeze.

Wrap as soon as frozen in aluminum foil and place in polyethylene bags. Do not keep over two months.

To serve: Unwrap and place canapés on a baking sheet. Allow to stand on sheet 20 minutes. Bake 10 minutes in a preheated hot oven (400°F.). Serve hot.

CHEESE WAFERS

½ pound American cheese, grated
¼ pound butter or margarine
½ cup enriched flour
1 teaspoon salt
Few grains red pepper

Cream cheese and butter together. Add flour, salt, and red pepper (be careful not to use too much red pepper). Mix well.

Place in refrigerator to chill as mixture may be too soft to handle. Then shape into roll (or rolls).

Wrap in aluminum foil and freeze immediately. Do not keep over two months.

To serve: Unwrap rolls and leave at room temperature 20 to 30 minutes. Slice thin.

Bake on a lightly greased cooky sheet from 10 to 15 minutes in a preheated moderate oven (375°F.). Serve hot or cold.

These may be sliced and baked, then frozen.

PAPRIKA CHEESE ROLL

½ pound sharp Cheddar cheese
½ pound pimiento brick cheese
2 3-ounce packages cream cheese
½ teaspoon Tabasco sauce
1 tablespoon Worcestershire sauce
1 teaspoon minced onion
½ clove garlic, finely minced
Mayonnaise to moisten
Paprika

Put Cheddar cheese and pimiento cheese through food chopper. Add cream cheese and seasonings. Blend well. Add just enough mayonnaise to moisten so roll is easily handled. Generously sprinkle a sheet of waxed paper with paprika. Shape cheese into two rolls and roll over paprika. Wrap in aluminum foil. Freeze immediately. Do not keep over two months.

To serve: Remove rolls from freezer and let stand at room temperature for 30 minutes. Slice and serve on canapé tray.

ROLLED CANAPÉS

Lightly butter a slice of bread from which the crusts have been removed.

Spread with filling such as deviled ham, cream cheese, or any kind of finely ground meat, fish, or egg.

Roll as for jelly roll. Seal edges securely by overlapping edges of bread, and pressing lightly with fingers.

Wrap in a slightly dampened tea towel and allow to stand for ½ hour. Cut in ½-inch slices.

SWEET PICKLE SLICES

Lightly butter a thin slice of bread, from which crusts have been removed. Then cover with a thin coating of cream cheese moistened with cream.

Wrap the bread around a whole 3-inch sweet pickle, making sure the edges of the bread are well overlapped and sealed.

Place in a slightly dampened tea towel for about 30 minutes.

Next slice through the pickle in ½-inch slices.

How to Freeze Cakes and Cookies

Frosted cakes should be frozen before wrapping for storage.

CAKES

Cakes may be frozen either frosted or unfrosted, as preferred. Both are satisfactory. While the uncooked batter may be successfully frozen, we prefer to freeze the cake after it has been baked. Saves considerable time when the cake is needed.

Also does not tie up the cake pans, because a piece of cardboard covered with polyethylene or aluminum foil can be used to support the cake.

Angel Food Cakes, and any of the other air-leavened cakes such as sunshine and lemon sponge, freeze beautifully. There is little, if any, change in texture of the cakes after freezing.

Butter Cakes also freeze well, though the texture may become a little finer and the cake more firm.

Fruit Cakes definitely improve with freezing. May be made well in advance of need. Fruit cakes which have been frozen do not crumble when sliced after they are thawed.

Frosted Cakes should be frozen before wrapping to prevent damaging the soft icing.

Bake cake, frost it, put in freezing compartment for a couple of hours, then wrap. This is particularly advisable for special birthday cakes with ornamental decorations.

Iced cakes must be unwrapped immediately after removing from freezer to prevent frosting from sticking to wrapping.

Unfrosted Layer Cakes should be separated by a round of polyethylene between each layer before wrapping and freezing. Or, layers may be wrapped separately.

Frostings That Are Excellent for Freezing

BUTTER FROSTING

4 tablespoons butter or margarine
3 cups sifted confectioners' sugar
3 tablespoons top milk (or cream)
1/2 teaspoon vanilla

Let butter stand at room temperature until softened.

Sift confectioners' sugar. Cream butter and sugar. Add top milk and vanilla. Beat well.

Makes enough frosting to generously frost an 8-inch layer cake.

CHOCOLATE FROSTING

3 squares (3 ounces) unsweetened chocolate
2 cups sifted confectioners' sugar
3 tablespoons hot water
3 egg yolks (freeze whites for other use)
4 tablespoons butter or margarine
1 teaspoon vanilla

Melt chocolate. Add sugar and hot water. Beat well (use electric mixer, if possible).

Beat in egg yolks one at a time, beating well after each addition.

Add butter, a tablespoonful at a time. Add vanilla. Continue to beat until butter is well blended and icing thoroughly mixed.

Makes enough to frost generously an 8-inch layer cake.

COOKIES

Some cookies freeze better than others. Cookies containing cereals such as corn flakes and bran do not freeze to advantage. Rich cookies such as sand tarts, sour cream cookies, or rich butter cookies, freeze satisfactorily.

However, there is little point in freezing baked cookies. Cooky dough may be kept in the refrigerator and cookies quickly baked as needed.

It is wiser to save freezer space for those foods which, when frozen, save time and energy for the homemaker.

PACKAGING, STORING AND THAWING CAKES AND COOKIES

FOOD	HOW PACKAGED	STORAGE TIME	HOW TO THAW
Plain Layer Cake, Iced		Not to exceed four months	Remove wrappings, let stand at room temperature 2 hours.
Chocolate Cake, Iced		Not to exceed four months	Remove wrappings, let stand at room temperature 2 hours.
Angel Food, Sunshine, Sponge Cake	Polyethylene laminated to aluminum foil, aluminum foil, or polyethylene bags are excellent for all packaging of cakes and cookies.	Six to eight months	Remove wrappings, let stand at room temperature 2 hours.
Fruit Cake		One year	Thaw in wrappings. Requires about 2 hours for 2 pounds of cake.
Baked Cookies		Two months	Remove wrappings, let stand at room temperature for 1/2 hour.

How to Freeze Pies and Pastries

Pies may be wrapped and frozen either before or after baking.

It is almost impossible to tell frozen pies from freshly baked pies.

You may freeze pies before or after baking. The majority of taste testers at the Institute voted for pies frozen *after* baking. When properly thawed, it is almost impossible to tell them from freshly baked pies.

Not all pies freeze to advantage. Mince pies and pies made of fruit or berries are most satisfactory. Double-crust pies freeze best. It is not worth the effort or storage space to attempt to freeze pies with meringue.

In making berry pies, it is essential to add extra thickening, since freezing develops more juice in the fruit. Otherwise, the pies will be too "runny." See recipes for fillings.

Such fruits as apples, peaches, and apricots do not generally require a great deal of thickening. However, especially in the case of apples, it is necessary to judge whether the fruit is juicy or dry and to add thickening accordingly. Even with the juiciest fruits, 4 tablespoons of flour or cornstarch are sufficient.

If frozen fruit is used for pie, add same amount of thickening recommended for fresh fruit pie to be frozen.

How to Wrap: Pies may be wrapped in polyethylene and aluminum foil; in polyethylene and stockinette; or in laminated paper.

Recommended Storage Time: Unbaked fruit or berry pies may be stored for 2 months—unbaked mince pies for 4 months. Baked fruit or berry pies may be stored for 4 months—baked mince pies for 4 months.

How to Thaw: All *baked* frozen pies are thawed by placing them unwrapped in a preheated 375°F. oven for 45 minutes.

Thaw *unbaked* pies, unwrapped, in preheated 375° F. oven for 1 hour.

To keep top crust from becoming too brown, place a piece of aluminum foil or brown paper over pie the last 20 minutes of baking.

How to Make Pie Fillings from Frozen Fruit: Place frozen fruit in a saucepan. Break gently with a table fork. Start over low heat.

Mix sugar and flour (cornstarch, if used) together. When fruit begins to melt, add sugar mix. Stir with fork to avoid breaking fruit. Cook until thickened.

Be sure to cool fruit before placing filling in pie shell. Bake pie the usual length of time. Serve pie hot or cold.

Do not freeze pie baked with frozen fruit filling . . . the second freezing will cause additional loss of flavor and juice.

Recipes for Fillings Using Fresh or Frozen Fruit

APPLE PIE FILLING

3½ cups apples, sliced
1¼ cups sugar
4 tablespoons flour (maximum)

BLUEBERRY PIE FILLING

3 cups berries
⅔ to ¾ cup sugar
2 tablespoons flour and
   2 tablespoons cornstarch OR
   4 tablespoons flour

CHERRY PIE FILLING

3½ cups pitted fresh cherries
⅔ to ¾ cup sugar
2 tablespoons flour and
   2 tablespoons cornstarch OR
   4 tablespoons flour

GOOSEBERRY PIE FILLING

4 cups berries
4 tablespoons cornstarch (or flour)
1½ cups sugar
2 tablespoons water

MINCE PIE FILLING

Follow your regular recipe. No extra thickening is required.

PEACH PIE FILLING

3½ cups peaches
¾ cup sugar
4 tablespoons flour (maximum)

RHUBARB PIE FILLING

3½ cups rhubarb
1½ cups sugar
2 tablespoons flour and
   2 tablespoons cornstarch OR
   4 tablespoons flour

How to Freeze Other Desserts

Treat Time—Any Time with
Food Freezer

You will find your home freezer can be a tremendous convenience in making desserts that will please your family and guests. You can prepare and freeze a wide variety of desserts at your leisure and use them when time is the most scarce commodity in your household.

Listed are a few of our favorites at the Institute, together with our tested recipes. Many of your own favorite recipes can also be frozen with great success.

Remember that while frozen desserts keep in good condition for two or three months, except in rare cases, it is not advisable to keep them longer.

FAVORITE FROZEN
DESSERT RECIPES

Ice Cream or Sherbet—either home-made or the commercial variety. Try the recipe for homemade economy ice cream given in this book or the variations.

Ice Cream Pie—use regulation pastry or graham cracker crust, fill with ice cream and freeze.

Another variation uses vanilla ice cream for crust, with contrasting flavor for filling. In making this variation, soften ice cream for crust sufficiently so that it can be flattened into regular pie pan, like any pastry.

Ice Cream Rolls—excellent surprise dessert in seasons when fresh berries are not available.

Chocolate Éclairs—filled with cream filling which tastes just like ice cream after it is frozen.

HOW TO MAKE FROZEN ÉCLAIRS

Make éclairs from a standard cream puff recipe (see Index). Shape oblong instead of round. Bake.

Cool. Fill with cream filling. Ice with chocolate icing.

Place on cooky sheet, and freeze until icing is firm.

Wrap and return to freezer for storage.

1. Batter is placed on pan or cookie sheet before baking.

Cream Filling for Éclairs:

2/3	cup sugar
5	tablespoons enriched flour
1/8	teaspoon salt
1/4	cup cold milk
3	egg yolks
1 1/2	cups scalded milk
1/2	teaspoon vanilla
3	egg whites

Mix sugar, flour, and salt together with cold milk. To this, add the well beaten egg yolks.

Pour slowly into scalded milk.

(To scald milk, place saucepan on heating unit of range and turn control to high heat for about 3 minutes.) Turn control to low and cook, stirring while cooking, until the mixture is thick.

Add flavoring, cool. Fold in stiffly beaten egg whites.

For chocolate filling, fold in one square (1 ounce) melted chocolate.

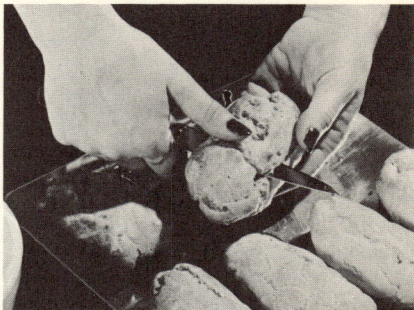

2. Cut tops off baked éclairs before filling with cream filling.

3. Replace tops on éclairs, cover with chocolate frosting.

ECONOMY ICE CREAM

2	eggs, separated
6	tablespoons sugar
4	tablespoons white corn syrup
1	cup top milk
1	cup coffee cream
1	teaspoon vanilla

Beat egg yolks, sugar, and corn syrup until thick and lemon-colored. Add milk, cream, and flavoring.

Pour into refrigerator dessert tray. Freeze until firm.

Remove to chilled bowl; add the unbeaten egg whites and beat until fluffy.

Package in tub or rigid carton and return to freezer. Serves 5.

Variations of Economy Ice Cream

Chocolate: Cook 2 ounces (2 squares) shaved chocolate with the sugar and milk of master recipe, stirring constantly until chocolate is melted.

Chill, add 1 teaspoon vanilla, then proceed as in master recipe.

Strawberry: Substitute 1 cup finely sieved strawberries for 1 cup of milk. Add 1/4 cup sugar. Combine as in master recipe.

STRAWBERRY ICE CREAM ROLL

3   eggs
1   cup sugar
1   cup cold water
¼   cup enriched flour
2   teaspoons baking powder
¼   teaspoon salt
1   teaspoon vanilla
Powdered sugar
1   quart vanilla ice cream
1½ cups sliced fresh strawberries

Beat eggs and sugar together until lemon colored. Add cold water and sifted dry ingredients. Add vanilla.

Bake in sheet pan 10 x 15 inches in hot oven (425°F.) 12 to 15 minutes.

Place tea towel on table, cover with waxed paper, sprinkle with powdered sugar.

Turn hot cake on waxed paper, cut off crisp edges of cake.

Hold paper and towel firmly, roll cake while hot. Cool.

Combine ice cream with berries, place in dessert tray and freeze until firm enough to spread without melting.

Unroll cake when cool and spread with ice cream and strawberry mixture. Roll up. Wrap and freeze.

Variations for Ice Cream Roll: Raspberries or peaches may be substituted for the strawberries. Also you may choose other flavors of ice cream and serve the ice cream roll with a sauce.

CRANBERRY SHERBET

1   pound cranberries
3   cups water
1½ cups sugar
1   tablespoon (1 envelope) unflavored gelatin
¼   cup cold water
Juice of 1½ lemons and orange juice
      to make 1 cup
2   egg whites

Cook cranberries with 3 cups water until berries are tender.

Strain through purée strainer, then add sugar and stir until sugar is dissolved.

To this hot mixture, add gelatin, which has been softened in ¼ cup cold water. Combine with fruit juices.

Allow to cool, pour into refrigerator tray and freeze almost to firm stage. Set control at "coldest."

Place unbeaten egg whites in a large bowl, then add nearly frozen sherbet. Beat until light and fluffy.

Return to refrigerator tray and finish freezing until firm.

Package in cartons and store in freezer.

PACKAGING, STORING, SERVING FROZEN DESSERTS

FOOD	HOW WRAPPED	STORAGE TIME	HOW TO SERVE
Eclairs	Polyethylene bag or wrapped individually in polyethylene or aluminum foil	Three months	Unwrap. Let stand 20 minutes at room temperature. Serve.
Homemade Ice Cream . . . or prepared in store carton	Rigid containers	One month	Thaw 10-15 minutes at room temperature.
Ice Cream Rolls	Polyethylene or aluminum foil	One month	Transfer from Freezer to Main Food Compartment of refrigerator for 1 hour or leave at room temperature for 15 minutes.

How to Freeze Ready-Cooked Poultry

Ready-Cooked Chicken from the Freezer

Meals can be quickly prepared when your food freezer has a supply of ready-cooked easy-to-warm dishes. Chicken pie and chicken à la king are particularly good and make excellent use of leftover chicken or turkey.

CHICKEN Ā LA KING

1	cup fresh mushrooms or 14-ounce can, sliced and drained
3	tablespoons chicken fat, butter, or margarine
4	tablespoons flour
1	cup chicken stock or milk
1	cup thin cream or top milk
1½	cups cooked chicken, cubed
1	whole canned pimiento, cut in strips
½	teaspoon salt
⅛	teaspoon pepper

Cook fresh mushrooms in fat about 4 minutes. (If canned mushrooms are used, they will be added later with chicken and pimiento.)

Add flour to fat and mushrooms and blend well. Add stock and cream or top milk.

Cook on low heat until thick, stirring constantly.

Add chicken (mushrooms, if canned), pimiento, seasonings.

Cool before packaging and place in freezer. Serves 5.

How to Package: Glass jars made for freezing, polyethylene bags, or rigid containers.

Storage Time: 6 to 8 months.

How to Reheat: If in glass jars, place jars in cold water until chicken mixture is soft enough to remove.

Cook in covered saucepan on low heat for 45 minutes to one hour, stirring occasionally.

In other containers, empty mixture at once into covered saucepan. Heat on low heat for about one hour.

CHICKEN OR TURKEY PIE

Use your favorite recipe. Place mixture into casserole or oblong dish. Cover dish with rich pastry, pressing it firmly to edges . . . or use rich biscuit dough, cut in rounds or squares.

For Flakier Crust: Roll pastry to desired thickness. Place casserole to be used, upside down, on top of pastry. Cut around the pastry with a knife. Perforate top of pastry with a table fork.

Now, carefully place pastry on a pastry rack (or cooky sheet) and bake about 10 minutes in 425°F. oven.

Do not let it become too brown. Cool.

Carefully place baked pastry on top of cooled chicken mixture in casserole. Wrap with aluminum foil and freeze.

Chicken or turkey pie may be baked before freezing, or frozen with unbaked topping. If baked first, cool before wrapping.

How to Package: Aluminum foil or polyethylene bags.

Storage Time: 4 months maximum.

How to Reheat: Do not thaw before reheating.

Remove wrapping and heat in 350°F. oven for about one hour.

Use 400°F. oven if pastry has unbaked topping.

How to Freeze Ready-Cooked Vegetables

There are only a few ready-cooked vegetables which freeze satisfactorily. Probably the two cooked vegetables which freeze to advantage, and actually improve after being frozen, are baked beans and candied sweet potatoes.

BAKED BEANS

Use your favorite recipe and be sure to cool beans before packaging.

How to Package: Glass jars suitable for freezing, polyethylene bags, or rigid cartons.

Storage Time: One year maximum.

How to Reheat: Remove from package and place in covered saucepan.

Heat on low heat for $1\frac{1}{2}$ hours or use a covered casserole in 350°F. oven for $1\frac{1}{2}$ hours.

CANDIED SWEET POTATOES

Select large, well shaped sweet potatoes . . . Nancy Hall or Puerto Rico varieties are the best to use.

Bake in 350°F. oven until done. This takes from 1 to $1\frac{1}{2}$ hours, depending upon the size of the sweet potato.

After the potato is baked, peel carefully and cut in halves or quarters, again depending on the size of the potato. Each slice should be at least $\frac{1}{2}$ inch thick.

Dip sliced sweet potato in lemon juice. Roll in granulated sugar.

How to Package: Package flat, with layers of waxed paper between each layer of potatoes. Wrap in aluminum foil.

Storage Time: Four months.

How to Reheat: Remove from wrappings. Spread in shallow pan. Heat for 30 minutes in 325°F. oven.

FRENCH FRIED POTATOES

Use your favorite recipe.

How to Package: Package in polyethylene bags.

Storage Time: Four to six weeks.

How to Reheat: Unwrap package. Spread frozen potatoes, in single layer, in shallow pan.

Place in preheated 400°F. oven. After 10 minutes, stir potatoes. Heat 10 minutes longer. Salt. Serve.

How to Freeze Ready-Cooked Meats

From the freezer: a complete company dinner in minutes.

Meats which require long, slow cooking, such as stews and meat sauces, can be frozen satisfactorily. However, cool all meat dishes before freezing. Partially cool in the kettle in which it was cooked and finish cooling mixture in the refrigerator.

Tests indicate that fried meats, such as steaks, chops, or fried poultry, do not freeze satisfactorily.

EXCELLENT FOR FREEZING

BEEF STEW

Use your favorite recipe, omitting the potatoes.

How to Package: Glass jars or casseroles suitable for freezing, polyethylene bags, rigid containers.

Storage Time: Not over 6 months.

How to Reheat: If packaged in glass jars, set jars in cold water until stew is soft enough to remove.

Place in covered saucepan. Add potatoes and heat on low heat or in casserole in 350°F. oven for one hour.

Chili Con Carne, Meat Sauce for Spaghetti and Chop Suey: Use your favorite recipe and follow same directions as for beef stew.

BAKED HAM

Use your favorite recipe for baking ham. Always remove ham from bone before freezing. Saves freezer space.

How to Package: Freezer foil, polyethylene or laminated aluminum foil.

Storage Time: Not over 3 months.

How to Reheat: Allow 20 minutes per pound in preheated 350°F. oven.

MARZETTI

4 ounces noodles
1½ quarts water
½ teaspoon salt

Bring salted water to rapid boil. Add noodles slowly so the water will maintain its rapid boil.

Cook uncovered, stirring occasionally. Cook until noodles are tender, about 10 to 15 minutes. Drain in a colander.

2 tablespoons shortening
1 pound ground beef
1 large onion, chopped fine
½ green pepper, chopped
1 8-ounce can mushrooms (stems and pieces)
1 teaspoon salt
¼ teaspoon black pepper
¼ teaspoon oregano
1 can condensed tomato soup
1 can tomato paste
⅓ cup water
1 tablespoon Worcestershire sauce
½ pound sharp cheese, grated

Melt shortening in skillet and brown beef. Add onion, green pepper, and mushrooms. Cook until tender. Add seasonings.

Combine tomato soup, tomato paste, water, and Worcestershire sauce.

Place a layer of noodles in a greased 3-quart casserole, then a layer of meat. Cover with sauce and half the cheese. Repeat layers and top with remainder of cheese.

Bake for 45 minutes in a preheated 375°F. oven. Cool thoroughly. Serves 4 to 5.

How to Package: Aluminum foil or polyethylene bag.

Storage Time: Not over 2 months.

How to Reheat: Unwrap casserole. Place casserole in 375°F. oven and heat for 45 minutes to one hour.

KEEP A FREEZER INVENTORY FILE

Know exactly what you have and when to use it. This can be done easily with a simple inventory kept on index cards, a separate card for each food. Note food name, quantity, cost, date frozen, and date of storage life limit. As food is used, note date and amount of withdrawal.

How to Freeze Ready-Cooked Soups

Soups with a milk base do not freeze satisfactorily. Vegetable, chicken, lentil and other dried legume soups are excellent when frozen. When making any of these soups which require long, slow cooking, make an extra amount and freeze whatever is not used immediately. Be sure to cool soups before starting to freeze them.

Clear broths (chicken, turkey, or beef) freeze satisfactory. Do not add noodles or rice when planning to freeze these broths . . . add when broth is reheating.

How to Package: When cool, soups may be poured into ice cube trays, frozen and cubes removed and packaged in polyethylene bags.

Or, package in glass jars suitable for freezing, polyethylene bags, or rigid cartons.

Storage Time: Not over 4 months.

How to Reheat: Remove from package. Heat in covered saucepan on low heat for 45 minutes to one hour.

Hint: Three of the frozen cubes will make one serving of soup when heated.

How to Freeze Fresh Vegetables

When to Gather or Buy Vegetables

Select only those which are in prime condition for freezing. In general, immature vegetables have not fully developed all their sweetness and flavor. Overripe vegetables will neither taste good nor keep satisfactorily. The best time to gather vegetables is in the cool of the morning when the dew is gone. Never pick vegetables at night and keep them in the refrigerator until the next day ... they lose that garden-fresh flavor.

If you do not raise your own vegetables, buy freshly picked ones from local gardens or nearby farms. The vegetables you buy are satisfactory for freezing only if you *arrange to get them within an hour or two after picking.* Vegetables which have stood longer will not be as tender, nutritive or well-flavored as garden-fresh ones. Freezing captures and preserves the flavor and goodness but it cannot improve them.

Frozen foods come from the freezer only as good as when they were frozen.

Speed Is Essential

Gather only as many vegetables as can be completely processed and placed in the freezer within two hours. The *"2 hours from vine to freezer"* rule is an excellent one to remember.

Wash, sort, scald, chill, drain, package, and freeze without wasting any time between steps.

Having all your supplies and materials ready before you begin is a big step toward accomplishing this "2-hour" rule.

Learn these steps, follow them closely and results will be excellent. Have all packaging materials ready before you start freezing. It saves valuable time.

1. Gather vegetables in the cool of morning, selecting the choice grades and only quantities that can be handled speedily.

2. Wash and sort vegetables carefully.

3. Scald according to directions for each vegetable.

4. Cool and drain quickly.

5. Pack in airtight containers.

6. Freeze at once.

7. Enter item in your freezer inventory file.

Which Vegetables to Select

Most vegetables can be frozen satisfactorily. Exceptions: salad greens, celery, radishes, and whole tomatoes. Certain varieties of vegetables freeze better than others. Directions for freezing specific vegetables rate varieties as to suitability for freezing. For success of freezing other varieties, consult your local seed company, county agent or State Agricultural College.

Wash and Sort Vegetables Carefully

Vegetables are prepared for freezing in much the same manner as for cooking. Wash carefully and thoroughly. While washing, sort for size and discard all inferior vegetables. For the best frozen vegetables, freeze only the choice fresh vegetables. Size-sorting of many vegetables (peas, beans, etc.) is important because you can obtain better uniformity.

Scald Vegetables Properly

Scalding is a must . . . never to be omitted! It retards enzymatic action, thus holds back the "growing process." Scalding "locks in" color, preserves flavor and saves vitamins so that, when served, the vegetable is as fresh as it was when taken from the garden.

Scald only one pound of any vegetable at a time. Live steam cannot penetrate evenly through larger amounts. Too many vegetables scalded at once may cause an inferior product.

Live Steam Scalding

This is the preferred method.

Necessary Equipment: Any large utensil with a tight-fittting cover, a trivet or rack, and a fine-mesh wire basket. If a wire basket is not available, a colander with small perforations may be used. It must not interfere with the cover's tight fit. If neither basket nor colander is available, loosely tie the vegetables in cheesecloth.

Procedure: Place rack in utensil. Add sufficient water to keep the utensil from boiling dry during scalding, but not enough to touch the vegetables.

Keep this water boiling vigorously throughout the entire scalding period.

Place vegetables into basket. When water is boiling violently, set basket in utensil and cover at once. Start counting scalding time when the lid is replaced.

Water Bath Scalding

Necessary Equipment: Large utensil with tight-fitting lid, (deep well cooker in electric range is ideal), fine-mesh wire basket or cheesecloth.

Procedure: Boil at least a gallon of water in the cooker or utensil. Have water boiling briskly so that temperature will not drop when vegetables are added.

Place vegetables in wire basket or tie loosely in cheesecloth. Lower basket into rapidly boiling water and cover immediately.

Start counting scalding time from the moment vegetables are placed in the boiling water.

Cool and Drain Quickly

Quick, effective cooling makes better frozen products. Draining is also most important. Moisture clinging to the vegetables when they are packed will form ice crystals and make it difficult to separate frozen vegetables when ready to cook.

Necessary Equipment: Large pan or sink filled with ice water, clean dish towels or absorbent paper toweling.

Procedure: Immediately after scalding, cool vegetables quickly in ice water.

With small vegetables (peas, beans, etc.) leave vegetables in container used during scalding and immerse it in ice water. Move basket back and forth to speed the cooling.

Drain thoroughly by placing several thicknesses of absorbent toweling on a tray. Carefully spread the vegetables on toweling. Shake tray slightly to bring all sides of vegetables in contact with toweling.

Package in Convenient Quantities

Determine the size packages that will best suit your family's needs. For instance, a pint carton of vegetables will usually serve 3 large or 4 small portions. A quart carton will serve from 6 to 8 portions. Containers larger than pints and quarts are not recommended for average-sized families because they waste valuable freezer space. Also food not eaten at one meal may be wasted as it is never advisable to refreeze thawed vegetables.

If freezing for a family of two, freeze in one bag just enough to serve two persons and enclose several of these bags in a larger one. Mark number of smaller bags on outside of larger one.

Never Skimp on Packaging

Buy only packaging materials that are both moistureproof and vaporproof.

Glass freezing jars and outer cardboard cartons may be used over and over again.

Polyethylene bags may be washed and reused providing they are free from pricks and holes.

Plain tin cans, which can be sealed airtight, may also be used except for asparagus and New Zealand spinach, which require enamel or lacquer-lined cans.

Freezing always results in expansion of the food; therefore it is necessary to leave head space to allow for this expansion.

Pint cartons: $\frac{1}{2}$-inch head space.
Quart cartons: $\frac{3}{4}$-inch head space.
Glass jars: 1- to $1\frac{1}{2}$-inch head space.
Tin cans: 1-inch head space.

Seal Carefully

Be sure all packages are airtight!

To close polyethylene bags: Put food in polyethylene bag. Then, starting at the bottom, *gently* press all the air out the bag. When the top of the food is reached, twist the bag tightly several times. Loop the top of the bag over and secure tightly with either a piece of string or an acetate band. Rubber bands do not hold at low temperatures.

Freeze at Once

When packages are filled, sealed and labeled, place them immediately in the freezer. If this is not practical, place packages in freezer compartment of refrigerator until you are ready to load the freezer.

Never allow filled packages to stand at room temperature.

A Hint for Mothers of Small Children

When sorting vegetables such as green beans, peas, carrots, or beets, you will find some that are too mature for freezing. Set these aside until after you have frozen the rest. These can be cooked, puréed, frozen, and used later for the baby and young children.

Here's how it's done: Steam the vegetable until it is well cooked . . . not overcooked. Purée in an electric food blender or by forcing through a food mill. Thoroughly cool the puréed vegetable.

After vegetable is cool, pour into refrigerator ice cube tray with the dividers in place. Freeze. When cubes are firmly frozen, remove them from the tray and package one or two cubes, enough for an individual serving, in small polyethylene bags.

To serve: Heat cubes in a covered saucepan. Start with low heat until food is thawed.

How to Prepare Vegetables for Freezing

Scald not more than one pound of any vegetable at one time.

Cool vegetable quickly by immersing in ice water.

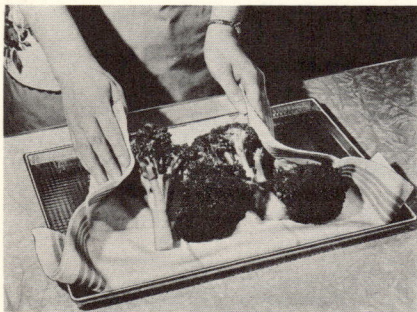

Drain vegetable thoroughly on absorbent toweling.

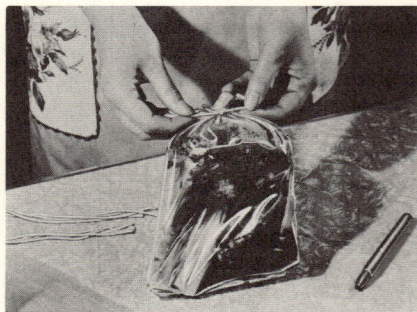

Package and gently force out any air pockets. Seal securely. Freeze immediately.

ASPARAGUS

(Do not use iron utensil . . . will discolor asparagus.)

Varieties suitable for freezing: excellent—Mary Washington and Martha Washington. 1½ pounds yield approximately 1 pint.

Scalding time:

Small Spears
By steam, 5 minutes.
By boiling water, 3 minutes.

Large Spears
By steam, 6 minutes.
By boiling water, 4 minutes.
Wash thoroughly. Discard all woody portions. Sort by size of butt end.

Cut stalks correct length to fit polyethylene bag—usually about 5 inches for quart-sized bag.

If you are planning to wrap asparagus in freezer foil, it is not necessary to cut all stalks a specific length.

Remove all scales by slipping sharp knife under scale and snipping off. Sand collects under these scales. Also, sweetness of frozen product is much improved if scales are removed. Do not bruise stem.

When scalding, stand asparagus with tips up. Cool and drain. Pack stalks parallel in polyethylene bags or freezer foil, placing heads in opposite directions. Freeze at once.

BEANS, GREEN SNAP OR YELLOW WAX

(Do not use iron utensil ... will discolor beans.)

Varieties suitable for freezing: Green snap, excellent—Tendergreen, Stringless Green Pod, Kentucky Wonder. Yellow wax, fair—consult your local seed man. 2/3 to 1 pound yields approximately 1 pint.

Scalding time:

By steam, 5 minutes.
By boiling water, 3 minutes.

Wash thoroughly. Sort for size. Remove the stem end. Leave blossom end on, it is particularly rich in vitamins and minerals.

For quick preparation, grasp as many beans as can be easily held in one hand. With small, sharp knife held in other hand, snip off stem end. Cut in 1-inch pieces, or in French style.

Do not scald small and large beans together. Cool, drain, pack and freeze. Package in polyethylene bags.

BEANS, LIMA

Varieties suitable for freezing: excellent—Fordhook (bush) and King of the Garden (pole). 2 to 2½ pounds in pods yield approximately 1 pint.

Scalding time:

Baby Lima Beans
By steam, 5 minutes.
By boiling water, 3 minutes.

Large Fordhook
By steam, 6 minutes.
By boiling water, 4 minutes.

Wash pods, shell beans. Sort for size. Overmatured beans are not recommended for freezing. Scald, cool and drain. Package in polyethylene bags. Freeze.

Lima beans still in their pods may be scalded in boiling water for 1 minute longer than shelled beans. Then cool, shell, drain, sort and package.

BEETS

Variety suitable for freezing: good—Detroit Dark Red. 1¼ pounds, without tops, yield approximately 1 pint.

Scalding time:

Young tender beets, up to 1½ inches in diameter, 3 minutes submerged in boiling water. **All other beets,** cook until tender.

Wash thoroughly before scalding or cooking. Immediately after scalding, cool beets and remove skin.

Small beets may be frozen whole. Large beets may be sliced, diced or quartered.

Cool, drain on absorbent paper toweling, pack in polyethylene bags. Freeze.

BROCCOLI

Variety suitable for freezing: excellent—Italian Green Sprouting. 2 pounds yield approximately 1 pint.

Scalding time:

Medium-Sized Pieces
By steam, 5 minutes.
By boiling water, 3 minutes.

Large Pieces
By steam, 6 minutes.
By boiling water, 5 minutes.

Select compact heads of uniform color. Immerse broccoli for ½ hour in a solution of salt water to remove any insects. Use 1 cup salt to 1 gallon of water. Wash carefully.

Remove woody portions. Separate heads in convenient size for packaging.

Scald, cool and drain. Package in freezer foil or polyethylene bags. Freeze.

BRUSSELS SPROUTS

Variety suitable for freezing: excellent—Long Island Improved. 1½ pounds yield approximately 1 pint.

Scalding time:

By steam, 5 minutes.
By boiling water, 4 minutes.

. Sprouts should be firm and dark green in color.

Immerse in salt water as for broccoli. Remove stem. If wilted, remove the outer leaves.

Scald, cool, drain, package in polyethylene bags. Freeze. Allow 5 to 6 sprouts to a serving.

CARROTS

Varieties suitable for freezing: excellent—Chantenay, Red Cored, Half Long. 1¼ to 1½ pounds yield approximately 1 pint.

Scalding time:

Sliced

By steam, 4 minutes.
By boiling water, 2 minutes.

Whole

By steam, 5 minutes.
By boiling water, 3 minutes.

Select only young, small carrots. Never attempt to freeze carrots which have grown to full maturity.

Wash and scrape. Sort for size. Scald, cool, drain and package in polyethylene bags.

Alternate top and tip of whole carrots when packaging. Package. Freeze.

CAULIFLOWER

Variety suitable for freezing: good—Snowball. 1 pound yields approximately 1 pint.

Scalding time:

By steam, 4 minutes.
By boiling water, 3 minutes.

Select compact, tender white heads. Trim and cut in pieces about 1 inch thick, or break small flowerets in medium-sized pieces.

Sometimes it is necessary to immerse cauliflower in a salt solution (as. for broccoli) to remove insects.

Allow 5 to 6 medium pieces for each serving.

Scald, cool, drain and package in polyethylene bags. Remove as much air as possible from the package. Freeze.

CORN ON THE COB

(Follow directions and corn will be just like fresh-picked.)

Varieties suitable for freezing: excellent—Golden Bantam Hybrids, Golden Cross Bantam, Cherokee, DeKalb Hybrid.

Scalding time:

By boiling water—ears 1½ to 2 inches at base, 8 minutes.
Larger ears require 11 minutes.

Select corn with kernels well formed, while milk is thin and sweet.

With sharp knife, cut a section about ½ inch wide from both ends. Husks will come off easier. Husk corn and remove silk.

If necessary, wash corn. Sort for size.

Scald for length of time indicated and cool in ice water the same length of time. Drain.

Package in freezer foil or polyethylene bags according to your family's serving needs . . . with not more than 6 ears to a package. Freeze.

CORN, WHOLE KERNEL

Varieties suitable for freezing: Same as corn on the cob. 6 ears yield approximately 1 pint when cut from cob.

Scalding time:

Same as for corn on the cob.

Scald corn. Cool. To remove kernels from cob: Impale base end of cob on large nail driven through a board.

Place in flat dish or on two thicknesses of waxed paper.

Cut corn from cob, holding knife not flat but at a sharp angle.

Examine kernels carefully, removing any bits of silk. Package in polyethylene bags. Freeze.

EGGPLANT

Variety suitable for freezing: good—Black Beauty. 1½ to 2 pounds yield approximately 1 pint.

Scalding time:

By steam, 5 minutes.
By boiling water, 4 minutes.

Select mature eggplant. Peel and cut into about 1/2-inch slices.

If boiling water method of scalding is used, add 4 1/2 teaspoons pure citric acid to 1 gallon of water.

If steam method is used, add same amount of citric acid, or 3 tablespoons lemon juice, to cooling water.

Put through another cold water rinse. Drain.

Place waxed paper between each slice. Package in polyethylene bags or aluminum foil. Freeze.

GREENS

(Spinach, Kale, Swiss Chard, Mustard Greens, and Turnip Tops)

Varieties suitable for freezing: Spinach, good—King of Denmark. Kale, excellent—Dwarf Green Curled. Swiss chard, excellent—Fordhook. Mustard, good—Mammoth. 1 to 1 1/2 pounds yield approximately 1 pint.

Spinach, Kale, Swiss Chard

Scalding time:

By steam, 2 1/2 minutes. Best method: Use wire basket, if possible.
By boiling water, 2 minutes.

Mustard Greens and Turnip Tops

Scalding time:

By steam, 3 to 3 1/2 minutes.
By boiling water, 2 minutes.

Use 2 gallons of water for each pound of greens.

Select young, tender greens. Discard all bruised leaves and cut off stems before washing.

Wash through several waters. *Lift* leaves from one pan of water to the other . . . don't pour off water . . . it may leave sand on the leaves.

Scald only a small amount of greens at one time, and wire basket is preferable. This is particularly true of spinach. Drain.

Complete draining of spinach is impossible, some water will remain in leaves.

If these suggestions are followed, there will be little matting of greens. Do not use pressure when packing. Polyethylene bags are excellent for greens of all kinds. Freeze.

MUSHROOMS

Scalding time:

Button Size—Steam 3 minutes.

Medium Size—Steam 4 minutes.

Sliced—Steam 3 minutes.

Warning: Unless you are completely familiar with wild mushrooms and can accurately identify edible ones, never attempt to freeze them.

Mushrooms must be handled quickly to prevent blackening.

Wash thoroughly. Remove tough portion of stem. Scald, cool quickly and drain.

Package in polyethylene bags. Start freezing immediately to avoid darkening.

OKRA

Varieties suitable for freezing: good—Clemson Spineless, White Lightning. 1 1/2 pounds yield approximately 1 pint.

Scalding time:

Small to Medium Pods—Steam 2 minutes. This is the only method recommended for okra.

Select young, tender pods. Scrub thoroughly. Rinse.

Remove stem end but do not cut into seed section. Care in cutting prevents the sticky juice from oozing out.

Scald, cool and drain. Pack compactly in polyethylene bags . . . alternating top and tip ends. Freeze.

PEAS

Varieties suitable for freezing: Green, excellent—Thomas Laxton and Alderman. Field, very good—Crowder and Black Eye. 1 1/2 to 2 pounds yield approximately 1 pint.

Scalding time:

By steam, 3 minutes.
By boiling water, 1 minute.

Select peas that are tender and are not fully matured.

Wash pods before shelling. Discard all immature and wrinkled peas while shelling. If pods are very full and difficult to shell, plunge pods in boiling water for 1 minute, then cool at once in ice water.

Scalding the pods does not take the place of scalding the peas. Scald, cool, drain and package in polyethylene bags. Freeze at once.

PIMIENTOS AND GREEN PEPPERS

Varieties suitable for freezing: Pimientos, excellent—Perfection. Green peppers, very good—California Wonder.

Sliced or Diced: Do not scald! Wash carefully, remove stem end and seeds.

Slice or dice and package in small polyethylene bags in amounts you will use at one time. Several small bags may be packaged in a pint or quart carton. Freeze at once.

Halved for Stuffing: Cut green pepper in half, lengthwise. Remove stem end and seeds.

Scald in boiling water 2 minutes. Cool in ice water, drain well.

When packaging, separate halves with waxed paper, place in polyethylene bags. Freeze immediately.

SQUASH

Variety suitable for freezing: excellent—Yellow Summer. 1 pound yields approximately 1 pint.

Scalding time:

By steam, 3 minutes.

Select squash not fully matured. Outer skin should be easily punctured with fingernail.

Wash thoroughly. Use a vegetable brush to remove dirt lodged in crevices.

Remove stem end. Do not peel. Cut in 1/2- to 1-inch slices. Do not remove seeds.

Scald. Cool 1 1/2 to 2 minutes. To avoid longer soaking, use quantities of ice in the water.

Drain carefully. Package in polyethylene bags. Freeze.

SUCCOTASH

Prepare corn and lima beans as given under directions for each. Use baby beans only.

Steam corn first, and while it is cooling and being cut from cob, scald and cool the beans.

Mix together in equal portions. Package in polyethylene bags. Freeze.

HOW TO PREPARE FROZEN VEGETABLES FOR SERVING

All vegetables . . . *except* corn on the cob and eggplant . . . are best cooked from the frozen state.

Break frozen vegetables into 3 or 4 chunks before placing in pan. Add about 1/4 cup of water. Salt to taste.

Cook about 1/3 to 1/2 of the time recommended for fresh vegetables. Frozen vegetables are scalded before freezing, so need less cooking time.

Corn on the cob and eggplant should be thawed before cooking. Thaw at room temperature. Thawing requires about 20 minutes for eggplant; 2 hours for corn on the cob.

Cook corn in boiling water 4 to 5 minutes.

Prepare eggplant according to your favorite method.

Caution: Do not overcook vegetables . . . either frozen or fresh. Overcooking causes loss of color and flavor, as well as vitamins.

How to Freeze Fruits

Fruit shortcake in-a-jiffy from the freezer.

Fruits are especially easy to freeze, so allow ample space in your freezer for a complete variety. Most fruits have a high sugar content and, for best results, should be frozen quickly.

Which Fruits to Select

Most fruits, berries and melons can be frozen satisfactorily, but some freeze better than others. In the same manner, certain varieties of each fruit freeze better than others. Directions for freezing specific fruits rate varieties as to suitability for freezing. If in doubt about freezing certain fruits, consult your local nurseryman, county agent or State Agricultural College for further information.

Whole citrus fruits should not be frozen, but serving slices, sections and juices are delicious and easy to freeze. Red raspberries are delicious when frozen.

When to Gather Fruits

The ideal time to freeze most fruits is at the height of maturity. It is best to allow most fruits to reach this stage on the vine, bush, or tree. However, fruits like peaches, plums, and figs are apt to become soft on the plant and are easily bruised in handling. Gather such fruits in the "firm ripe" stage and store overnight . . . insures more even ripening and, with peaches, they are easier to peel.

Gather fruit in the cool of the morning. Sun-heated fruit may bruise excessively from handling and result in an inferior frozen product. Gather no more fruit than can be quickly prepared, packaged, and frozen at one time.

While speed of handling is not so critical with fruits as with vegetables, the shorter the holding time after gathering for most fruits, the better the frozen fruit will be.

Wash Fruit Thoroughly

This is one of the most important steps in preparing fruits for freezing. Low-growing fruits and all wild fruits should be washed twice or more to remove sand and dust.

Wash no more than one quart of small fruit (berries or cherries) at one time. This can be done in a colander, using a spray when possible. Never allow fruit to stand in water more than one minute as water-soaked fruit will not freeze successfully.

After washing, drain fruit thoroughly. Spread fruit carefully on a tray or large utility dish on which several thicknesses of absorbent paper toweling have been placed. If possible, set tray in refrigerator about one hour to cool and firm the fruit.

Stem Fruits Carefully

Never squeeze the stems off berries. The stems of raspberries, dewberries, and gooseberries may be lifted off with the fingers. Use a sharp knife to stem strawberries.

Peel Fruits Rapidly

Apples, apricots, peaches, nectarines, and pears oxidize and discolor rapidly after the skin is removed.

To prevent this, peel and slice fruit directly into a solution of 3 tablespoons lemon juice (or 3 tablespoons salt OR 4½ teaspoons citric acid) to each gallon of cold water.

Don't allow fruit to remain in solution longer than one minute, so do no more than one package at a time.

Rinse in cold water and drain before packaging. Then continue to peel, slice, and package until all fruit has been prepared.

Remove Seeds Carefully

Fruits with seeds (plums, prunes, peaches, apricots, and nectarines) must have the seed removed before freezing. Avoid bruising fruit.

Pulp

Fruit to be pulped (puréed) may be cooked before forcing through a purée strainer or electric food blender. Such fruits as strawberries, grapes, raspberries, peaches, and plums may be forced through purée strainer or food blender without cooking.

Sweeten Fruits Properly

Many fruits retain better flavor if sweetened before freezing. There are two methods of sweetening fruit: dry sugar method and syrup method.

DRY SUGAR METHOD

Method #1: After the fruit has been washed, drained, and cooled, carefully transfer fruit to a bowl. Sprinkle sugar over fruit. Sweeten one quart at a time to avoid bruising.

A clean flour sifter will give more even distribution of sugar.

To mix sugar through fruit, use wooden slotted spoon and gently lift fruit through sugar. Package at once.

Method #2: Wash, cool, and drain fruit. Fill package about ¼ full. Sprinkle in ¼ of sugar, about one or two tablespoons. Continue filling container in this way.

Container may be shaken occasionally to distribute sugar, but avoid pressure on container. Seal at once.

SYRUP METHOD

Syrup is the most satisfactory sweetening agent if fruit is to be used for sauce. Syrup is preferable for apricots, pears, and figs.

The simplest way to add the syrup to the fruit is to first fill the container with fruit and then add syrup to cover. Seal at once.

The syrup must always be cold before using . . . a good idea is to make the syrup a day in advance and store it in a covered container in the refrigerator.

SUGAR SYRUP

Add sugar to boiling water and cook until sugar is thoroughly dissolved.

The sweetness desired in the frozen fruit should govern the syrup to be used. See specific directions for recommended syrup with each particular fruit.

Very Thin: 1 cup sugar to 4 cups boiling water.

Thin: 1 cup sugar to 3 cups boiling water.

Medium: 1 cup sugar to 2 cups boiling water.

Heavy: 1 cup sugar to 1 cup boiling water.

Package Fruits Carefully

Polyethylene bags are excellent, but care should be taken when sealing and handling the bag before the fruit is frozen. Rigid cartons, tin cans (if lacquered inside), and special glass freezing jars may be used.

Containers must also be moisture-vaporproof because air leakage causes destruction of vitamins and minerals and also spoils the appearance of the fruit.

Package According to Use

Decide how the frozen fruit is to be used and then package the fresh fruit accordingly. For instance, fruits to be used for pies or jams need not be sweetened before freezing, with the exception of apricots and peaches which sometimes discolor unless sugar or syrup is added.

As a sauce, a pint carton of fruit will serve 3 or 4. A pint will make a skimpy 8-inch pie but a quart will make four generous individual shortcakes. But if used as a topping over ice cream, a pint of strawberries will serve 5 or 6.

Select package sizes that adequately take care of a meal, with no save-overs. Frozen fruits lose their flavor if left standing several hours after thawing. *Never refreeze fruit.*

Allow for Expansion and Seal Carefully

Package fruit firmly but do not use pressure or crush the fruit. If using a rigid container, there should be sufficient air space to allow for some expansion. Fill container to within 1/2 inch of top for dry sugar packs and 1/2 to 3/4 inch for syrup packs. Make packages airtight.

Label Clearly and Freeze at Once

After sugar or syrup has been added to fruit in container, package should be sealed, labeled clearly, and placed immediately on quick-freeze shelf with the sealed side up to prevent leakage. If this is not practical, place packages in freezer compartment of refrigerator until ready to load the freezer.

A Hint for Mothers of Small Children

When sorting fruits for freezing, use only those which are firm and ripe. Those which are overripe but still usable can be puréed for the baby and young children. Peaches, apples, apricots, plums, and pineapple are easy to purée and will save both time and money in the preparation of the children's meals.

How It's Done: Peel (or pare) the fruit and then cook thoroughly ... be careful not to overcook. You may want to add a bit of sugar as the fruit cooks. Then force it through a sieve or food mill or put it through an electric food blender. Cool thoroughly.

After the fruit is cool, pour into refrigerator ice cube tray with the dividers in place. Freeze. When cubes are firmly frozen, remove them from the tray and package one or two cubes, enough for an individual serving, in small polyethylene bags.

To serve: Let cubes stand at room temperature until suitable for serving.

A CAUTION FOR DIABETICS

If you must take sugar precautions when freezing fruits for your family, you'll want to set aside a certain proportion of the mature fruit and prepare it separately.

Among fruits which freeze well without sugar are: red raspberries, strawberries, pineapple, blackberries, and dewberries. Use the same procedure as for regular fruit freezing and **don't add sugar or syrup.**

A syrup may be made from Sucaryl, available at drugstores. Be sure to label packages carefully and make a separate entry in your freezer inventory file.

How to Prepare Fruits for Freezing

Wash fruit in cold running water or use a gentle spray.

Use a sharp knife and gently remove strawberry cap.

Drain fruit on tray with absorbent paper toweling.

Fruit may be sweetened by mixing with sugar before packaging.

Sugar may be added alternately with fruit as it is packaged.

Seal tightly by twisting polyethylene. Fasten with acetate bands.

APPLES FOR SAUCE

Varieties suitable for freezing: good—Baldwin, Greening, Northern Spy, and Yellow Transparent. 1¼ pounds yield approximately 1 pint.

Peel and core the apples. Cut into eighths. Place in saucepan and add only enough water to start the apples cooking. Bring to a quick boil. Reduce heat to simmer and cook about 10 minutes until apples are mushy. Add sugar to taste and stir.

Some apples cook to a fine mush without straining, but if straining is necessary, force the sauce through a purée strainer. Cool thoroughly. Package in polyethylene bags. Freeze.

APPLES FOR PIE

Varieties suitable for freezing: good—any high-acid variety. 1 pound yields about 1 pint.

Freeze enough in one container for a pie . . . a quart container holds apples for a 9-inch pie. *Do not freeze apples which have turned brown on the inside or have started to mold.*

Peel and core the apples. Cut into slices for pie. Apples discolor rapidly after the skin has been removed, so slice apples directly into a solution of 3 tablespoons lemon juice (or 3 tablespoons salt OR 4½ teaspoons citric acid) to 1 gallon cold water. Never allow apples to remain in solution more than one minute. Rinse in cold water before draining.

Place slices on a tray covered with several thicknesses of absorbent paper toweling. Place tray in refrigerator and allow to drain. Thorough draining before packaging makes slices easier to separate for making pies.

Immediately after draining, pack into polyethylene bags and freeze. Add sugar, if desired, in the proportion of 1 part sugar to 4 parts apples.

APRICOTS

Varieties suitable for freezing: good—any tree-ripened variety. ¾ to 1 pound yields approximately 1 pint.

With skins: Select firm, fully ripened fruit of bright apricot color, with no traces of green. Wash thoroughly. Remove stem. Cut in half and remove pit.

Dip pitted halves in a solution of 1 tablespoon lemon juice and 1 quart water. Drain by placing cut side down on a tray covered with several thicknesses of absorbent toweling.

Place in polyethylene bags or rigid containers. Cover with cold, medium syrup. Seal. Freeze at once.

Without skins (Preferred): Place about 20 apricots in a wire basket. Plunge into boiling water to cover for 1 minute. Remove and plunge into cold water to cover for 1 minute . . . or until cool.

Remove skin. Cut in half and remove pit. Dip pitted halves in a solution of 1 tablespoon lemon juice to 1 quart water. Drain by placing cut side down on a tray covered with several thicknesses of absorbent toweling.

Place in polyethylene bags or rigid containers. Cover with cold, medium syrup. Seal. Freeze at once.

BLACKBERRIES

Variety suitable for freezing: fair—Wild Eldorado. 1 quart berries yields about 1 quart frozen fruit.

Select firm, fully matured fruit. Immature blackberries, even though a good black in color, turn reddish black when frozen.

Wash carefully in cold water, never more than 1 quart of berries at a time. Gently move the berries through the water by hand, then lift them to a tray covered with several thicknesses of absorbent paper toweling. Spread them only one layer thick.

Place immediately in refrigerator to cool before packaging. If you wish to add sugar to berries, use the same method as for red raspberries. Package in polyethylene bags, seal and freeze.

For use as a sauce, pack berries in polyethylene bags or rigid containers and cover with a thin or medium syrup. Seal and freeze immediately.

BLUEBERRIES

Variety suitable for freezing: excellent—any small-seeded variety. 1 pint berries yields approximately 1 pint frozen fruit.

Carefully remove leaves, foreign matter and immature berries. Wash thoroughly. Remove stems. Drain on absorbent paper toweling. Place in bowl. Add sugar in proportion of 2 tablespoons sugar to 1 cup berries. Stir gently to avoid bruising the fruit.

Package in polyethylene bags or rigid containers. Seal. Freeze.

CANTALOUPE

Variety suitable for freezing: good—any fully ripened, deep yellow variety. 1 cantaloupe yields approximately 3 pints.

Good for fruit cups or salads during the winter months. Select firm, fully ripened cantaloupe. Cut in half and remove seeds. A French potato ball cutter is ideal for scooping out the cantaloupe. If one is not available, remove rind, cut melon in slices and cube. Drain before packaging.

Package in polyethylene bags. Seal and freeze. Once thawed, cantaloupe must be used immediately.

CHERRIES, SOUR

Variety suitable for freezing: excellent—Montmorency. 1 quart cherries yields about 1 pint frozen fruit.

Wash thoroughly and quickly. Remove from water at once. Remove stems. Place on tray covered with several thicknesses of absorbent paper toweling.

Set tray in refrigerator until cherries are firm again.

Then remove pits. A salad fork or three-pronged kitchen fork is excellent to do this. With the fork, gently press prong into stem end and lift out the pit. Squeezing the pit out bruises the fruit. Work with only 1 quart at a time because juice accumulates and the cherries may have to be drained again.

Add 2 tablespoons sugar to 1 cup cherries and package in polyethylene bags. Freeze.

Cherries for pies may be frozen without sugar.

CHERRIES, SWEET

Varieties suitable for freezing: fair—Bing and Lambert. 1 quart cherries yields about 1 pint frozen fruit.

Select fully tree-ripened cherries. Proceed as for sour cherries. A medium syrup may be used if the sweet cherries are to be used as a sauce.

Package in polyethylene bags or rigid containers. Seal and freeze at once.

CITRUS JUICES

Select juicy, well-matured oranges and grapefruit. Extract juice. Remove seeds and strain, if desired. Pour into rigid containers. Seal. Freeze at once.

CRANBERRIES

Variety suitable for freezing: excellent—Howes. 1/2 pound yields approximately 1 pint.

Sort berries carefully. Remove stems and all spongy or poorly formed cranberries. Wash berries carefully. Drain.

Package in polyethylene bags. Freeze. Cranberries do not need sugar for successful freezing.

CURRANTS

Varieties suitable for freezing: good—any large variety. 3/4 pound yields about 1 pint.

Wash and drain currants before removing from stem. Then remove stem and place currants in a bowl. Mix with sugar in proportion of 1 part sugar to 4 parts currants.

Place in polyethylene bags. If currants are to be used as a sauce, place in rigid containers and cover with a medium syrup. Seal and freeze.

DEWBERRIES

Variety suitable for freezing: fair—Boysenberries. 1 quart berries yields about 1 quart frozen fruit.

Same procedure as for blackberries.

FIGS

Varieties suitable for freezing: excellent—Magnolia, Brown Turkey, and Celestial.

Gather figs that are completely ripe but not bruised or softened. Figs may be frozen with or without skin.

Peeled Figs: Wash thoroughly. Remove stem. Using a sharp knife, peel very thin. Package according to size of family, allowing 4 or 5 figs per serving. Freeze.

Place figs in polyethylene bags. When bag is ¼ filled, sprinkle sugar over figs. Continue alternating figs and sugar. Use 1 part sugar to 4 parts figs. Seal and freeze. Prepared this way, figs are delicious served with cream.

Or fill container. Cover figs with a medium syrup. Seal and freeze.

If figs are to be used as a topping over ice cream, use a heavy syrup.

Unpeeled Figs: Sprinkle 6 quarts of figs with 1 cup baking soda. Pour 6 quarts boiling water over them. Let stand 10 minutes. Rinse in clear, cold water. Drain thoroughly on absorbent paper toweling on a tray. Set tray in refrigerator to chill.

Package in polyethylene bags. Add medium syrup. Seal and freeze.

GOOSEBERRIES

Varieties suitable for freezing: excellent—wild, any large-sized variety. 1 pint fresh berries yields approximately 1 pint frozen fruit.

Frozen gooseberries are excellent for pie. Select fully matured green gooseberries. Wash thoroughly. Remove stem and blossom end. Drain. Place berries in bowl. Add sugar, if desired, in proportion of 2 tablespoons sugar to 1 cup gooseberries. Package. Freeze.

GRAPEFRUIT AND ORANGE SECTIONS

Chill fruit thoroughly. Then, peel and section the fruit, making sure all skin and membrane are removed. Drain on absorbent paper toweling. Prepare only enough for 3 or 4 packages at one time as a protection against vitamin loss.

Package in polyethylene bags with rounds of waxed paper between layers. Seal and freeze. Sugar may be added to grapefruit sections, if desired.

HUCKLEBERRIES

Same procedure as blueberries.

NECTARINES

Practically all varieties suitable for freezing.

Same procedure as for peaches.

PEACHES

Varieties suitable for freezing: Yellow, excellent—Hale Haven, J. H. Hale, and Red Haven. White, excellent—Golden Jubilee and Georgia Belle. 1 to 1½ pounds yield approximately 1 pint.

Select tree-ripened peaches. Peel, rather than scald peaches . . . doing only a few at a time.

Slice peaches directly into the polyethylene bag in which they are to be frozen.

Add sugar alternately with the peaches in proportion of 2 tablespoons sugar to 1 cup peaches. Seal and freeze. This method helps to retard browning or oxidation of peaches.

Or, you may peel and slice about one quart at one time. Place in a bowl and sprinkle 1 tablespoon lemon juice over them to retard discoloring.

Add sugar in proportion of 2 tablespoons sugar to 1 cup peaches. Turn peaches over and over in bowl with wooden spoon.

Handle gently. If you desire, peaches may be packed in medium syrup in polyethylene bags or rigid containers.

Note: Sometimes, due to growing season and the variety of peaches selected for freezing, the peaches may discolor in spite of anything that can be done.

PEARS

(Not especially recommended for freezing.)

Varieties suitable for freezing: fair—Kieffer and Baldwin. 1 to 1¼ pounds yield approximately 1 pint.

Select tree-ripened fruit. Wash, peel and cut into desired sizes. Place peeled and cored fruit in a solution of 1 tablespoon lemon juice (or 1 tablespoon salt OR 1 teaspoon citric acid) to 1 quart of cold water. Drain on tray covered with several thicknesses of absorbent paper toweling. Set tray in refrigerator to chill pears.

Pack in polyethylene bags or rigid containers. Add medium syrup to completely cover pears. Seal and freeze.

PINEAPPLE

Excellent for freezing. 1 pineapple yields approximately 3 pints or 12 to 14 slices.

An easy way to peel pineapple is to lay the fruit, side down, on a good cutting board. Grasp the stem end with one hand. With a sharp knife, cut bottom end off pineapple. Place pineapple upright on cutting board and, while holding by stem, remove peeling by slicing downward. When peeling is removed, return pineapple to its side and cut in ½-inch slices. Discard stem when last piece is sliced. Remove any "eyes" remaining in each slice. Cut out core

These slices may be frozen whole. Place in freezer foil (use drugstore wrap) or in polyethylene bags. Pineapple may be shredded and 2 tablespoons of sugar added to each cup. Or, a thin syrup may be used. Place in polyethylene bags or rigid containers. Seal. Freeze.

Note: If frozen pineapple is to be used in gelatin dessert, it must be brought to the boiling point and cooked a minute or two before using, otherwise gelatin will not congeal.

PLUMS

Varieties suitable for freezing: Plums, very good—Damson and Red June. Prunes, very good—Italian. 1¼ pounds yield approximately 1 pint.

Select fully ripened fruit, not yet brown around the pit. Wash, sort, stem and cut in half, removing the pit. Drain on tray with several thicknesses of paper toweling. Set tray in refrigerator to chill fruit.

Place fruit in bowl. Add sugar in proportion of 1 cup sugar to 5 cups fruit or use medium syrup. Package in polyethylene bags. Freeze.

RED RASPBERRIES

Varieties suitable for freezing: excellent—Cuthbert, Latham, and Viking. 1 pint fresh berries yields approximately 1 pint frozen ones.

Raspberries are exceptionally fragile. Great care should be used in washing them, as they bruise easily.

If possible, wash raspberries in water which has been cooled, with ice, to about 40°F. Wash only a few berries at a time and do not allow them to remain in the water more than 30 seconds.

Use the same procedure as strawberries (see below). Drain thoroughly. Then place berries on tray covered with several thicknesses of absorbent paper toweling.

Set tray in refrigerator to cool and firm the fruit... about one hour.

Package raspberries in polyethylene bags or rigid containers. When container is ¼ filled with berries, add ¼ of the sugar (use proportion of 2 tablespoons sugar to 1 cup raspberries). Continue alternately adding berries and sugar until container is filled. Seal. Freeze immediately.

Raspberries make their own syrup when sugar is added. A pint of raspberries makes 4 servings. Purple varieties may also be frozen by this procedure.

RHUBARB

Variety suitable for freezing: excellent—Victoria. 1¼ pounds yield approximately 1 pint.

Freeze rhubarb as early in the spring as possible, before the rhubarb becomes tough and stringy.

Wash under running water. Remove stem and leaf end.

Cut in 1-inch pieces (cuts much easier with scissors). Drain. Package in polyethylene bags. Seal and freeze.

Rhubarb keeps beautifully without sugar or syrup. A quart makes one 9-inch pie.

STRAWBERRIES

Varieties suitable for freezing: excellent—Marshall, Sparkle, Gem, Senator Dunlap, and Fairfax. ⅔ quart yields approximately 1 pint.

Do not remove cap from fruit until after berries are washed. Sort and place in colander. Wash strawberries with fine spray, if possible. If not, dip colander in large container filled with very cold water. Gently lift colander up and down in water two or three times. Drain thoroughly.

To remove cap, use a sharp paring knife. Do not squeeze cap off with fingers. Slip knife directly under the cap, taking care not to cut through into the center of the fruit. Pry cap off.

Place fruit on tray covered with several thicknesses of absorbent paper toweling and put tray in refrigerator to chill the strawberries. Strawberries may be frozen in syrup or by adding sugar.

Add sugar in proportion of 2 tablespoons sugar to 1 cup strawberries. The drained and cooled strawberries may be placed in a bowl and the sugar sprinkled over them, or they may be sweetened in container in which they are to be frozen. When container is ¼ full, add ¼ of the sugar, repeating until container is filled.

Package in polyethylene bags or rigid containers. Seal and freeze at once.

WATERMELON

Variety suitable for freezing: any variety is fair for freezing if thoroughly ripened. Centers of melons are best to use.

Same as for cantaloupe.

Note: The freezer is an ideal place for quickly cooling a watermelon for picnics. Place whole melon in freezer for 3 or 4 hours.

HOW TO PREPARE FROZEN FRUITS FOR SERVING

Always thaw fruit in the container in which it was frozen. This usually requires about 2 to 3 hours at room temperature.

Do not open the container until the fruit is nearly thawed . . . since frozen fruit, once thawed, collapses quickly.

Remove from freezer only the quantity of fruit you plan to use at one time.

Frozen fruit cannot satisfactorily be refrozen once it is thawed.

Before freezing cherries, remove the pits with a salad fork or three-pronged kitchen fork.

When using glass freezer jars, or other types of containers especially designed for freezing, always be sure to follow manufacturer's directions carefully for sealing.

How to Freeze Meat and Game

WRAPPING MEATS FOR THE FREEZER

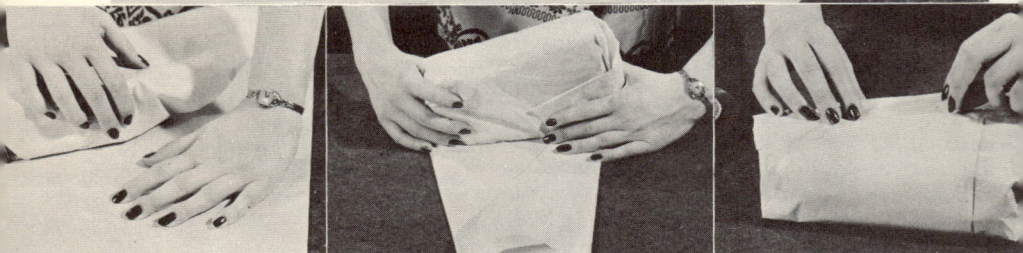

Fasten the loose end securely with freezer tape.

Freezing meat is quite easy. Only a few simple rules must be followed to assure a delicious product.

When selecting or specifying animals for freezing, choose healthy ones of the size and finish which will produce the weight and quality of cuts preferred by the family.

Excessive finish or fatness is unnecessary, but an ample fat covering increases the desirability of the meat and protects the lean from drying out during the frozen storage. This does not apply to veal which rarely has surplus fat.

The same general rules apply to meats purchased from a meat market or produce house. Ask for quality cuts from prime cattle. If the meat dealer knows you intend to freeze the meat, he may be more careful in his selection and will trim it to your preference.

Proper Wrapping of Meat Is Important

The quality of frozen meat is partly determined by the proper selection of wrapping material and the method of wrapping.

Improper wrapping results in "drying out" of meat and game which affects both the appearance and flavor. This condition is called "freezer burn."

It is unwise to attempt to economize on wrapping materials. Regular butcher paper, ordinary waxed paper, or grocery bags must never be used.

Polyethylene laminated to aluminum foil is best. Aluminum foil with a stockinette outer wrap is also satisfactory.

If a bone protrudes, use a double thickness of waxed paper as "padding" over the bone, then wrap all in aluminum foil. Be sure to work as much air as possible out of the packages before sealing.

Wrapping of meat is simple, yet requires care. Wrappings for meats must be moisture-vaporproof, easy to handle, tough enough to resist tearing and easy to label.

Keep meat cool both during and immediately after wrapping.

When wrapping, the foil must be pulled tightly around the meat to eliminate all posssible air. The finished package should be smooth and firmly packed to conserve storage space.

Place two sheets of waxed paper or polyethylene between chops, steaks, or hamburg patties (if they are to be wrapped together) to facilitate separating them when ready to use. This also makes it easier to broil or pan fry meat from the frozen state.

In general, each package should contain the meat needed for a single meal for the family.

Which Meats to Select

When selecting or specifying meats for freezing, choose healthy ones which will produce the weight and quality of cuts preferred by the family.

Excessive fatness is unnecessary, but an ample fat covering is desirable and protects the lean from drying out during frozen storage. This does not apply to veal since it rarely has surplus fat.

As often as possible, try to select quality meat that is U. S. Government graded. A stamp (a harmless vegetable dye) will appear on all major portions of the carcass. Grading classifies meat according to relative tenderness and quality. Beef and veal grades are: Prime, Choice, Good, Commercial, and Utility. Lamb is graded Prime, Choice, and Good. Pork is of such uniformity that it is not generally graded.

Chill Meat Thoroughly

Meat should be chilled promptly, once the carcass has been prepared. Chilling removes body heat and arrests the destructive growth of bacteria, molds and yeasts which multiply rapidly at temperatures around 70°F., but slowly at temperatures between 30°F. to 40°F. Improper chilling may ruin the flavor of the meat or even render it unfit for use.

Cut Meat to Family Preferences

Again, this is no job for the novice. Most locker plants employ expert meat cutters or can direct you to one. Specify the cuts your family enjoys most and have the meat cut in family-sized portions. This eliminates waste.

Boning meat is recommended because less storage space is required and the danger of bones puncturing the wrapping is eliminated.

Label Clearly

After the meat is packaged, the next important step is proper labeling. Write on the package the type meat enclosed, the approximate number of servings and the date of the packaging. If meat is to be used with a definite recipe, label accordingly.

Start Freezing Immediately

Just as soon as the meat is packaged and labeled, it should be placed in the freezer. If this is not practical, place the packages in the freezer compartment of your refrigerator until ready to load the freezer. Do not allow packaged meat to remain at room temperature any longer than is absolutely necessary.

Do Not Refreeze
Thawed Uncooked Meat

Never refreeze thawed uncooked meat! The meat will still be good but some of the flavor will be lost. Uncooked meat, that you wish to refreeze, must be cooked first.

Approximate Yield of Beef Carcass

Live weight .... 750 lbs.
Whole carcass .... 420 lbs.

Trimmed cuts from whole carcass:	Live Weight	Carcass Weight	
Steaks and oven roasts	23%	40%	172 lbs.
Pot roasts	11%	20%	83 lbs.
Stews and ground meat	11%	20%	83 lbs.
	45%	80%	338 lbs.*

Forequarters will yield:

Steaks and oven roasts		25%	55 lbs.
Pot roasts		32%	70 lbs.
Stews and ground meat		27%	59 lbs.
		84%	184 lbs.

Hindquarters will yield:

Steaks, oven roasts and pot roasts		58%	117 lbs.
Stews and ground meat		18%	37 lbs.
		76%	154 lbs.

("Freezing Meat," U.S. Dept. of Agriculture Bulletin AW1-75)

* The loss of 82 pounds between the actual yield of finished product and the dressed carcass is due to bones which are removed before packaging, plus normal shrinkage, fat and meat trimming, and the liver, tongue and heart. To conserve freezer space, it is advisable to remove as much bone as possible, as well as unnecessary fat.

A Guide to Remember: Meat may be frozen successfully once when raw and once after it has been cooked.

Consult a Skilled Beef Cutter

For meat of high quality, it is imperative that the carcass be properly prepared and chilled. Few persons, except skilled meat cutters, know how to do this correctly.

If weather is not cold enough to do a proper job of chilling, make advance arrangements to have the cleaned and dressed carcass removed immediately to a chilling room. The temperature of slaughtered meat is around 100°F. and body temperature of the carcass must be reduced to between 33°F. and 40°F. within 24 hours after slaughtering.

Beef should be aged, but that is a job for the expert. Aging or ripening tenderizes and improves the flavor of the beef. Prime beef with a one-inch coating of fat all over should be aged a little longer than the poorer qualities of beef.

Cutting the Beef

If the beef carcass is from a reasonably young, well-bred and well-fed animal, the rib and top round can be cut into satisfactory steaks and the first cuts of the rib and arm side of the chuck are usually sufficiently tender to be cooked as oven roasts.

If the animal was old and thin, even the loin steaks may not be sufficiently tender for broiling or frying, but should be cut for braising.

If there is any doubt as to the suitability of the meat for various cuts and methods of cooking, it is advisable to engage an expert cutter who will help you in classifying the meat cuts.

Roasts are usually boned and rolled to save space. Also the bone may be removed from the rump and arm pieces cut from the chuck.

Less-tender cuts such as shank, brisket, plate, neck and flank are most often boned, then ground, or cut into one-inch cubes without gristle or too much fat, and packaged in suitable amounts for stews and casserole dishes.

Ground meat is not salted before freezing. If it is to be broiled or fried, make into patties before wrapping. A pound of meat makes 6 generous-size hamburg patties. If this is done before freezing, it is not necessary to thaw the patties before cooking.

The liver may be sliced before freezing. The heart and tongue may be cleaned and frozen whole.

Packaging and wrapping of beef is same as for all meats. Freeze at once.

LAMB

Lamb may carry a fat covering which is comparable to the various grades of beef. Since it comes from an animal which is less than a year old, any longer than a five-day holding or aging period would result in excessive shrinkage.

The weight of the dressed carcass is usually about half that of the live animal.

As with all other meat, rapid chilling is extremely important. Since the lamb is small, the temperature of the carcass should reach between 33°F. and 40°F. in 24 hours or less. Longer first chilling is apt to destroy the fine flavor of the meat.

Lamb is packaged as other meats. Label and freeze at once.

VEAL

The calf should weigh from 110 to 200 pounds. As with beef, it is desirable to cut veal to suit the immediate needs of the family.

The veal carcass will yield about 80 to 90 pounds of roasts, chops, stew and ground meat.

The hindquarter of the veal is cut into round, rump, loin and flank.

The forequarter is cut into shank, shoulder, rack and breast. Cutlets are made from the round. The loin and rack may be cut into chops.

The rump, shoulder and breast may be boned, rolled and tied for roasting. The flanks and shanks are usually ground.

Veal is slaughtered and cared for in the same manner as beef. However, because veal has little or no fat, it is packaged immediately after the chilling period is finished, and does not go through any aging process.

Veal must be chilled to 33°F. to 40°F. within 24 hours after slaughtering.

Veal should be packaged or wrapped immediately after chilling. Freeze at once.

Approximate Yield of Lamb Carcass

	Live Weight	Carcass Weight	
Live weight			85 lbs.
Whole carcass			41 lbs.
Trimmed cuts:			
Legs, chops, shoulders	37%	75%	31 lbs.
Breast and stew	8%	15%	7 lbs.
	45%	90%	38 lbs.

("Lamb and Mutton on the Farm," U.S. Dept. of Agriculture Bulletin 1807)

PORK

Pork is a highly perishable meat, and great care must be exercised in caring for the carcass after the hog is slaughtered.

Pork may sour in 12 hours if hung at warm air temperatures; therefore, *rapid chilling is essential.* The carcass must cool to between 33°F. and 40°F. in a maximum of 24 hours.

Immediately after the chilling, the carcass should be cut, wrapped and frozen.

Pork does not require aging; on the contrary, the speedier pork can be frozen after chilling, the better the quality of the frozen meat.

When to Butcher Pork

On the farm, butchering should be done when the weather is as favorable as possible. Temperatures between 33°F. and 40°F. are best.

Should the weather be extremely cold, hang the carcass in a shed and protect it from freezing by wrapping with a sheet.

If the hog is butchered in warm weather, and chilling facilities are not available at home, arrangements should be made with your local locker plant or meat market to hang the carcass in their chilling rooms immediately after the carcass is cut and cleaned. These arrangements should be made in advance.

Cutting the Pork

As with beef, pork should be cut in family-sized pieces.

Chops should be cut in size desirable for frying.

The hams and bacon are usually cured, but the shoulders may be sliced for frying, or cut into roasts for freezing. Fresh ham may be sliced for frying or cut into roasts.

Spareribs consume considerable room in a storage compartment due to their bony structure. However, frozen spareribs are excellent and keep as satisfactorily as any other portion of the hog.

Speed Chilling of Pork

Split the warm hog and pull the leaf fat as soon as the internal organs have been removed. It also aids chilling to remove the head before hanging.

Unless care is taken, the fat bellies and hams of warm, freshly slaughtered hogs often overlap each other during the cooling process, which closes the body cavity to air circulation. Warm hogs, carelessly hung, will frequently show spoilage the next day, even when held at low temperature.

Whole or half carcasses should be suspended to chill so they do not touch. Never lay hog carcasses on floor to chill. When hams touch each other, chilling is frequently delayed too long and spoilage is the result.

If warm carcasses are held overnight

Approximate Yield of Pork Carcass

Live weight			225 lbs.
Whole carcass			176 lbs.

Trimmed cuts:	Live Weight	Carcass Weight	
Fresh hams, shoulders, bacon, jowls	40%	50%	90 lbs.
Loins, ribs, sausage	15%	20%	34 lbs.
	55%	70%	124 lbs.
Lard, rendered	12%	15%	27 lbs.

("Freezing Meat," U.S. Dept. of Agriculture Bulletin, AWI-75)

at temperatures slightly above freezing, the internal temperature of the hams will not always be below 40°F. It is suggested that cuts from such meat be spread out during the second night to permit complete chilling.

It is imperative that pork be completely chilled before freezing, even though it delays the wrapping of the meat an additional 12 to 24 hours.

If a ham thermometer is available, test the temperature of the large pieces with it. The need for prompt and thorough chilling of warm carcasses cannot be overemphasized. The heavier and fatter the hog, the greater is the need for careful handling.

SAUSAGE, CURED HAMS, BACON

These pork products do not lend well to freezing and should not be kept over 3 weeks. The salt used as a seasoning and preservative activates oxidation which, in turn, results in rancidity.

Sausage

Freezing seasoned sausage is a controversial subject at present. Many authorities state that sausage is the only meat which may be seasoned before freezing. Seasoning includes the addition of salt, black pepper, red pepper, sage, smoking or the addition of cereals. According to Dr. J. G. Woodroof of the Georgia Experiment Station, smoking improves flavor, stabilizes color, partially sterilizes the meat, improves appearance, increases tenderness, prevents rancidity and drives off up to 20% of the water.

Cured Hams and Bacon

Cured hams may be frozen either sliced or whole. Bacon also may be frozen, but does not adapt itself as well to freezing as does ham.

If the bacon is sliced before freezing, dehydration may occur.

If the supply of bacon is greater than can be used within a limited time,

it may be desirable to freeze a portion of it.

It is advisable to cut the smoked bacon into 1- or 2-pound slabs, wrap, freeze, take out packages as needed and slice after thawing.

RABBITS AND OTHER SMALL GAME*

Freeze rabbits and other small game in much the same way as poultry.

Immediately after killing, skin, behead and remove entrails. The carcass should then be thoroughly and carefully washed, chilled and cut into pieces for cooking.

Package as for chicken fricassee.

VENISON AND OTHER LARGE GAME*

Prepare, package and freeze in much the same way as beef or veal.

*Note: Some states do not permit game to be kept more than 10 days. Consult your game warden or State Conservation Department before freezing game for longer storage.

How Long May Meat Be Held at 0°?

This also is a controversial subject and depends upon many factors, such as proper slaughtering, chilling, aging, wrapping and the speed with which the meat starts on its way to being frozen, after wrapping. However, the Government Bulletin, "Freezing Meat and Poultry Products" AWI-75, gives the following times at 0°F:

Product	Storage Period
Ground meat	1 to 3 months
Fresh pork and fish	3 to 6 months
Lamb and veal	6 to 9 months
Beef, poultry and eggs	6 to 12 months

HOW TO COOK FROZEN MEATS

There are two satisfactory methods of cooking frozen meats: (1) remove from frozen storage, unwrap and cook from the frozen state or (2) thaw before cooking the meat.

Cooking meats from the frozen state is preferred as there is a minimum loss of weight and juices, resulting in better flavor and a more tender piece of meat . . . but it is necessary to add extra minutes to the cooking time.

Roasting: A five-pound roast thaws completely in about 24 hours at room temperature.

If placed in the food compartment of a refrigerator, it requires from 36 to 48 hours to thaw.

If roasts are thawed, and if there is any doubt of the complete thawing of the meat, allow longer roasting time than for fresh meat.

In roasting meat from the frozen state, add an additional 15 to 20 minutes per pound of meat.

The ideal method is to place the meat in the oven immediately after removing from the freezer.

When the meat is completely thawed, place a meat thermometer through the thickest part and cook by temperature. The meat thermometer is the most accurate method of cooking meat whether it is frozen or fresh.

Broiling: Broiling steaks from the frozen state requires an additional 10 to 15 minutes per side, depending upon the degree of broiling desired.

From tests which we have conducted, we have found broiling from the frozen state gives a juicier and better-flavored steak.

Caution About Cooking Pork

Pork must be thoroughly cooked whether it is cooked from the frozen or thawed state.

Allow an additional 15 to 20 minutes per pound of pork.

One may become infected with a serious disease called Trichinosis through the eating of pork which has not been thoroughly cooked. There is some belief that freezing kills trichinae, but until that fact is definitely proved, frozen pork should be given the same thorough cooking as fresh pork.

How to Freeze Poultry

Poultry is one of the high protein foods that keeps exceedingly well in the frozen state. The methods described in this book have produced frozen poultry of excellent quality, taste and appearance.

Look ahead and decide what your family will want. Then plan to freeze poultry in season and enjoy special treats the year 'round. Here are some suggestions for choosing poultry for freezing.

CHICKEN

The size of the chicken determines how best it may be used.

Broilers—Weight not over 2½ pounds dressed, not over 12 weeks old.

Frying Chicken—Weight 3 to 3½ pounds, about 20 weeks old.

Fricassee—Weight 4 to 6 pounds, can be from 1 to 2 years old and reasonably fat.

Roasting Chicken—Weight 4 to 5 pounds, reasonably fat, not over a year old.

Capon—Weight 7 to 10 pounds, reasonably fat, not over 8 to 10 months old.

HOW TO WRAP POULTRY FOR FREEZING

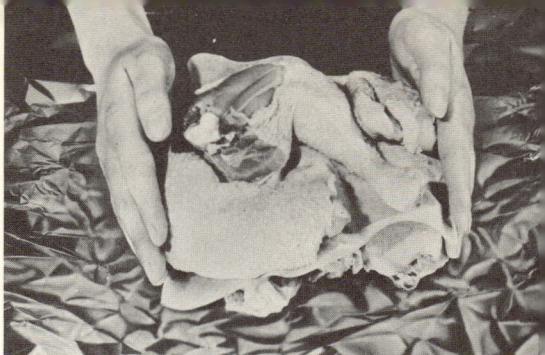

Arrange cut-up poultry so it will make compact, airtight package.

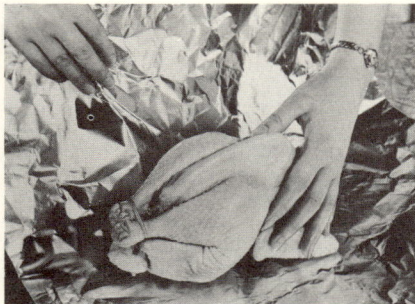

Center whole bird on sheet of wrapping material.

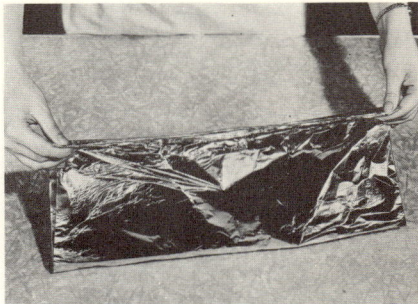

Make tight fold of foil and roll the fold down against bird.

Expel excess air by molding foil to shape of food.

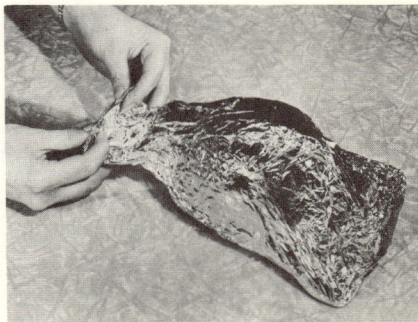

Crimp ends tightly to provide airtight seal.

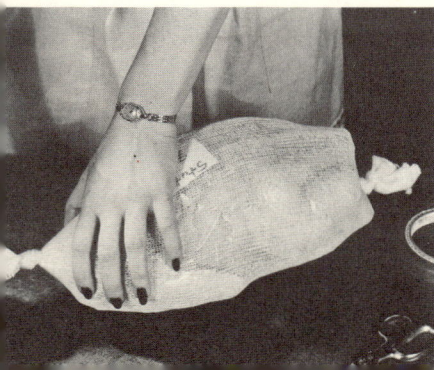

If regular freezer-weight aluminum foil is used instead of polyethylene-backed aluminum foil, cover sealed package with stockinette, outer protective covering.

Game Birds

Handle same as other poultry.

Consult your game warden or State Conservation Department before freezing game birds for storage more than 10 days. Some states limit the length of time game birds may be kept.

Turkey

May be frozen at any time the bird has reached maturity, but most turkeys are at their prime during October, November, December and January.

Wrap Poultry Carefully

Poultry must be protected so that it will not lose moisture or flavor during freezing or storage.

Poorly wrapped birds dry out and are tough and dry when cooked. This condition is often referred to as "freezer burn."

Birds may also become rancid or take on foreign flavors if not properly wrapped.

Polyethylene laminated to Aluminum Foil (best)—Can be molded easily to shape of bird. No outer wrap necessary.

Aluminum Foil (recommended)—Can be smoothed to conform to the shape of the bird, thus eliminating air pockets. Use outer wrap for extra protection.

Polyethylene (recommended)—Wrap polyethylene sheets or bags carefully around the bird and force out any air pockets which might form during wrapping. Secure tightly. Use outer wrap of stockinette for extra protection.

To Freeze Giblets

Clean giblets thoroughly and package in polyethylene bags for freezing.

Cut-Up Poultry

Cut-up poultry can be packed in aluminum foil, polyethylene bags or wrapped in laminated paper to form a neat, compact package.

Seal Securely

Inner wrappings should be securely sealed with acetate tape.

Protective sheet wrappings should also be sealed with acetate tape. If stockinette is used, knot ends tightly against bird.

Aluminum foil is sealed securely if edges are tightly folded and pressed firmly against bird. No further sealing is necessary.

Label Informatively

With china marking pencil or waterproof ink, make notation of kind of poultry, how prepared, weight and date of freezing.

If a stockinette outer covering is used, the information can be written on a slip of paper and placed between the stockinette and inner wrapping before ends are secured.

Thaw Poultry Before Stuffing

Frozen poultry must be thawed completely before stuffing.

It may be thawed in one of three ways: (1) at room temperature, (2) in the refrigerator for slow defrosting, or (3) in a 300°F. oven for quickest defrosting.

Do not soak frozen poultry in water to speed thawing.

A whole chicken requires 6 to 8 hours to thaw at room temperature or 3 to 5 hours per pound if thawed in the main food compartment of refrigerator.

An average-sized turkey requires 24 to 36 hours to thaw at room temperature. This same turkey will thaw in about 2 hours in a 300°F. oven.

Caution When Freezing Poultry

The American Institute of Baking states that poultry (chicken, duck, turkey, and other birds) should never be stuffed before it is frozen!

Extensive research done by the

American Institute of Baking indicates that three different organisms which are frequently found in poultry can cause extreme illness—even death. While it is true that a sufficiently high oven temperature will destroy most of these organisms, the thawing time of a frozen stuffed bird is so slow that it makes a perfect "breeding ground" for these bacteria.

Therefore, the American Institute of Baking recommends that all poultry be frozen without stuffing . . . and then, after thawing, the bird may be stuffed just before it is placed in the oven for roasting.

The Institute also recommends a dry stuffing in preference to a moist one.

The stuffing may be made the evening before it is to be used, and stored in the refrigerator overnight.

The frozen bird, if kept at room temperature overnight, will be thawed sufficiently by morning to permit easy stuffing. In this way, the bird may be stuffed quickly on the morning it is to be roasted.

It is important that . . .

1. Stuffed poultry should not be allowed to stand for more than four hours at room temperature . . . either before or after roasting.

2. After stuffed poultry has been roasted and served, the stuffing should be removed from the carcass and placed in a covered container . . . and refrigerated as soon as possible.

3. Place uneaten portion of cooked poultry in refrigerator immediately after removing it from the table.

If uneaten portion of turkey is to be frozen, trim or slice meat from carcass and wrap for freezing.

HOW TO COOK FROZEN POULTRY

For Frying or Fricassee: Frozen pieces of chicken or young turkey may be rolled in seasoned flour and fried immediately without any preliminary thawing. Or, pieces may be thawed and fried the same as unfrozen chicken.

For Stewing: Remove wrapping and place frozen chicken in kettle. Cover with boiling water and cook as unfrozen chicken.

For Broiling: Broil without any preliminary thawing. Put broiler pan at least 5 inches away from broiling unit.

Allow 20 to 30 additional minutes for each half chicken.

Otherwise, thaw broilers overnight and cook as unfrozen broilers.

How to Freeze Fish and Shellfish

Fish is an exceptionally perishable food. Contamination by bacteria from the air and water begins within a few hours after they are caught.

Chilling fish with ice or placing in the household refrigerator retards bacterial action but does not prevent it. Organisms which attack fish normally live at lower temperatures than those which attack meats. Speed in preparing and freezing fish is, therefore, essential.

The storage period for frozen fish is relatively short. One to three months usually is considered the maximum.

Selection for Freezing

Fish that contain a high fat content, such as salmon, mackerel, carp, and herring, do not keep as long or as satisfactorily as the non-oily varieties, such as halibut, haddock, and trout.

Preparation for Freezing

Fish to be frozen should be prepared for freezing immediately after catching. Or, in case of delay, it should be promptly packed in quantities of ice.

Prepare as for cooking. Remove fins, tails, entrails, and scales, if any. Fillet large fish. Rinse or dip in salt water,

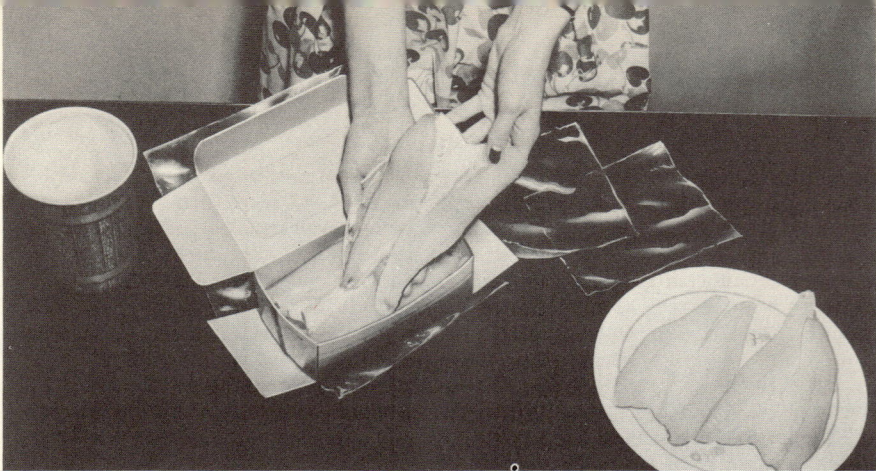

Place two sheets of waxed paper between fillets so they will be easy to separate when frozen.

about 1 cup pickling salt to 1 gallon of water.

Individual servings of fish are more convenient to use if first wrapped in polyethylene or aluminum foil.

To prevent any possible exchange of odors with other foods during storage, the individually wrapped packages should be wrapped in a second layer of aluminum foil, polyethylene bag, or laminated papers.

Two pieces of waxed paper between the individual fillets or slices of fish will not only aid the retention of the original quality, but facilitate handling when preparing for cooking.

HOW TO FREEZE CLAMS

Razor clams are of the best quality if dug between September and April, although they may be taken the year around.

Dead clams should not be used; and care in cleaning clams for freezing should be exercised.

1. Rinse off external sand by hosing or washing under water tap.

2. Place clams in cold water to which salt has been added in the proportion of 3 ounces (about 4 tablespoons) to each gallon of water. Allow to stand for about an hour so that the clams will clean themselves of most of the sand held within the body.

3. Open or shuck as follows in order of preference:

a. Shuck raw, saving liquid.

b. Steam open; subject to live steam until majority of shells open.

c. Immerse in boiling water for 2 to 3 minutes to open shells.

4. Wash clams well under running water, having slit the neck and digger lengthwise to remove any dirt, sand or foreign material and stomach contents. Drain off excess water.

5. If desired, the necks may be cut off, ground and packed separately for use in chowder.

6. Pack body, whole or minced, in glass freezing jars, waxed tubs or polyethylene-lined cartons.

Cover with clam liquid. A salt solution (1 level tablespoon to a quart of water) may be substituted for the clam liquid.

The meats should be thoroughly covered with the liquid or brine to prevent "freezer burn" and off-flavor development during storage. Leave head space for expansion. Seal well.

7. Freeze.

Note: If there is any question about "mussel poisoning" or "clam poisoning" during the late spring or summer months, consult the nearest city or county health officer.

For more detailed information regarding clam freezing, see Oregon Agricultural Experiment Station Circular of Information No. 301, Freezing Razor Clams.

HOW TO FREEZE OYSTERS

Oysters are more susceptible to various types of spoilage than are some of the other marine foods. They must be handled with care and *as rapidly as possible*.

Assemble everything needed before starting.

1. Use only live oysters.
2. Hose off or wash under tap to remove external debris from shell.
3. Shuck or open raw in usual manner, saving oyster liquid.
4. Wash thoroughly in salt brine (1 level tablespoon salt to a quart of water). Leave oysters in brine for one hour but no longer.
5. Drain off excess water or brine.
6. Package in polyethylene-lined carton, waxed tubs or glass jars.
7. Cover surface with oyster liquid to prevent exposure to air. Leave head space for expansion.
8. Seal and freeze.

HOW TO FREEZE SHRIMP

The procedure for freezing shrimp varies according to location. For complete information, consult your local State Agricultural College.

HOW TO FREEZE CRABS AND LOBSTERS

In sections of the country where crabs and lobsters are available, it is often desirable to freeze their meat. Frozen meat is excellent, makes delicious salads.

Lobsters are handled the same as crabs.

1. Use only live crabs.
2. Remove back shell. (Note: Iced or chilled crabs will be less active than those fresh out of the water.)
3. Eviscerate and wash. Be sure to remove the jelly-like substance which is the newly forming shell.
4. Break crabs in half. Pre-cook by placing in a pressure cooker, a steamer or a large kettle containing an inch of vigorously boiling water.

When using a pressure cooker, exhaust steam from petcock 7 to 10 minutes, then tighten the petcock and raise the pressure to 2 pounds. Cook from 12 to 15 minutes.

When using a steamer or large kettle, count time from when steam flutters the lid or escapes rapidly. Steam the crabs 20 to 22 minutes.

5. Remove meat. A small amount of cold water may be used to cool down a few crabs to start with, but it is better if the meat does not come in contact with water at this point. Keep leg and body meat separate to facilitate packing.
6. Pack meat for freezing in rigid containers or polyethylene-lined containers.
7. Cover meat with a salt brine (1 level tablespoon of salt for each quart of water), leaving head space for expansion. Seal.
8. Freeze immediately.

Optional Method for Killing and Cooking

Live crabs may be killed and cooked by dropping into a large amount of vigorously boiling salted water and boiling 20 to 25 minutes.

The method outlined above, however (killing and cleaning before cooking), is preferred, since it produces a more desirable meat.

Note: The information on clams, oysters, and crabs was prepared by Dr. E. W. Harvey of the Seafood Laboratory at Astoria, Oregon; State Circular No. 164, Oregon State College.

HOW TO COOK FROZEN FISH AND SHELLFISH

Fish is best when cooked from the frozen state. Cook just as you would unfrozen fish but allow a little extra time.

For stews, chowders and soups, seafood is cooked from the frozen state.

For use in appetizers and salads, or for frying and scalloping, seafood is thawed in food compartment of the refrigerator. Thaw in sealed freezing container in which seafood was frozen.

Serve whipped cream while still frozen as it will thaw quickly.

BUTTER

Butter may be frozen satisfactorily. Recommended storage period is approximately 3 months.

Butter for freezing should be made from freshly pasteurized cream, well salted and thoroughly worked to remove all traces of buttermilk.

Butter made from unpasteurized cream will turn rancid rapidly and should _never_ be frozen.

Wrap butter in double thickness of aluminum foil to prevent transfer of odor.

It is not advisable to freeze more than two pounds of butter in any one package.

COTTAGE CHEESE

Cottage cheese may be frozen and kept in rigid containers for 2 to 3 months.

It should be of good quality and made from pasteurized milk, the curd washed and salted but not creamed.

In packaging, be sure to leave head space for expansion.

Thawing cottage cheese takes $3\frac{1}{2}$ to 4 hours at room temperature.

CREAM

Pasteurized cream may be frozen and kept for 2 to 3 months. Unpasteurized cream does not keep satisfactorily for more than 2 to 3 weeks.

When sweet cream is frozen, the water and milk solids separate so, after thawing, do not mix to their original form. For that reason, frozen cream

How to Freeze Dairy Products

does not ship as satisfactorily as fresh cream.

Cream may be frozen in polyethylene bags or rigid containers. Leave 1-inch head space for expansion.

WHIPPED CREAM

Whip, season and flavor cream as usual.

Spoon out, in serving-size portions, onto cooky sheet that has been covered with waxed paper.

Set cooky sheet in freezer. When whipped cream is frozen solid, remove cream with a spatula and package in polyethylene bags. Seal and freeze immediately.

This is an excellent way to use an overabundant supply of whipped cream. Will thaw in about 30 minutes.

HOW TO FREEZE EGGS

Eggs are among the most satisfactory of all foods to freeze. They keep well for 6 to 8 months and, when used, it is impossible to tell them from fresh eggs.

The volume of the frozen egg white is equal to fresh egg whites and, if frozen properly, they continue to keep their fresh taste.

There is one important fact to remember when freezing eggs. They must be strictly fresh, for the frozen product is only as good as the fresh or original product.

However, we do not recommend freezing quantities of eggs in one container, unless that full amount will be used at once when the eggs are re-moved from the freezer.

Eggs do not hold up long after they have thawed and there may be consid-erable waste of the frozen product if more eggs are frozen in one container than will be used at one time.

In the Institute, we have found it ad-visable to freeze in one envelope only the amount of whole eggs, egg yolks, or egg whites that will be used at one time.

For example, if you make 3-egg cakes frequently, package three eggs to an envelope. Then when you want to make a cake, lift out one envelope.

Freeze egg whites for angel food cake the same way.

For omelets, separate the egg whites and yolks, put them in separate poly-ethylene bags, then package several of each together. Then when you want to make an omelet, take out one package containing the proper assortment of whites and yolks.

WHOLE EGGS

Beat eggs slightly with fork, just enough to mix yolk and white.

Add 1/4 teaspoon salt for each 3 eggs.

Pour into small polyethylene bags, seal package in rigid carton and freeze.

EGG WHITES

Measure out the amount needed in a specific recipe which you prepare often.

Pour into polyethylene bag, seal package in rigid carton and freeze. Egg whites do not need any mixing before freezing.

EGG YOLKS

Egg yolks should be slightly beaten, but not enough to make them fluffy or lemon colored.

To each 3 egg yolks, add 1/4 teaspoon salt. The addition of salt prevents co-agulation of yolk solids during storage. Package and freeze.

How to Thaw Frozen Eggs and Cottage Cheese

Place sealed envelope of eggs in a bowl of cold water. They will defrost in about 30 minutes. Or, they can be left in the sealed envelope at room temperature which requires about 2 hours to thaw.

Cottage cheese should be thawed slowly in the refrigerator. If thawed at room temperature, it will take 3 1/2 to 4 hours. When thawed, add cream and use immediately.

What to Do When Your Home Freezer Stops

If your home freezer stops running and will be off for some time, you can take several steps to keep food from spoiling.

Keep the freezer closed.

Move the food to a locker plant.

Add dry ice if you can get it. To prevent burns, wear gloves when you handle dry ice.

Can the food if necessary.

Keep Freezer Closed

Open the freezer only to take out the food for moving to a locker plant, or to add dry ice.

Estimate How Long Current Will Be Off

Don't worry if you know you can have the freezer running again in a few hours.

When the freezer stops running, the power supply may be off or the freezer itself may be out of order.

1. Try to find how long the power will be off.

2. Consult the instruction book to determine if there is something you can do to put the freezer back into operation. Or——

3. Try to find out how long it will take to get a serviceman to put the freezer back in running order.

Estimate How Long Food Will Keep

Try to estimate about how long the food will stay frozen. With the freezer closed, food will usually stay frozen in a fully loaded cabinet 2 days; in a cabinet with less than half a load, not more than a day. Tests in a warm room show that after the freezer stops running——

Food in well-filled, well-insulated 4-cubic-foot home freezers will not begin to spoil in less than 3 days.

Food in well-filled, well-insulated 12- to 36-cubic-foot home freezers will not begin to spoil in less than 5 days.

How long the food in your freezer will stay frozen depends on——

1. The amount of food in the freezer. A full freezer will stay cold many hours longer than a freezer only a quarter full.

2. The kind of food. A freezer full of meat will not warm up so fast as a freezer full of baked food.

3. The temperature of the food. The colder the food, the longer it will stay frozen.

4. The freezer itself. A well-insulated freezer will keep food frozen much longer than one with little insulation.

5. Size of freezer. The larger the freezer, the longer the food will stay frozen.

Consider the Freezer-Locker Plant

Make arrangements well in advance with your local locker plant to take care of food in an emergency. Then if an emergency occurs:

1. Call the locker plant to see if it is operating and, if so, whether it has room for your food. If space is available——

2. Wrap the food in plenty of newspapers and blankets, or use insulated boxes.

3. Rush the food to the locker plant.

Use Dry Ice If You Can Get It

If locker space is not available and it looks as though the freezer would be stopped for longer than a day, use dry ice if you can get it. The more dry ice you use, the longer the food will keep frozen. Fifty pounds will keep the temperature down to 15°F. for about 2 days in an average-size freezer. You may be able to buy dry ice from a local dairy or a cold-storage warehouse.

Move any food from the freezing compartment to the storage compartment of the freezer. Put heavy cardboard directly on the packages of frozen food and then put the dry ice on top of the cardboard.

Should You Cover the Freezer With Blankets?

If you have put dry ice into the cabinet, you may cover the freezer with blankets, quilts, or some other covering. It will help to put crumpled newspaper or excelsior between the cabinet and the blankets.

If you put blankets or other coverings on the freezer, be sure to pin or fasten them so that they will not cover the air-vent openings. The power may go on unexpectedly and ventilation will be needed.

What Should You Do with Food If It Thaws?

You can refreeze thawed fruits.

Fruits usually ferment when they start to spoil. A little fermentation will not make fruits dangerous to eat, but it may spoil their flavor. So you can refreeze thawed fruits if they still taste and smell good. Or you can use them in cooking and baking or for making jams, jellies, and preserves.

Be careful when you refreeze thawed meats and poultry.

Meats and poultry become unsafe to eat when they start to spoil. Therefore, examine each package of food before you decide what to do with it. If the food still contains some ice crystals, it may safely be refrozen, even though the quality may suffer. It is often wiser to eat food that is completely thawed than to refreeze it. Be sure to cook it thoroughly, however. If the odor of thawed food is poor or questionable, get rid of the food. It may be dangerous!

Be careful when you refreeze vegetables, shellfish, and cooked foods.

Often, you can't tell by the odor whether vegetables, shellfish, and cooked foods have spoiled. Bacteria multiply rapidly in these foods, even at 50°F. So don't refreeze any of these foods when they have thawed completely. If ice crystals are still in the food, you can refreeze it immediately. Usually it is safe to do so, even though the quality may suffer. If the condition of the food is poor or questionable, get rid of it. It may be dangerous!

Refreeze Food Quickly

When you refreeze thawed food, freeze it quickly. If your freezer is full of warmed foods, to get a quick refreeze it is best to take the food to a commercial locker plant. Chill to 0°F. or below before taking the food back to your home freezer. Wrap the food well with newspapers and blankets before moving it to or from the freezer plant.

To refreeze food in your own freezer, rearrange the food to get the warmer packages against the refrigerated surface, if possible. Pile the packages so that the air can circulate around them. This means quicker freezing. If the freezer cabinet is too full, move some of the colder packages to the refrigerator, and return them gradually to the freezer.

Be Prepared

1. Find out about your nearest locker plant. Arrange to take your food there in an emergency.

2. Try to locate a source of dry ice in your community.

3. Keep canning supplies on hand, and keep canning equipment in good working order. At times, the only practical solution is to can thawed food to save it.

4. During the seasons when power failure is frequent in your community, it's good insurance to run the freezer between 10° and 20° below zero.

5. Clean and cool the freezer before refilling it if you have found it necessary to remove stored food.

6. In choosing a freezer, select one with good insulation. A well-insulated freezer keeps food cold hours longer than a poorly insulated one, when the power goes off.

7. Use care in preparing, packaging, and freezing food. The more sanitary you are in preparing food for the freezer, the better it will be able to withstand a stoppage of the freezer. Sanitary preparation means fewer bacteria to cause spoilage. Frozen bacteria are not dead bacteria; when they warm up they become active.

FROSTINGS AND FILLINGS BOOK

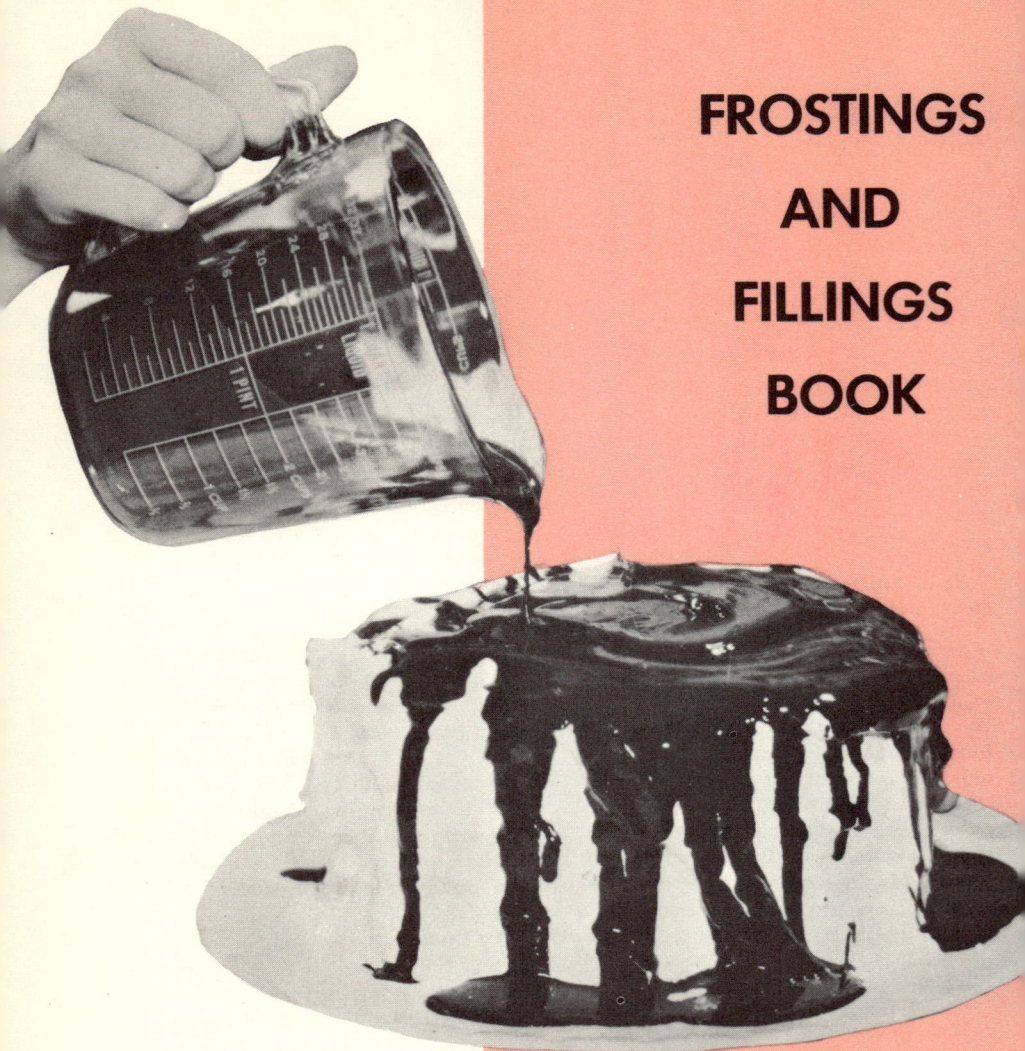

For a chocolate veneer, pour melted chocolate over frosted cake, allowing it to run down the sides.

The "How To's" of Cake Decorating

Delicious cake is always welcome, no matter how simple and unadorned. But anyone who takes pride in baking wants to add those final distinctive touches to cakes that will make them as lovely to look at as they are delicious to eat. Frostings not only make lovely cakes doubly tempting. They also keep cakes moist and delectable.

CHOOSING A FROSTING

A frosting should complement or flatter the flavor or color of your cake. A rich frosting should be chosen for a simple economy cake, a fluffy frosting for a light moist cake, and so on. A sponge cake, angel food, or a pound cake may be served unfrosted or finished off with a simple icing or glaze or with a topping. For good looks, frostings must be soft and manageable, yet not the least "runny."

Uncooked butter frostings call for confectioners' sugar (XXXX). Coarser sugar will make them grainy. If too soft these frostings can be thickened by the addition of a little more sugar. If too stiff, thin with a few drops of cream or other liquid.

Fluffy frostings such as the 7-minute, boiled, and uncooked meringue types are luscious and lavish looking. Make these the day the cake is to be served. Overcooking gives these frostings sugary texture. Undercooking leaves them too soft.

Creamy cooked frostings are fudge-like in consistency, creamy, and delicious. They harden more quickly than uncooked frostings, so need to be spread more quickly. The bowl of frosting may be placed over warm water to keep the frosting soft and workable.

CAKE DECORATING WITH FROSTING

A plain cake is a pleasant dessert—but a decorated cake is a party. The difference is simply a skillful hand with frosting. Special decorating may consist of the simple decorative touches described below, arranged in an appropriate design, or it may include more elaborate borders, rosettes, and festoons made with frosting and a cake decorator. Even the elaborately decorated cakes which are seen in caterers' windows are not so difficult to do as might be supposed. A few simple rules and practice with cake decorating equipment will soon give you artistically

Spread frosting carefully on lower layer, then fit top.

Start frosting at the sides, then fill in the top.

Light strokes with a spatula will vary the decorative effect.

decorated cakes. The equipment may consist merely of homemade paper cornucopias with a few inexpensive basic metal tubes or it may include a special cloth, rubber, or metal holder and a large variety of tubes. These may be purchased at most house furnishing stores.

Preparing the Cake

First, frost cake as directed, but spread frosting smoothly over the top and sides unless a rough surface or swirl pattern is part of the desired decorative effect.

Not all frostings can be used for decorating. The frosting must be stiff enough to hold its shape and yet be soft enough to pass through the small opening of a decorating tube. Butter frostings are usually preferred as they keep well; a frosting must be one that will not harden or dry too quickly because the decorating process often takes some time.

The frosting may be tinted delicately as desired. Pastel tints are usually best, but brighter colors may be used for color accents.

HINTS AND STEPS IN FROSTING A CAKE

1. Have the cake thoroughly cool. Brush or rub off all loose crumbs. Trim off ragged edges with a scissors.

2. Choose a flat plate or tray that will "frame" the cake. A 9-inch cake looks best on a plate or tray 12 to 13 inches in diameter. This allows a border of about 2 inches all around the cake. If the plate is too large or too deep, it dwarfs the cake. If too small, it make the cake appear clumsy and overbalanced.

3. To keep the plate clean while frosting, cover the outer area of the plate with pieces of waxed paper extending beyond the edge of plate.

4. If your cake is quite moist, a little powdered sugar sprinkled on the plate will keep it from sticking.

5. Place cake in position (on the papers) on the cake plate. If there is any difference in cake layers, choose the thicker layer for the bottom layer, and keep a smooth-crusted layer for the top.

6. Use a flexible spatula to spread frosting.

7. For a layer cake, place some frosting on the bottom layer. Spread it smoothly, almost to the edge. With a soft filling, spread to 1 inch from the edge. Then adjust the second layer so that edges are even and cake uniform in height. If top layer slides, insert a wire cake tester or slender knitting needle through both layers to anchor. This can be removed before frosting the top.

8. To frost outside of cake, spread frosting over edge and sides. Then pile remaining frosting on top and spread lightly to the edges. Swirl the frosting attractively as you frost.

9. Work quickly so that the frosting will not crust over before you finish. Let frosting set slightly, then draw out the pieces of waxed paper carefully from under cake.

10. For very special cakes, it pays to frost smoothly first with a thin layer of frosting to hold down any crumbs and to give an even base coat. When set or firm, the final frosting may be spread more easily.

11. For cupcakes, hold each cake, turning as you spread frosting on the top. To frost the sides as well, hold cake, top and bottom, while frosting sides, then place on cake rack or hold on a fork while frosting the top (or the bottom).

HOW TO COLOR FROSTINGS

To tint frostings, add a few drops of food coloring at a time and work or mix into frosting until evenly tinted.

HOMEMADE CAKE DECORATOR

If you have no cake decorating set, you can make your own decorator bag for special borders and writing. For the bags, cut squares or 10x8- or 12x9-inch rectangles of sturdy waxed or thin parchment paper into two triangles (step 1).

Roll each triangle into a cone shape, making sure it is tightly rolled so as not to give under pressure (steps 2, 3, and 4). Fold down the top point of the cone to keep it from unfolding (step 5).

Washable bags may be shaped similarly from muslin or light canvas, then stitched.

For writing, snip off the tip of the paper cone to give a small opening. Designs can be made by cutting this tip. An inverted "v" cut will shape leaf designs or flutings; a series of tiny "y's" will form shell designs and ridged borders.

If preferred, metal tips may be inserted at the bottom of the canvas bag or paper cone. Cut the tip off on the dotted line and drop the metal tube in as shown in steps 6 and 7.

For best results, fill cake decorator tube, bag, or cone only half-full of frosting at a time. Use one hand to guide the tip, the other to force out frosting gently.

Practice on paper or an inverted pan before attempting to decorate a cake in order to make sure that the frosting is of the right consistency.

If it is too soft it will not spread and the design will not be clear cut, and it will be difficult to break off the flow of frosting at the right point. If it is too stiff it will be difficult to push through the tube and will tend to break or crack.

SIMPLE DECORATIVE TOUCHES

Confectioners' Sugar: (1) Sprinkle the sugar through a small sieve onto unfrosted cake. (2) For special designs, place a fancy paper doily or a cut-out pattern, or letters on top of the cake. Then sprinkle with confectioners' sugar. Carefully lift the pattern up and away. The design will be embossed on the cake.

Candies: Use colored or silver candies for forming letters, festoons, or simple borders. With a toothpick, draw or space out the design lightly on frosted cake. Then place candies carefully on design. If necessary, use a tweezers to place each candy in position.

Chocolate: Melt chocolate over boiling water with 1 teaspoon butter for each square (ounce) of chocolate. Use to dribble over fluffy frosting from a teaspoon. Or paint the chocolate onto a smooth frosting to form a design, greeting, or name.

Frosting Sculpture: Frost cake with 7-minute frosting. Then tint more frosting with food coloring and use to form swirls or "ferns" at intervals on top and sides of cake.

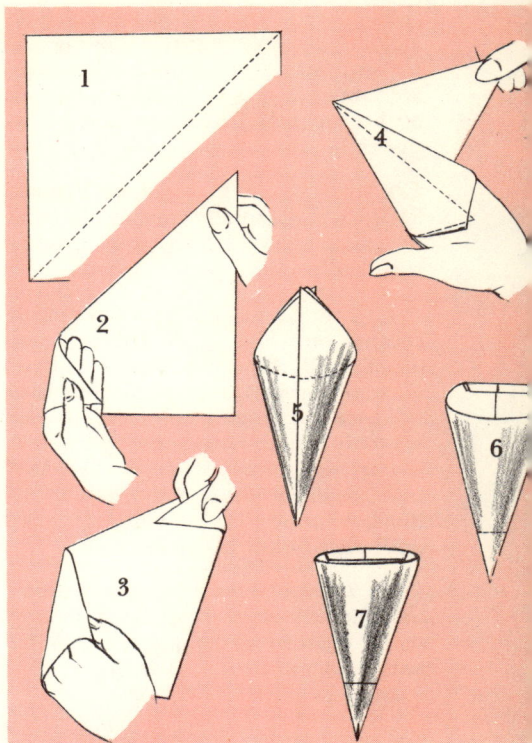

Fruit and Nuts: For flower and leaf designs, colored candies may be used with citron cut in leaf shapes. Other fruits such as raisins, candied cherries, citron, etc. may be arranged on cakes in designs. Try cluster raisins with toasted almonds, cherry bits with strips of citron.

Pecan or walnut halves may be centered on cupcakes or cake squares. Chopped pecans, walnuts, or pistachios are attractive pressed against sides of frosted cakes or around top edge in a border or scattered freely on the top.

To Toast Nuts: Place nuts in a shallow pan with a little butter (1 teaspoon butter for each cup of nuts). Heat in moderate oven (350°F.) until lightly browned, 15 to 20 minutes. Or heat and stir in a heavy skillet.

To Sliver Almonds: Blanch shelled almonds by covering with boiling water and letting stand until skins wrinkle, about 3 minutes. Drain and rub off brown skins. Split nuts and cut in slivers.

Coconut, Plain, Toasted, or Tinted: Sprinkle it over fluffy frostings or press it against sides of cake while frosting is still soft.

To Tint Coconut: Sprinkle shredded coconut on white paper. Dilute a tiny bit of food coloring in a small amount of water; sprinkle over coconut and rub evenly through it until the coconut is evenly tinted. Or put the coconut in a glass jar, filling no more than half full. Sprinkle with a few drops of diluted coloring. Cover jar and shake until all coconut is tinted.

To Toast Coconut: Spread shredded coconut in a thin layer on a baking sheet. Toast in moderate oven (350°F.) until golden brown, stirring it frequently to toast evenly.

Flowers: Dainty fresh flowers or a spray of green leaves are an especially inviting garnish on a simply frosted cake. Place small flowers and feathery greens in a small glass and insert in center of a frosted tube cake. Place matching flowers around the cake. Use tiny rosebuds or nosegays tied with ribbon for small cakes. Flowers around cakes should be grouped low enough so that the base of the cake can be seen.

Jelly: Use beaten or melted jelly for designs; for example, a red jelly heart or a green shamrock. Use a toothpick to mark the design on the cake, then spread the jelly inside the design.

Candles: Select candles and holders in the right color and size for the cake. A single large candle or candle-flower may be used in the center or a few medium-sized candles near the center instead of many small candles for older birthdays.

HOW TO CUT CAKES

Use a long, sharp knife for cutting cakes and cut with a gently sawing motion. Do not press down. For best results with frosted cakes, rinse the knife frequently in hot water. (This cannot be done at the table but it is an excellent aid when cutting cakes in kitchen for a party.)

Round layer cakes may be cut in wedges so that each piece has equal frosting. To serve sponge cake and angel food, cut lightly with a very sharp or serrated knife, or "tear" off each piece, using two forks or a cake breaker.

To Cut a Tiered Cake: First slice the bottom tier to edge of the second tier around cake. Then slice the second tier to edge of top tier. This uncovers another circle of bottom tier to slice.

The top tier of cake should now be removed to pack away for the bride's own souvenir. Then you can finish slicing the center of the second tier, which in turn uncovers the center of bottom tier. This is sliced last. You can adapt this procedure to almost any size or shape of tiered cake.

Candies become butterflies on this butterfly cake.

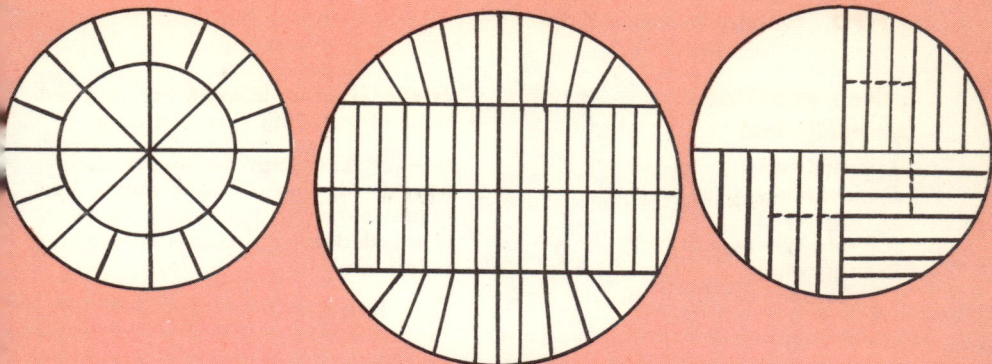

Here are diagrams for cutting round cakes when serving a crowd. Use the largest one for deep, single-layered cakes or try the other two for 9- or 10-inch layer cakes.

To cut a square cake 8 x 8 x 2 inches or larger.

Cooked Frostings

FLUFFY COOKED FROSTING

1¼ cups sugar
¼ teaspoon cream of tartar
½ cup water
3 egg whites
½ cup confectioners' sugar
½ teaspoon vanilla

Combine 1 cup sugar, cream of tartar, and water; stir over low heat until thoroughly dissolved. Bring to a boil and cook to the medium-hard ball stage (250°F.).

Beat egg whites until stiff but not dry. Fold in remaining ¼ cup sugar, a tablespoon at a time, beating after each addition.

Slowly pour syrup into egg whites, beating constantly. Beat in sifted confectioners' sugar and vanilla.

Makes frosting to cover top and sides of two 9-inch layers.

CREAMY CHOCOLATE FROSTING

1 cup firmly packed brown sugar
3 squares (3 ounces) chocolate
¼ teaspoon salt
⅓ cup evaporated milk or ⅓ cup cream
3 tablespoons butter or margarine
1 teaspoon vanilla
Confectioners' sugar

Combine brown sugar, chocolate, salt, and milk or cream in a saucepan. Bring to boiling point. Cook on medium heat until slightly thickened, about 5 minutes. Remove from heat.

Add butter and vanilla. Cool slightly. Add enough sifted confectioners' sugar for proper consistency to spread. Beat until smooth.

Spread between layers and on top and sides of cake.

BOILED FROSTING
(Master Recipe)

1½ cups sugar
Dash of salt
½ cup water
3 tablespoons corn syrup
2 egg whites
½ teaspoon vanilla

Cook sugar, salt, water, and corn syrup to the soft ball stage (238°F.). Remove mixture from heat.

Beat egg whites quickly with a rotary beater. Pour hot syrup slowly in a fine stream over egg whites, beating constantly.

Add vanilla and continue beating until frosting stands up in peaks. Quickly spread on cake.

On a rainy or humid day, boil syrup to higher temperature. If frosting hardens before spreading, beat in a few drops of hot water.

Makes frosting for top and sides of 2 9-inch layer cakes or 24 cupcakes.

Boiled Frosting Variations

Apricot Frosting: Fold ½ cup cooked apricot pulp into beaten frosting.

Brown Sugar Frosting: In master recipe, substitute brown sugar for granulated. Omit corn syrup and cook to 250°F. instead of 238°F.

Chocolate Frosting: In master recipe, add ¼ cup cocoa or 2 squares (2 ounces) melted chocolate to sugar, and cook with sugar and water.

Coconut Frosting: Sprinkle plain, tinted, or toasted shredded coconut over frosting.

Coffee Walnut Frosting: In master recipe, substitute coffee for water. Omit vanilla. Add ½ cup chopped walnuts to beaten frosting.

Colored Frosting: Tint frosting with food coloring as desired. Flavor as desired.

Fruit Frosting: Prepare master recipe. Fold chopped candied cherries, chopped candied pineapple, or other chopped candied fruit into beaten frosting.

Ginger Frosting: In master recipe, use ¼ cup brown sugar and 1 cup granulated sugar. Fold in ½ cup finely chopped, drained preserved ginger just before spreading.

Lady Baltimore Frosting or Filling: Prepare master recipe. Chop and fold ¼ cup each of dried figs, pitted dates, seedless raisins, walnuts, and blanched almonds into beaten frosting. If desired, substitute almond extract for vanilla.

Lemon Frosting: Prepare master recipe. Fold into frosting 2 tablespoons lemon juice and 1 teaspoon lemon rind just before spreading.

Lord Baltimore Frosting or Filling: Prepare master recipe. Fold ½ cup toasted coconut, ¼ cup chopped candied cherries or chopped maraschino cherries, ¼ cup chopped, toasted, blanched almonds or chopped pecans into beaten frosting.

Marshmallow Frosting: Prepare master recipe. Cut marshmallows into quarters. Arrange on top of cake. Spread frosting over them, or fold in half-melted marshmallows just before spreading.

Molasses Frosting: In master recipe, substitute 3 tablespoons molasses for corn syrup.

Nut Frosting: Sprinkle whole or chopped nuts over frosting.

Peppermint Frosting: Flavor master recipe with a few drops of peppermint instead of vanilla.

Strawberry Frosting: Prepare master recipe and fold ½ cup crushed strawberries into beaten frosting.

SHADOW FROSTING

Spread cake with white mountain frosting.

When the frosting has set, melt 2

squares (2 ounces) chocolate in double boiler over hot water, heating only until the chocolate is melted. Pour the chocolate over top of cake slowly and let it trickle down the sides.

For use on small tea cakes, frost the top only with the white mountain frosting. Smooth the frosting in the center and make a rim around the outside edge.

Pour the chocolate in the center to be held in place by the rim until it sets.

WHITE MOUNTAIN FROSTING

2   egg whites
1½ cups sugar
½   cup cold water
1   tablespoon light corn syrup or ¼ teaspoon cream of tartar
1   teaspoon vanilla

Put the egg whites in a mixing bowl. Combine sugar, water, and corn syrup or cream of tartar in a small saucepan. Stir over low heat until the sugar has dissolved. Boil rapidly until a small amount of syrup forms a soft ball when dropped into cold water (238°F.). Remove from heat.

Beat the egg whites quickly until stiff. Continue beating while pouring the hot syrup in a fine stream over the egg whites. Add the flavoring and continue beating until the mixture is stiff enough to spread.

EASTER EGG CAKE

To make an Easter egg cake, stir up your favorite layer cake batter and pour half into an inverted melon mold.

Tint the rest pale pink and pour into a duplicate mold. Baked, the two layers go together with a filling and a few toothpicks to hold them firmly in the egg shape.

Prepare frosting and tint it a nice Easter egg color with food coloring and frost egg carefully all over.

Remember to reserve a little of the frosting to use white or tinted in a contrasting shade for writing "Happy Easter" on your lovely confection.

Note: If you have no melon molds, deep bowls of oven-proof ware will do. The halves will be round but when still warm can be pressed into oblong shape.

Easter Egg Cake

SEVEN MINUTE FROSTING
(Master Recipe)

2   egg whites, unbeaten
1½ cups sugar
⅛   teaspoon salt
⅓   cup cold water
1   tablespoon light corn syrup
1   teaspoon vanilla

Place egg whites, sugar, salt, water, and corn syrup in top of double boiler.

Place over boiling water and beat constantly with a large double rotary beater or electric mixer at high speed until frosting will stand in peaks, about 7 minutes.

Remove from heat; beat in vanilla. Quickly spread on cake.

Makes enough frosting for top and sides of 2 9-inch layer cakes or 2 dozen cupcakes.

Seven-Minute Frosting Variations

Chocolate Frosting: Stir into beaten frosting 2 ounces (2 squares) melted chocolate.

Coconut Frosting: Sprinkle plain, tinted, or toasted coconut over frosting while still soft.

Coffee Frosting: In master recipe, omit vanilla. Substitute coffee for water.

Colored Frosting: Tint frosting as desired with food coloring. Flavor as desired.

Fruit Frosting: Prepare master recipe. Fold ½ cup chopped candied cherries, chopped candied pineapple, or other candied fruit into beaten frosting.

Lemon Frosting: In master recipe, substitute 2 tablespoons lemon juice and grated rind of 1 lemon for 2 tablespoons water, the corn syrup, and vanilla.

Orange Frosting: In master recipe, substitute 3 tablespoons orange juice and grated rind of 1 orange for 3 tablespoons water, the corn syrup, and vanilla.

Marshmallow Frosting: Follow master recipe and fold in 1 dozen quartered marshmallows with flavoring.

Peppermint Candy Frosting: Prepare master recipe. Fold ¼ cup crushed hard peppermint candy into beaten frosting. Garnish sides of cake with additional ¼ cup of crushed hard peppermint candy.

Sea Foam Frosting: Omit corn syrup in master recipe. Substitute 1½ cups brown sugar for granulated sugar.

FOUR MINUTE FROSTING

1   egg white, unbeaten
¾   cup sugar
Dash of salt
3   tablespoons water
1   teaspoon light corn syrup
½   teaspoon vanilla

Prepare as for the seven-minute frosting, beating only 4 minutes.

Frosts tops and sides of two 8-inch layers (thinly) or two 8 x 4 x 3-inch loaves, or top and sides of 9 or 10-inch tube cake.

Jelly Heart Decoration

EASY FUDGE FROSTING

3   1-ounce squares unsweetened chocolate
2   tablespoons butter or margarine
2¾ cups sifted confectioners' sugar
7   tablespoons light cream or top milk
Dash of salt
1   teaspoon vanilla

Melt chocolate and butter over boiling water and blend.

Add 1½ cups confectioners' sugar, cream, and salt, all at once and beat until smooth. Cook and stir over low heat until mixture bubbles up well around edges.

Remove from heat; add vanilla and remaining sugar in thirds, beating after each addition until smooth.

Place over bowl of ice water until thick enough to spread on cake.

Frosts tops and sides of two 8-inch layers or two 8-inch square cakes.

To make this bride's cake, cover cake with a white fluffy frosting and trim with a decorating frosting in a pastry tube. Attach a silver bell to a white covered wire entwined with small white flowers. Insert in center of cake. Garnish with additional flowers.

STRAWBERRY FLUFF

2   egg whites, unbeaten
1   cup sugar
Dash of salt
1⅓ cups sliced fresh strawberries or 1 package frozen sliced strawberries, thawed and drained

Combine egg whites, sugar, salt, and ⅔ cup strawberries in top of double boiler. Beat about 1 minute to blend.

Place over rapidly boiling water and beat constantly with rotary egg beater or at high speed with electric mixer 7 minutes, or until frosting will stand up in stiff peaks.

Remove from boiling water and beat until cool. Fold in remaining drained berries and spread at once.

Frosts tops and sides of two 9-inch layers; top and sides of 13 x 9 x 2-inch cake. Or fills 16 x 10 x 2-inch cake roll.

CARAMEL FROSTING

1½ cups firmly packed brown sugar
1   cup top milk or light cream
2   tablespoons butter or margarine
½   teaspoon vanilla
⅛   teaspoon salt

Combine sugar and milk and bring to boil, stirring constantly.

Stirring occasionally, boil to soft ball stage (236°F.).

Remove from heat and add butter, vanilla, and salt. Cool to lukewarm and beat until of spreading consistency.

Makes frosting for top and sides of two 8-inch layers or 24 cupcakes.

MAPLE FROSTING

¾   cup firmly packed brown sugar
2½ tablespoons water
1   egg white
¼   teaspoon maple flavoring

Cook sugar, water, and egg white in top of double boiler, beating constantly until mixture stands up in peaks (about 7 minutes).

Remove from heat and add maple flavoring. Beat until of spreading consistency.

Pretty finishing touches are easy to add to your frosted cupcakes. Just keep a few garnishes on hand and you're ready for any party cakes.

FONDANT FROSTING

2 cups sugar
1 cup water
½ teaspoon cream of tartar or 2 tablespoons light corn syrup

Combine the ingredients in a saucepan and stir over low heat until sugar is dissolved. Cover and bring to a rapid boil.

Uncover and continue to boil, without stirring, until a small amount of syrup forms a soft ball when dropped into cold water, or to 238°F. on a candy thermometer. Remove from heat and allow to cool to lukewarm.

Then beat with wooden spoon until syrup becomes white and creamy. Spread quickly over cake.

If it becomes too dry for smooth spreading, add a little hot water and beat until smooth. The fondant may be delicately tinted with food coloring and flavored as desired.

Dipping with Fondant: Make fondant frosting and keep it soft over boiling water, stirring in a few drops of boiling water if mixture becomes too stiff.

Add flavoring or food coloring desired, but stir as little as possible to avoid crystallization.

Lower small cakes or cookies into the liquid fondant on a dipping fork. Raise cake and draw the dipping fork lightly across the edge of the pan to remove any excess fondant, then invert the dipped cake onto a platter or waxed paper.

Work quickly so that the fondant will not become too thick. If it should thicken, however, add a few more drops of boiling water to bring it back to the right consistency.

Decorate the little cakes with a bit of candied fruit or rind, nuts, or tiny sugar flowers.

PENUCHE (PANOCHA) PECAN FROSTING

1½ cups firmly packed light brown sugar
1½ cups granulated sugar
2 tablespoons light corn syrup
¾ cup milk
¼ cup shortening
¼ cup butter or margarine
¼ teaspoon salt
1 teaspoon orange extract
1 cup chopped pecans

Place both sugars, corn syrup, milk, shortening, butter, and salt in saucepan. Bring slowly to full rolling boil, stirring constantly, and boil briskly 2 minutes. Cool to lukewarm.

Add orange extract and beat until thick enough to spread. Add pecans and mix.

Makes frosting to cover tops and sides of two 9-inch layers.

A pumpkin of orange frosting tops this cake; face is painted on with chocolate.

PRALINE FROSTING

1 cup firmly packed light brown sugar
½ cup granulated sugar
¼ cup corn syrup
½ cup top milk or ½ cup light cream
2 tablespoons butter or margarine
¾ cup chopped pecans
1 teaspoon vanilla

Combine sugars, syrup, and milk or cream in saucepan and cook to soft ball stage (236°F.).

Remove from heat. Add butter but do not stir. When cool, beat until spreading consistency is reached. Add nuts and vanilla.

Makes frosting for top and sides of two 9-inch layers.

BOILED MARSHMALLOW FROSTING

2½ cups granulated sugar
½ cup light corn syrup
¼ teaspoon salt
½ cup water
2 egg whites
1 teaspoon vanilla
8 marshmallows, cut in quarters

Place sugar, corn syrup, salt, and water together in a saucepan and cook to the firm ball stage (250°F.).

Pour the hot syrup slowly into the well beaten egg whites, beating constantly.

Add vanilla and continue beating until the frosting will hold its shape when tossed over the back of a spoon. Add marshmallows.

This frosting recipe will stand in swirls an inch or more high.

BURNT SUGAR

Heat and stir 1 cup sugar over medium heat until it foams up dark orange in color. Remove from heat. Slowly add 1 cup hot water.

Return to heat and boil until sugar is dissolved.

Keep and use as needed for flavoring frostings and whipped cream.

PETIT FOURS FROSTING

2 cups granulated sugar
1 cup water
1/8 teaspoon cream of tartar
1 to 2 cups sifted confectioners' sugar

Combine granulated sugar, water, and cream of tartar. Cook over direct heat to 226°F., or a thin syrup. Stir only until sugar is dissolved. Remove from heat.

Pour into top of double boiler and cool to somewhat above lukewarm (110°F.). Gradually add 1 to 2 cups sifted confectioners' sugar until frosting is of proper consistency to pour.

Place a few cakes in rows on a wire rack over a cooky sheet, allowing considerable space between cakes. Pour frosting over cakes, covering tops and sides and allowing frosting to drip onto cooky sheet. Keep over hot water when not pouring.

If it becomes too thick, add a few drops of hot water. If too thin, add a little more sifted confectioners' sugar. Scrape frosting from cooky sheet, reheat, and use for other cakes. Repeat the process until cakes are completely coated.

Decorate with ornamental frosting, colored sugar, candied fruit, or nuts.

HONEY ALMOND FROSTING

2 egg whites, unbeaten
1/4 cup honey
1 cup toasted, chopped almonds

Combine egg whites and honey in top of double boiler, beating with rotary egg beater until thoroughly mixed.

Place over rapidly boiling water, beating constantly with rotary egg beater, and cook 7 minutes, or until frosting will stand up in peaks.

Remove from boiling water. Add 1/2 of nuts. Spread on cake, sprinkling remaining nuts over top of cake while frosting is still soft.

Makes frosting to cover tops and sides of two 8- or 9-inch layers.

HUNGARIAN CHOCOLATE FROSTING

3 1-ounce squares unsweetened chocolate
1 1/2 cups sifted confectioners' sugar
2 1/2 tablespoons hot water
3 egg yolks
1/4 cup softened butter or other shortening

One whole egg may be substituted for the 3 egg yolks; use only 2 tablespoons water.

Melt chocolate. Remove from heat; add sugar and water, and blend. Add egg yolks, one at a time, beating well after each. Add butter gradually, beating well after each addition.

Makes frosting for tops and sides of two 8- or 9-inch layers, or top and sides of 8-, 9-, or 10-inch square cake, 10 x 5 x 3-inch loaf, a 9-inch 3-layer cake, or 24 cupcakes.

BUTTERSCOTCH FROSTING

1 cup firmly packed light brown sugar
1/3 cup granulated sugar
1/3 cup hot water
1 beaten egg white
1/2 teaspoon vanilla
Few grains salt

Mix together brown sugar, granulated sugar, and water over low heat until thoroughly dissolved. Bring to a boil and cook until syrup spins a long thread.

Pour syrup slowly over egg white, beating constantly. Add vanilla and salt.

If desired, 1/3 cup chopped nuts may be added.

TUTTI-FRUTTI FROSTING

2 egg whites
1 1/2 cups sugar
1/4 cup maraschino cherry juice
1 tablespoon lemon juice
3/4 cup toasted, chopped, blanched almonds
1/4 cup macaroon crumbs

⅛ teaspoon grated orange rind
20 cut up maraschino cherries

Combine egg whites, sugar, and fruit juice. Cook over boiling water, beating constantly until frosting will stand in peaks.

Fold in remaining ingredients and spread over cake.

MOCHA FROSTING

About ⅓ cup strong coffee
4 cups firmly packed sifted confectioners' sugar
½ cup shortening
⅛ teaspoon salt
1 teaspoon vanilla

To make strong coffee, add ½ cup medium-ground coffee to 1 cup cold water. Heat to boiling. Remove from heat and let stand 2 minutes. Strain and cool slightly.

Combine sugar gradually with shortening and add coffee as needed to make a creamy-smooth mixture. Add salt and vanilla. Spread on cooled cake.

Makes frosting for tops and sides of two 9-inch layers.

Mocha Chocolate Frosting: To above recipe, add 1 square (1 ounce) melted unsweetened chocolate. A little more coffee may be needed for good spreading consistency.

COCONUT MOROCCO FROSTING

2 unbeaten egg whites
1½ cups firmly packed brown sugar
Dash of salt
5 tablespoons water
1 square (1 ounce) unsweetened chocolate, melted and cooled
1 teaspoon vanilla
1½ cups moist, sweetened coconut

Combine egg whites, sugar, salt, and water in top of double boiler, beating with rotary egg beater until thoroughly mixed. Place over rapidly boiling water.

Beat constantly with rotary egg beater and cook 7 minutes or until frosting will stand in peaks. Remove from boiling water. Fold in chocolate and vanilla. Do not beat mixture.

Spread on cake. Sprinkle with coconut while frosting is still soft.

For holiday cupcakes, frost devil's food cupcakes with white mountain frosting. Place a candle atop each cake and set on a white paper doily.

Uncooked and Quick Frostings

Pineapple and gumdrops make an attractive, easy decoration.

PLAIN CONFECTIONERS' FROSTING
(Master Recipe)

    2 cups sifted confectioners' sugar
    2 tablespoons soft butter or marga-
       rine
    1 teaspoon vanilla or almond extract
    About 2 tablespoons boiling water,
       hot milk, hot cream, or fruit
       juice

Combine sugar, butter, and vanilla in a bowl. Add liquid, a little at a time, beating well with fork or spoon between additions.

Add only enough liquid to give the mixture easy spreading consistency.

Variations of Confectioners' Frosting

Glossy Chocolate Frosting: Add 1½ ounces (1½ squares) unsweetened chocolate melted over hot water, or ⅓ cup cocoa, sifted in with the sugar.

Coconut Confectioners' Frosting: Just before spreading plain confectioners' frosting or glossy chocolate frosting, add ½ cup moist shredded coconut. Garnish top of cake with more coconut.

Coffee Confectioners' Frosting: Use strong hot coffee for the liquid.

Maple Confectioners' Frosting: Use maple syrup for the liquid.

Nut Confectioners' Frosting: Add about ½ cup chopped nuts just before spreading. Garnish cake with nut halves or finely chopped nuts.

Raspberry Confectioners' Frosting: Omit flavoring in plain confectioners' frosting and use crushed raspberries and their juice as the liquid.

Raisin Confectioners' Frosting: Add about ½ cup chopped raisins to plain confectioners' frosting just before spreading.

Rum Confectioners' Frosting: Substitute rum or rum flavoring for other flavoring.

Strawberry Confectioners' Frosting: Omit flavoring in plain confectioners' frosting and use crushed strawberries and their juice as the liquid.

Simple Lemon Confectioners' Frosting: Substitute lemon juice for 1 tablespoon of the water. Add ½ teaspoon grated lemon rind.

Simple Orange Confectioners' Frosting: Omit flavoring. Use orange juice for the liquid. Add 1 teaspoon grated orange rind.

LEMON CONFECTIONERS' FROSTING
(Master Recipe)

1   egg yolk
1½ tablespoons lemon juice
1   tablespoon grated orange rind
⅛   teaspoon salt
2   cups confectioners' sugar

Combine egg yolk, lemon juice, orange rind, and salt. Beat until smooth.
Gradually mix in sugar and beat until of spreading consistency.
Makes frosting for 2 layers or 20 cupcakes.

Variations:

Lime Confectioners' Frosting: Substitute lime for lemon juice and ¼ teaspoon grated lemon rind for orange rind. Tint lightly with green food coloring.

Orange Confectioners' Frosting: Substitute 2 tablespoons orange juice for lemon juice and omit grated orange rind.

CREAM CHEESE ICING
(Master Recipe)

1   package (3 ounces) cream cheese
1   tablespoon milk
1½ cups sifted confectioners' sugar
1   teaspoon vanilla

Soften cheese with milk. Gradually add confectioners' sugar and vanilla. Beat until creamy.

Variations:

Cream Cheese Chocolate Icing: Increase milk to 3 tablespoons, and confectioners' sugar to 2½ cups. Add 2 ounces (2 squares) melted unsweetened chocolate and ⅛ teaspoon salt. Omit vanilla.

Orange Cream Cheese Icing: Substitute 2 tablespoons orange juice and 1 teaspoon grated orange rind for milk and vanilla.

FLUFFY LIME FROSTING

6   tablespoons butter or margarine
¼   teaspoon salt
1   teaspoon vanilla
1   egg white, unbeaten
3½ cups sifted confectioners' sugar
2½ tablespoons lime juice
2½ teaspoons grated lime rind

Cream together butter, salt, and vanilla. Add egg white. Then add sugar, alternately with lime juice, beating well after each addition. Add lime rind and beat well.
Makes frosting for tops and sides of two 8-inch layers, or top and sides of a 9- or 10-inch angel food cake.

Fluffy Orange Frosting: Use above recipe, substituting orange rind and juice for lime rind and juice.

QUICK FRUIT FROSTING

3   cups sifted confectioners' sugar
3   teaspoons grated orange rind
About ¼ cup lemon juice
Dash of salt
¼   cup butter or other shortening, melted

Combine sugar, rind, juice, and salt in small bowl. Add melted butter and beat.
Makes frosting for tops and sides of two 8-inch layers (thinly). Use half recipe for top of 8 x 8 x 2-inch square cake.

BROILED FROSTING

½   cup butter or margarine
1   cup firmly packed brown sugar
6   tablespoons cream
1   cup shredded coconut
1   cup chopped nuts

Heat butter and brown sugar together until melted and well blended. Add cream, coconut, and nuts, and spread on warm cake immediately.
Place under broiler until delicately brown, about 3 minutes.

HEART'S DELIGHT CAKE

1. Soften one 8-ounce package cream cheese at room temperature.

2. Blend 4 cups sifted confectioners' sugar into cream cheese. Add 2 tablespoons maraschino cherry juice and blend again.

3. Add 2 tablespoons chopped maraschino cherries, mixing them in lightly.

4. Spread frosting on bottom layer of your favorite cake baked in 2 heart-shaped pans.

5. Cover with second layer of cake and spread remaining frosting on sides and top of cake.

BUTTER FROSTING
(Master Recipe)

- ¼ cup butter or margarine
- 2 cups sifted confectioners' sugar
- ⅛ teaspoon salt
- 3 tablespoons cream
- 1 teaspoon vanilla

Cream butter until soft. Slowly stir in 1 cup sugar and the salt. Add additional sugar alternately with cream, beating thoroughly after each addition until creamy and smooth. Beat in vanilla.

Additional cream may be added to give frosting spreading consistency.

Makes frosting to cover top and sides of two 8-inch layer cakes or 2 dozen cupcakes.

Butter Frosting Variations

Almond Butter Frosting: Omit vanilla in master recipe. Add 1 teaspoon almond flavoring.

Apricot Butter Frosting: Omit cream in master recipe. Add ¼ cup cooked apricot pulp and 1 teaspoon lemon juice.

Chocolate Butter Frosting: Melt 2 ounces (2 squares) unsweetened chocolate over hot water. Blend with 2 tablespoons boiling water. Add vanilla reduced to ½ teaspoon and salt. Substitute 2 tablespoons milk for cream.

Cinnamon Butter Frosting: Substitute cinnamon for vanilla in master recipe.

Coffee Butter Frosting: Substitute strong coffee for cream in master recipe.

Lemon Butter Frosting: Substitute lemon juice and 1 egg yolk for the cream and vanilla in master recipe. Add 1½ teaspoons grated lemon rind.

Maple Walnut Butter Frosting: In master recipe, substitute maple flavoring for vanilla. Add ½ cup chopped walnuts with the last of the sugar.

Mint Butter Frosting: Prepare master recipe. Color frosting green. Substitute mint flavoring for vanilla.

Or melt peppermint candy and add to frosting for flavor and color.

Mocha Butter Frosting: In master recipe, substitute coffee for cream. Add 1½ tablespoons cocoa with the creamed butter.

Orange Butter Frosting: In master recipe, substitute 1 egg yolk and 2 tablespoons orange juice for the cream. Substitute grated orange rind for vanilla.

Pineapple Butter Frosting: In master recipe, omit cream. Add about ¼ cup drained crushed pineapple. Use lemon juice for flavoring.

Pistachio Butter Frosting: Prepare master recipe. Color frosting pale green. Add a few drops of almond extract.

Strawberry Butter Frosting: Omit liquid in master recipe. Add about ¼ cup crushed strawberries.

Use lemon juice for flavoring. Decorate with whole strawberries.

CREAMY VANILLA FROSTING

- 2 tablespoons shortening
- 2 tablespoons soft butter or margarine
- ⅛ teaspoon salt
- 1 teaspoon vanilla
- 2 cups firmly packed confectioners' sugar
- 2 tablespoons warm cream

Cream shortening and butter together. Add salt, vanilla, and 1 cup sugar. Stir in warm cream.

Add remaining sugar and beat until thoroughly blended.

Spread on top and sides of cake. Makes frosting for two 8-inch layers.

Creamy Lemon Frosting: In above, substitute 1 tablespoon lemon juice and ¼ teaspoon grated lemon rind for vanilla.

MOLASSES MOCHA FROSTING
(Master Recipe)

2 cups sifted confectioners' sugar
1/4 cup butter or margarine
1 egg white, unbeaten
1 tablespoon cold coffee
1 tablespoon molasses
1 teaspoon vanilla

Add 1 cup sugar gradually to butter and egg white. Mix well.

Add remaining sugar alternately with coffee, molasses, and vanilla. Beat well.

Makes enough for tops and sides of two 8-inch layers or tops of two 9-inch layers.

Variations:

Molasses Chocolate Frosting: Add 3 tablespoons cocoa or 1 square (1 ounce) melted chocolate.

Molasses Orange Frosting: Omit coffee and vanilla. Add 2 tablespoons orange juice, 1 teaspoon grated orange rind, and 1/2 teaspoon grated lemon rind.

BUTTERFLY FROSTING

2 tablespoons butter or margarine
2 1/2 cups sifted confectioners' sugar
1 egg white, unbeaten
About 1 tablespoon cream
3/4 teaspoon vanilla
1/8 teaspoon salt
Coloring

Cream butter; add part of sugar gradually, blending after each addition. Add remaining sugar, alternately with egg white, then with cream, until of right consistency to spread. Beat after each addition until smooth.

Add vanilla and salt. Tint delicately with coloring.

For assorted frostings, divide untinted frosting into four small bowls. Use one plain or flavor with 1/2 square (1/2 ounce) melted unsweetened chocolate. Tint the remaining frostings to give delicate, yet decided shades of yellow, green, and pink.

While using assorted frostings, keep bowls covered to avoid crusting. If necessary, one or two drops of cream or milk may be added to keep frostings of right consistency to spread. Use for decorating, if desired.

SUPREME CHOCOLATE NUT FROSTING

1/2 cup butter or margarine
1 egg
2 ounces (2 squares) chocolate
1 1/3 cups confectioners' sugar
1/8 teaspoon salt
1 teaspoon vanilla
1 cup chopped nuts

Cream butter until soft and creamy. Beat in egg.

Melt chocolate and add to butter-egg mixture. Add confectioners' sugar, salt, and vanilla. Beat until smooth and creamy. Stir in chopped nuts.

Makes frosting for 1 large loaf cake or 24 cupcakes.

ALMOND PASTE FROSTING

Blanch or skin 1 pound of almonds and put through food chopper, using medium blade.

Mix in 1 pound confectioners' sugar, sifted very well.

Beat 3 egg whites slightly, then mix them in. Finally, add 1 teaspoon almond extract.

Because this makes a heavy and stiff paste, you have to place it on the cake and work it into a smooth, even layer with your hands.

ALMOND FROSTING

Cream 1/2 cup butter. Add dash of salt. Blend in 1 3/4 cups sifted confectioners' sugar gradually.

Add 1 unbeaten egg yolk, 1/2 teaspoon almond extract, and 4 teaspoons milk. Beat until of spreading consistency.

Add few drops of yellow food coloring, if desired.

ORNAMENTAL FROSTING

Cream 2 tablespoons butter. Blend in 2 cups sifted confectioners' sugar, mixing well.

Add 1/2 teaspoon vanilla and 2 to 4 tablespoons hot cream, a little at a time, until frosting is of right consistency to press through a cone made from heavy brown paper.

Divide into 3 or more parts and tint each a different pastel color by adding food coloring, a drop at a time.

Decorate cakes by pressing frosting through paper cones.

GOLDEN CREAM FROSTING

1/4 cup shortening
1/4 cup butter or margarine
1/2 teaspoon salt
1 teaspoon vanilla
1 egg yolk
1 3/4 to 2 cups sifted confectioners' sugar
1 tablespoon milk

Cream shortening and butter until soft and fluffy. Beat in salt, vanilla, and egg yolk. Add sugar alternately with milk, beating constantly.

Makes frosting for top and sides of two 9-inch layers.

BROILED TOPPING, HAWAIIAN STYLE

1 baked cake, 9 x 13 x 2 inches, warm or cold
8 pineapple slices, drained (No. 2 1/2 can)
1/2 cup firmly packed brown sugar
2 tablespoons flour
3 tablespoons soft butter or margarine
Red currant jelly

Arrange the drained pineapple slices on the baked cake.

Make a crumbly mixture of the brown sugar, flour, and butter and sprinkle evenly over pineapple slices.

Fill the center of each pineapple slice with a spoonful of jelly and broil carefully for several minutes until topping is bubbly and warm.

Broiled Topping, Hawaiian Style

"NO-COOK" MARSHMALLOW FROSTING

1/4 teaspoon salt
2 egg whites
1/4 cup sugar
3/4 cup corn syrup, light or dark
1 1/4 teaspoons vanilla

Add salt to egg whites and beat with electric or rotary beater until mixture forms soft peaks.

Gradually add sugar, about 1 tablespoon at a time, beating until smooth and glossy. Continue beating and add corn syrup, a little at a time, beating thoroughly after each addition, until frosting peaks. Fold in vanilla.

Makes enough to frost top and sides of two 9-inch layers.

Variations:

Coffee Frosting: Omit vanilla; add 1 tablespoon instant coffee with corn syrup.

Lemon or Orange Frosting: Omit vanilla; fold in 2 teaspoons grated lemon or orange rind.

Spice Frosting: Omit vanilla; add 1/2 teaspoon ginger, 1/4 teaspoon cinnamon, and a few grains of cloves with dark corn syrup.

Coconut Frosting: Sprinkle 1 cup shredded coconut over top and sides of frosted cake, or fold in 1 cup shredded coconut with vanilla.

MOLASSES BUTTER FROSTING

2 tablespoons shortening
2 tablespoons butter or margarine
1/4 teaspoon salt
1/4 cup light molasses
1/4 cup cream
4 cups firmly packed sifted confectioners' sugar

Cream shortening and butter. Add salt, molasses, and cream; mix well. Add confectioners' sugar gradually and stir until smooth.

Spread between, on top and sides of two 9-inch layers. Use with spice cake.

BANANA BUTTER FROSTING

1/2 cup mashed ripe banana
1/2 teaspoon lemon juice
1/4 cup butter or margarine
3 1/2 cups sifted confectioners' sugar

Mix together banana and lemon juice.

A shower cake is easy with this white mound cake baked in one bowl and covered with a fluffy white frosting.

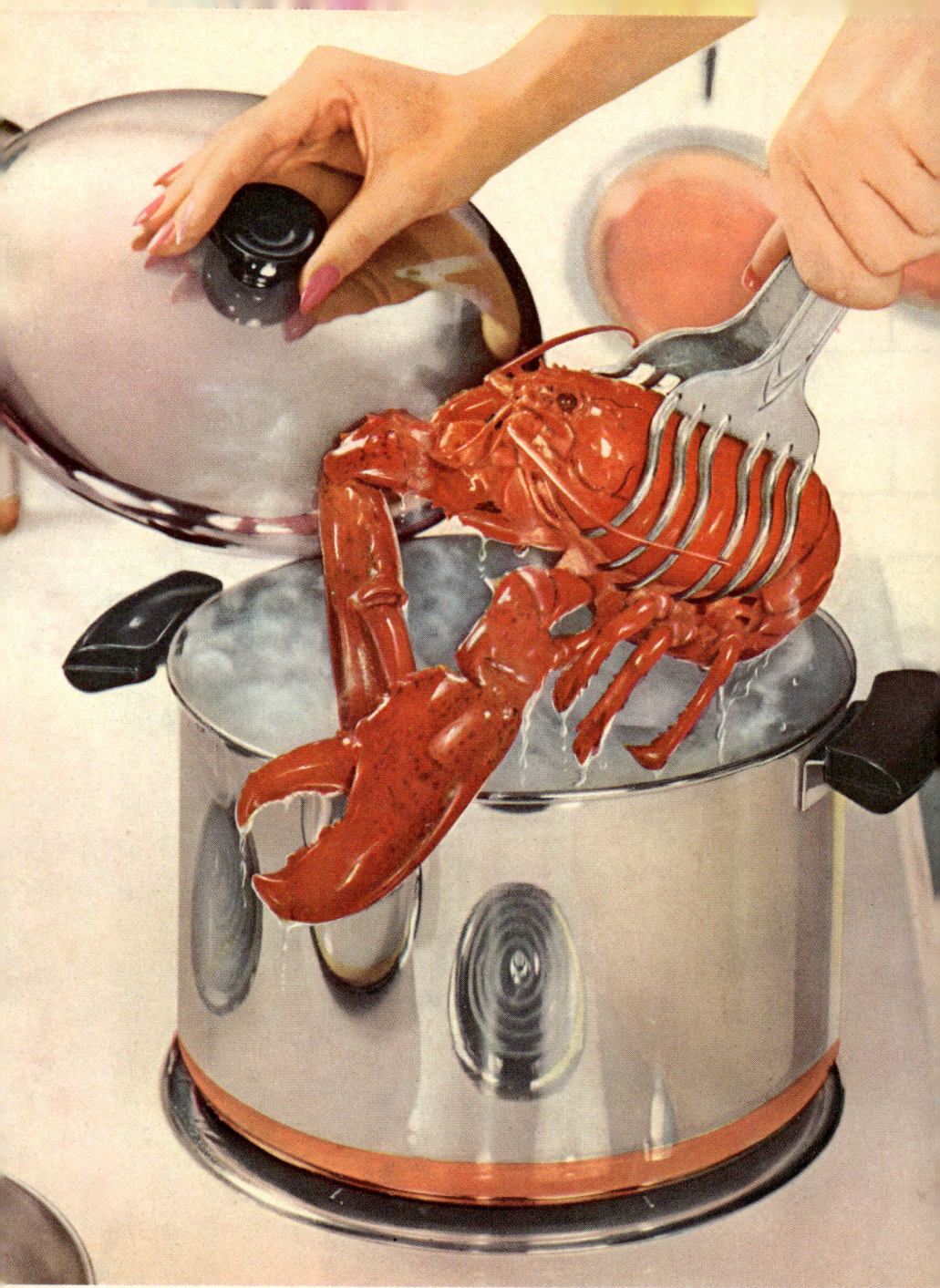

Be it Lobster à la Newburg or just plain, boiled lobster with a butter sauce, you're headed for sumptuous, tasteful eating with freshly cooked Maine lobster.

LOW CALORIE ORANGE-PINEAPPLE SHERBET

1   6-ounce can frozen unsweetened
    orange juice concentrate
1   6-ounce can frozen unsweetened
    pineapple juice concentrate
3½ cups cold water
2   tablespoons Sucaryl solution or 48
    tablets, crushed
1   cup nonfat dry milk solids

Set refrigerator at coldest setting. Put all ingredients into a 2-quart mixing bowl in order given. Beat just enough to blend.

Pour into ice cube trays; freeze 1 to 2 hours until half frozen.

Remove to large chilled mixer bowl; beat on low speed until mixture is softened, then beat on high speed 3 to 5 minutes until creamy but not liquid.

Pour into freezer containers or ice cube trays. Freeze. Makes 20 servings of 58 calories each.

Beat butter until creamy. Add sugar and banana alternately, a small amount at a time, beating until frosting is light and fluffy.

Makes enough frosting for top and sides of two 9-inch layers.

QUICK FUDGE FROSTING

6   to 8 ounces semisweet chocolate
1/4   cup butter or margarine
1 1/2 cups sifted confectioners' sugar
1/2   teaspoon cinnamon
1/8   teaspoon salt
1/2   cup warm milk
1   teaspoon vanilla

Melt chocolate over hot water. Blend in butter.

Combine sugar, cinnamon, and salt. Add alternately with milk to chocolate-butter mixture, beating after each addition. Add vanilla and cool.

Makes frosting for 24 cupcakes or tops and sides of two 9-inch layers.

CHOCOLATE MOCHA FROSTING

1/4 cup butter or margarine
1/4 cup strong coffee
2   cups confectioners' sugar
1/4 cup cocoa
1/2 teaspoon salt
1   teaspoon vanilla

Have butter and coffee at room temperature. Sift together sugar, cocoa, and salt.

Combine all ingredients and beat until smooth and fluffy. Spread on cake.

Makes enough frosting for two 9-inch layers.

EASY CHOCOLATE FROSTING

3   tablespoons butter or margarine
2   squares (2 ounces) chocolate
2 3/4 cups sifted confectioners' sugar
1   teaspoon vanilla
1/3 cup hot milk

Combine butter and chocolate in top

of double boiler. Cook over boiling water until chocolate is melted.

Combine sifted confectioners' sugar with vanilla and hot milk and blend well.

Add melted chocolate and beat until smooth and thick.

SPICY RAISIN FROSTING

1 3/4 cups confectioners' sugar
1   tablespoon cocoa
1/2 teaspoon cinnamon
1/2 teaspoon cloves
1/2 teaspoon nutmeg
1/2 cup sweetened condensed milk
1/2 teaspoon vanilla
1/2 cup raisins

Combine ingredients in order given. Use to frost spice cakes.

FLUFFY UNCOOKED FROSTING

2   egg whites
1   tablespoon vinegar
1   teaspoon lemon juice
Few grains salt
2   teaspoons cornstarch
About 2 1/2 cups sifted confectioners'
     sugar

Beat egg whites until stiff. Add vinegar, lemon juice, salt, and cornstarch. Continue beating.

Gradually add sugar until of consistency to spread.

FLUFFY HONEY FROSTING

1   egg white
Dash of salt
1/2 cup honey

Beat egg white with salt until stiff enough to hold up in peaks, but not dry.

Pour honey in fine stream over egg white, beating constantly until frosting holds its shape. (Beat about 2 1/2 minutes with electric mixer, or about 4 minutes by hand.)

Makes frosting to cover tops of two 8-inch layers.

Glazed Fruit Cake

Glazes

APRICOT GLAZE

Wash and drain 1 cup dried apricots. Put in saucepan with $2\frac{1}{2}$ cups water and boil uncovered 10 minutes.

Put through sieve or food mill. There should be 2 cups apricot purée; if not, add water to make that amount.

Combine purée with $2\frac{1}{2}$ cups sugar. Bring to a boil and boil gently 5 to 8 minutes, stirring constantly until purée is as thick as marmalade.

Cool and use for tarts, pastries, and under frostings of decorated cakes to give a smooth surface over which to spread the outer frosting.

To Store: Keep unused glaze in covered container in refrigerator. When ready to use again, warm slightly to facilitate spreading.

CHOCOLATE GLAZE

1   tablespoon butter or margarine
1   1-ounce square unsweetened chocolate
$1\frac{1}{2}$ tablespoons hot milk
$\frac{1}{2}$ cup sifted confectioners' sugar
Dash of salt

Melt butter and chocolate together. Combine milk, sugar, and dash of salt in bowl. Blend in chocolate mixture gradually.

Pour over cake and spread with spatula. Makes enough glaze to cover cake roll or 8- or 9-inch layer.

COFFEE GLAZE

$2\frac{1}{2}$ tablespoons water
1   tablespoon butter or margarine
$1\frac{1}{3}$ cups sifted confectioners' sugar

Dash of salt
2   teaspoons instant coffee

Heat water and butter together. Measure sugar, salt, and instant coffee into bowl. Add hot liquid and stir until smooth.

Pour over cake, letting it run down sides. Makes glaze to cover tube cake.

LEMON GLAZE

$1\frac{1}{2}$ tablespoons milk
1   tablespoon butter or margarine
1   cup sifted confectioners' sugar
$1\frac{1}{2}$ tablespoons lemon juice
$\frac{1}{2}$ teaspoon grated lemon rind

Heat milk and butter together. Measure sugar into bowl. Add liquid and stir until smooth. Then add juice and rind.

Pour over cake, letting it run down sides. Makes enough glaze to cover a 9-inch or 10-inch tube cake.

ORANGE GLAZE

1   teaspoon grated orange rind
1   tablespoon orange juice
1   cup firmly packed sifted confectioners' sugar
About 1 tablespoon water

Combine orange rind and juice; let stand 5 minutes. Strain and discard rind.

Stir juice into sugar and add enough water to make a good spreading consistency.

Spread on slightly warm cake. Makes enough glaze for top of one 9-inch square cake.

For a quick decoration, confectioners' sugar is sprinkled through a paper doily.

Cake Fillings

CREAM FILLING
(Master Recipe)

3/4 cup sugar
5 tablespoons flour
1/4 teaspoon salt
2 cups scalded milk
2 slightly beaten eggs
1 teaspoon vanilla

Combine sugar, flour, and salt. Slowly stir in scalded milk. Cook in double boiler over boiling water for 15 minutes, or until thick.

Add a little of the hot mixture to eggs. Stir in remaining hot mixture. Cook over simmering water for 3 minutes. Cool and add vanilla.

For a richer filling, add 2 tablespoons butter to hot cooked custard.

Makes filling for 4 large layers or 24 large cream puffs or 24 éclairs.

Cream Filling Variations:

Banana Cream Filling: In master recipe, substitute 1 teaspoon lemon juice for vanilla. Add medium-sized mashed banana to filling.

Butterscotch Cream Filling: In master recipe, substitute 3/4 cup brown sugar for granulated sugar. Add 2 tablespoons butter to cooked filling.

Chocolate Cream Filling: In master recipe, increase sugar to 1 cup. Add 2 ounces (2 squares) unsweetened chocolate to milk before cooking. Beat until smooth.

Coconut Cream Filling: In master recipe, add 1 cup shredded coconut to filling.

Coffee Cream Filling: In master recipe, substitute 1/2 cup strong fresh coffee for 1/2 cup milk. Proceed as directed.

Creamy Custard Filling: Prepare master recipe. Fold 1/2 cup whipped heavy cream into chilled filling.

Pineapple Cream Filling: In master recipe, substitute lemon juice for vanilla. Add 1/2 cup crushed, drained pineapple to filling.

APPLE FILLING

¾ cup sugar
1 tablespoon flour
3 tablespoons lemon juice
1 tablespoon water
1 beaten egg
1 cup grated apple

Combine all ingredients. Cook over very low heat until thick, 8 to 10 minutes. Cool.

Spread between layers. Frost cake with seven-minute frosting.

Pineapple Coconut Filling: In above recipe, substitute 1 cup drained crushed pineapple for the grated apple, and add ½ cup freshly grated coconut.

DATE FILLING

1 pound chopped, pitted dates
1 tablespoon lemon juice
½ cup water
⅓ cup sugar
⅛ teaspoon salt
1 cup finely chopped nuts

Combine all ingredients except nuts and bring to boiling point, stirring constantly until thick.

Add nuts and cool. Spread between layers.

FRUIT CAKE FILLING AND FROSTING

2 cups sugar
6 tablespoons cornstarch
1 cup drained, crushed pineapple
1 cup chopped maraschino cherries
1 cup liquid (pineapple juice plus water)
2 tablespoons butter or margarine
Juice of 2 lemons
1 cup chopped nuts
1 4-ounce can coconut
¼ cup brandy or rum (optional)

Combine sugar, cornstarch, pineapple, cherries, liquid, and butter in a saucepan. Stir until well blended. Cook over low heat until very thick, stirring frequently.

Remove from heat; add lemon juice, nuts, coconut, and liquor. Blend well. Cool.

Spread between layers and on top and sides of cake.

Halloween
Fig
Faces

WHIPPED CREAM FILLING
(Master Recipe)

½ teaspoon unflavored gelatin
1 tablespoon cold water
3 tablespoons confectioners' sugar
¼ teaspoon vanilla
½ cup heavy cream

Soften gelatin in cold water. Place over boiling water. Stir until dissolved. Let cool.

Mix with sugar, vanilla, and cream. Whip until stiff. Chill thoroughly before spreading. Makes filling for two 9-inch layers.

Variations of Whipped Cream Filling

Applesauce Filling: Omit vanilla in master recipe. Decrease cream to ⅓ cup. Before chilling, fold in ½ cup chilled, thick applesauce and ½ teaspoon cinnamon.

Chocolate Filling: In master recipe, increase sugar to 4 tablespoons. Mix with 2 tablespoons cocoa before adding cream.

Coffee Filling: Substitute coffee for water in master recipe.

Pineapple Filling: Omit vanilla in master recipe. Decrease cream to ⅓ cup. Before chilling, fold in ½ cup drained, crushed pineapple.

STRAWBERRY WHIPPED CREAM FILLING

¼ cup powdered sugar
½ cup mashed strawberries
1 cup cream, whipped
1 stiffly beaten egg white

Add sugar to strawberries. Combine whipped cream and beaten egg white. Fold in strawberries.

If too sweet, add a few drops of lemon juice. If too tart, add more sugar.

PINEAPPLE FILLING

¾ cup sugar
2½ tablespoons cornstarch
⅛ teaspoon salt
Grated rind of 1 lemon
¼ cup lemon juice
3 slightly beaten egg yolks
½ cup canned pineapple juice
2 tablespoons butter or margarine

Mix sugar, cornstarch, and salt in top of double boiler. Add lemon rind and lemon juice and mix well. Add egg yolks, pineapple juice, and butter and blend.

Place over boiling water. Cook until thick and smooth, stirring constantly, about 15 minutes.

Makes filling for two 8-inch layers.

GOLDEN CREAM FILLING

1½ tablespoons (1½ envelopes) unflavored gelatin
4 tablespoons cold water
8 egg yolks
⅛ teaspoon salt
1 cup confectioners' sugar
4 tablespoons strong fresh coffee
1 pint cream, whipped

Soften gelatin in cold water.

Beat egg yolks with salt until thick. Beat sugar in gradually.

Dissolve softened gelatin in hot coffee. Add to egg-sugar mixture.

Let stand until partially set. Fold in whipped cream.

Makes filling and topping for two 9-inch layers.

CARAMEL FILLING

½ cup firmly packed brown sugar
2 cups granulated sugar
1 cup buttermilk
½ teaspoon baking soda
½ cup butter or margarine
1 tablespoon vanilla

Combine sugars, buttermilk, baking soda, and butter. Cook until syrup forms a soft ball when a small amount is dropped into cold water (238°F.).

Cool. Add vanilla. Beat until creamy. Spread over cake.

SOUR CREAM FILLING

2 eggs
⅔ cup sugar
1 cup sour cream
Pinch of salt
½ teaspoon vanilla

Beat eggs until thick. Gradually add sugar, beating constantly. Add sour cream and salt.

Cook over boiling water until thickened, stirring constantly, about 15 minutes.

Cool. Add vanilla. Makes filling for two 9-inch layers.

BANANA FILLING

1 cup sugar
¼ cup water
3 large bananas, mashed
2 lightly beaten egg yolks

Heat sugar and water until syrup spins a thread when dropped from fork or spoon (234°F.).

Banana cream filling can be used on top as well as between layers.

Combine mashed bananas with beaten egg yolk. Add syrup gradually, beating thoroughly.

Place over hot water. Heat through, beating thoroughly. Cool before spreading.

Banana Nut Filling: Add about ½ cup chopped nuts just before spreading.

APRICOT FILLING

½ pound dried apricots
½ cup sugar
½ cup crushed pineapple
1 cup chopped nuts

Wash apricots and place in a saucepan. Barely cover with water. Add sugar. Cover and simmer over low heat about 30 minutes.

Strain. Add well drained crushed pineapple, then add nuts. Cool. Spread between layers.

Our famous date got on this cake just where the sugar didn't.

WALNUT TORTE FILLING

2 beaten egg yolks
1/2 cup sugar
3/4 cup milk
1/2 teaspoon vanilla or rum flavoring
1 pound chopped walnuts

Mix egg yolks and sugar; add milk and cook in top of double boiler until thick.

Cool; add vanilla or rum and nuts. Spread between layer of walnut torte.

MAPLE CREAM FILLING

4 egg yolks
3/4 cup confectioners' sugar
3/4 cup milk
1/2 cup butter or margarine
2 teaspoons maple flavoring

Beat egg yolks until thick and lemon colored. Add sugar and milk and cook in double boiler, stirring constantly, until thick, about 10 minutes. Cool.

Cream butter until fluffy. Add thoroughly cold custard and maple flavoring. Beat with rotary beater until smooth.

Makes filling for 3-layer 8-inch cake.

RUM NUT FILLING AND FROSTING

1/4 cup enriched flour
3/4 cup milk
1/4 cup butter or margarine
1/2 cup shortening
3/4 cup granulated sugar
1/2 teaspoon salt
1/2 teaspoon vanilla
3/4 cup chopped nuts
3 tablespoons rum flavoring
4 cups tightly packed sifted confectioners' sugar

Measure flour into saucepan. Add milk gradually, stirring until smooth. Cook to thick paste over slow heat, stirring constantly. Cool to lukewarm.

Cream butter, shortening, granulated sugar, and salt thoroughly. Add lukewarm paste and beat with rotary beater until fluffy. Fold in vanilla and nuts.

Spread 1/3 of mixture between layers of 9-inch layer cake.

Add rum flavoring and confectioners' sugar to remaining mixture and stir until well blended.

Spread over top and sides of cake. Makes filling and frosting for two 9-inch layers.

CHOCOLATE BRAZIL NUT FILLING

2 squares (2 ounces) chocolate
3/4 cup milk
4 tablespoons flour
1/2 cup sugar
1 tablespoon butter or margarine
1/2 teaspoon vanilla
1/2 cup ground Brazil nuts

Add chocolate to milk in double boiler. Beat over low heat until chocolate is melted and well blended.

Add a small amount of the chocolate mixture to the flour, which has been sifted with the sugar.

Return to double boiler. Stir until smooth and cook until thickened. Add butter and vanilla.

When cool, add Brazil nuts and spread on cake.

SOUR CREAM RAISIN FILLING

1 cup sour cream
1 cup sugar
1 cup seedless raisins

Combine ingredients. Cook in top of double boiler until thickened.

FIG FILLING

1/3 cup sugar
2 tablespoons cornstarch
1/2 cup boiling water
1/4 pound chopped figs
2 tablespoons lemon juice
1 tablespoon grated lemon rind

Mix sugar and cornstarch in a saucepan; add water. Cook until thick and smooth.

Add figs, lemon juice, and rind. Cool. Spread between layers.

LEMON FILLING
(Master Recipe)

3/4 cup sugar
5 tablespoons flour
1/8 teaspoon salt
2/3 cup water
1 slightly beaten egg
1 tablespoon butter or margarine
1 teaspoon grated lemon rind
1/3 cup lemon juice

Combine sugar, flour, and salt in top of double boiler. Add water and blend thoroughly. Cook over boiling water until thickened, stirring constantly.

Cover and cook additional 10 minutes, stirring occasionally.

Stir in a little of the hot mixture into slightly beaten egg. Slowly stir into the remaining hot mixture. Cook over simmering water for 2 minutes, stirring constantly.

Cool slightly. Add butter and lemon rind. Chill and add lemon juice. Makes filling for two 9-inch layers.

Lemon Filling Variations

Lemon Cream Filling: Fold 1/2 cup whipped, heavy cream into chilled lemon filling.

Orange Filling: Proceed as for lemon filling. Decrease sugar to 1/2 cup, water to 1/2 cup, lemon juice to 1 tablespoon, lemon rind to 1/2 teaspoon.

Add 1 tablespoon orange rind. When chilled, add 1/2 cup orange juice.

Orange Date Filling: Add 1/2 cup chopped dates to orange filling.

Orange Coconut Filling: Add 1/2 cup shredded coconut to orange filling.

Orange Cream Filling: When orange filling is chilled, fold in 1/2 cup whipped heavy cream and 1/2 cup plain or toasted shredded coconut.

LORD BALTIMORE FILLING AND FROSTING

1 1/2 cups sugar
1/2 teaspoon cream of tartar
Dash of salt
1/2 cup hot water
3 egg whites
1/2 teaspoon vanilla
2 teaspoons lemon juice
1/2 cup macaroon crumbs
12 candied cherries, chopped
1/2 cup chopped blanched almonds
1/4 cup chopped pecans

Blend sugar, cream of tartar, salt, and hot water. Cook, without stirring, to soft ball stage or 240°F. on candy thermometer.

Beat egg whites until stiff. Pour syrup in a fine stream over beaten whites, beating constantly. Add vanilla.

Add lemon juice to crumbs. Fold crumbs, cherries, and nuts into 1 1/2 cups of frosting and use this for cake filling.

LIME FRUIT FILLING

To 1/2 cup of fluffy lime frosting (see Index), add 2 tablespoons each of chopped raisins, nuts, candied cherries, and citron.

Spread between layers of cake. Use remaining frosting to cover top and sides of cake. For a gay effect, sprinkle silver dragées or tiny colored candies on top of cake.

FROZEN DESSERT BOOK

Ice cream gets top TV reception.

In Nero's time, the Romans flavored snow from the Alpine passes with fruit juices, and served it as a summer dessert. Several centuries later, Marco Polo brought back a recipe for "milk ice" as one of the treasures from his travels in the East. Still later, "cream ice" became the favorite dessert of Charles I.

In our own country, Dolly Madison, the gracious wife of our fourth President, introduced ice cream at the Presidential reception in the early 1800's.

Today, ice cream and its frozen relatives are no longer reserved for special occasions or privileged persons. Instead, they are among the most popular and most typical of American desserts.

The family of frozen desserts includes many kinds of delicacies which are divided into several classes.

CLASSES OF FROZEN DESSERTS

1. Ice Cream

a. Plain or Philadelphia ice cream: Milk or cream is sweetened, flavored and frozen. It may or may not contain either gelatin or eggs.

b. French, New York or cooked ice cream: Cream is folded into a custard foundation containing many egg yolks and the mixture is frozen.

c. American ice cream: Similar to French ice cream except that flour or cornstarch is substituted for part or all of the egg yolks.

d. Parfait: Whipped cream and flavoring are folded into a foundation of beaten egg whites or yolks cooked with hot syrup, and the mixture is frozen.

e. Frozen pudding: Actually French ice cream which has the egg whites added separately. Contains generous amounts of fruit or nuts.

2. Frozen Custard

Similar to New York ice cream except that the egg whites are added separately. Usually has a lower fat content than is legal for ice creams.

3. Ice

Fruit juice, sweetened with sugar, diluted with water and frozen. May or may not contain gelatin or eggs. Frappés are ices frozen to a slushy consistency.

4. Sherbet

Frozen mixture of fruit juice, sugar and milk, cream or ice cream. Usually contains a stabilizer such as gelatin. A sorbet is a sherbet made with a combination of fruit juices; a lacto is a sherbet made with sour milk; soufflés are sherbets made with whole eggs.

5. Mousse

Still-frozen dessert of sweetened, flavored whipped cream. May or may not contain fruits.

General Directions for Preparing Frozen Desserts in Refrigerator

1. Rapid freezing is important to make refrigerator ice creams that are smooth. Speed up freezing by turning temperature control to coldest point 1/2 hour before preparing dessert. Allow control to remain at this point until dessert is frozen.

2. The dessert is apt to freeze more rapidly if ice cubes are not being frozen at the same time.

3. Measure sugar or any other sweetening agent carefully; excess sugar retards freezing.

4. Remove ice cubes from tray to be used and replace empty tray in refrigerator to chill while preparing dessert.

5. Pour mixture into cold tray and place tray in fastest freezing position in the unit. Usually this is the bottom of freezing unit.

6. For more rapid freezing, moisten inside bottom of freezing unit with a little water before replacing tray. This way the tray will contact the freezing unit immediately.

7. Most frozen desserts are smoother when beaten once during the freezing process. Freeze mix to consistency of mush (don't let it get too hard if you want a smooth product); empty into a chilled bowl and beat until fluffy but not melted. Return quickly to chilled tray moistened on bottom and continue to freeze.

8. When mix is frozen sufficiently, turn thermostat halfway between the coldest setting and normal.

9. When beating cream or egg whites for folding into half-frozen mixtures, beat them only until they hold a soft peak, not until stiff.

10. When beating egg whites, reserve 2 tablespoons sugar for each egg white to add gradually to the egg whites after the foamy stage is reached. This meringue-like mixture holds up better during the folding-in process than plain egg white does.

General Directions for Hand-Turned or Motor-Driven Freezers

1. A 1-quart freezer requires about 6 pounds of ice to freeze the dessert and pack it for 2 hours. A 2-quart freezer requires about 10 pounds. Allow a few extra pounds for the ice that melts while the dessert is being frozen.

2. Be sure ice is chipped from the top of the block in an ice refrigerator. Modern ice boxes are regulated so that ice must cover the bottom of the ice chamber to insure correct food compartment temperature.

3. Ice cubes from an automatic refrigerator can be used as an ice supply. Two cups of water yield about 1 pound of ice.

4. Put pieces (or cubes) of ice into a canvas bag and crush with a mallet.

5. Finely crushed ice melts faster and hastens the freezing of ice cream.

6. Scald and cool the can, the cover and dasher of the freezer.

7. The ice cream mixture should be cold when it is put into the freezer. A warm mixture may result in a coarser-textured dessert.

8. Fill the can only two-thirds full. As the dasher turns, air is whipped into the dessert, causing it to "swell."

9. Ice cream freezes as heat from it is absorbed by the ice and salt. Ice alone is not cold enough to freeze foods; therefore, salt is added which lowers the temperature of the ice.

10. Use 8 parts ice to 1 part ice cream salt. This allows for a moderate rate of freezing so that a rather large amount of air may be incorporated. This helps to produce a smooth ice cream. In addition, this proportion of ice to salt prevents waste of ice due to too rapid melting.

11. Crank the freezer a few times before adding the ice to be sure the freezer turns freely. Then, turn the crank while adding the ice and salt.

12. Turn the crank slowly for the first 3 minutes to chill the mixture thoroughly. Then crank rapidly to make desserts creamier.

13. When the crank becomes too difficult to turn, the dessert is frozen.

14. To improve flavor, let frozen desserts "ripen" 1 to 2 hours before serving. To do this, remove dasher, press down mixture in can with a spoon, place a cork in the hole of the lid and put the lid in place. Repack the freezer with a mixture of 3 parts crushed ice to 1 part ice cream salt, and cover the freezer with newspapers or a heavy cloth.

15. The dessert can be ripened, also, in the tray of an automatic refrigerator. Pack the dessert firmly in tray, cover with a double layer of waxed paper and turn the control of the refrigerator to the coldest point. The dessert will remain smooth for several hours.

General Directions for Molded Frozen Desserts

1. Use a regular ice cream mold, or an ordinary tin can, such as a baking powder or coffee can with a tightly fitting cover.

2. Chill mold thoroughly before filling with cold ice cream mixture.

3. Fill mold to overflowing. Cover with waxed paper and put on lid.

4. Seal lid edge with a piece of adhesive tape or a strip of cloth dipped in melted fat or paraffin, covering the crack completely. When fat or paraffin cools it hardens, making a seal to keep out the salty water.

5. Bury the mold in a mixture of 3 parts crushed ice to 1 part ice cream salt. Cover ice mixture with newspaper or heavy cloth. Allow about 3 hours to freeze a quart-sized mold. Drain off water and add more ice and salt in same proportions, if necessary.

6. When frozen, remove mold, dip in warm water for a few seconds, or wrap in a cloth wrung out of hot water. Remove the strip around lid, the cover and waxed paper. Invert on a serving dish.

Baked Alaskas

Baked Alaska

BAKED ALASKA
(Master Recipe)

- 1- to 1½-inch layer sponge or layer cake
- ⅛ teaspoon salt
- 5 egg whites
- ⅔ cup sugar
- 1 quart or 2 pints firm, brick ice cream

Cover a wooden cutting board with a strip of heavy wrapping paper. If a thick wooden board is not available, a heavy baking sheet may be used. The wood is preferred because it is an extremely slow heat conductor, an advantage when "cooking" ice cream.

Arrange cake on the paper. (The paper will help slide dessert onto plate.)

Add salt to egg whites and beat until soft peaks form. Add sugar gradually and continue to beat until meringue holds stiff peaks.

After making meringue, center ice cream on cake. The layer of cake should be large enough to extend ½ to 1 inch beyond edge of ice cream.

Spread meringue over entire surface of ice cream and cake edge, carefully sealing to edges of cake. Sprinkle top with granulated sugar for a snowy effect.

Bake in very hot oven (450°F.) until golden brown, about 5 minutes.

To serve, slide from board to plate. Slice at the table in front of guests. Garnish servings with whole berries. Serves 6.

Baked Alaska in Pie Shells: Fill baked pie shell or individual tart shells with firm ice cream. Cover with meringue and finish as directed in Baked Alaska.

Individual Baked Alaska: Cut individual rounds or squares of sponge cake. Cover and bake as above.

Fruit Alaska: Cover cake with a layer of fresh or stewed fruit. Arrange ice cream on top. Cover with meringue. Bake as above.

Rum Alaska: Place 2 half egg shells open side up in top of meringue before baking. Bake. Fill shells with rum. Set aflame and serve.

Alaska with Nuts: Sprinkle chopped nuts over meringue.

Strawberry Alaska: Use 2 pint bricks of vanilla or strawberry ice cream.

Place 1 pint brick on the cake. Cover with a 1-inch layer of sliced and chilled strawberries; place the other pint brick on top.

Proceed as in master recipe.

Orange Alaska: The procedure is the same as in the master recipe but the ice cream is replaced by orange ice.

Remove the Alaska from the oven and surround by orange sections which have been cooked in a thin syrup until glazed.

PINK LADY ALASKA
Crumb Crust:
20 graham crackers, finely rolled (about 1⅔ cups crumbs)
¼ cup softened butter or margarine
¼ cup sugar

Blend together graham cracker crumbs, butter or margarine, and sugar. Press firmly against bottom and sides of 9-inch pie plate.

If desired, bake in moderate oven (375°F.) 8 minutes. Chill.

(Make the crumb crust early in the day—ready to fill at serving time.)

Filling:
16 marshmallows
2 tablespoons crushed strawberries
2 stiffly beaten egg whites
¼ cup sugar
¼ teaspoon salt
1 pint vanilla ice cream, very firm
1 cup fresh sliced strawberries

Stir and melt marshmallows and crushed strawberries over low heat until smooth. Beat sugar gradually into stiffly beaten egg whites until they hold a peak.

Add salt. Gradually beat in cooled marshmallow mixture.

Fill crumb crust with ice cream, cover with sliced strawberries. Top with gay swirls of marshmallow meringue (be sure meringue completely covers ice cream). Brown quickly in broiler and serve at once. Serves 6 to 8.

Pink Lady Alaska

Surprise Alaska

SURPRISE ALASKA

1   cooled 9-inch sponge cake
6   egg whites
½ teaspoon cream of tartar
1   cup sugar
1   quart vanilla or strawberry ice-cream

Place cooled cake on several thicknesses of waxed paper (trimmed to size of cake) on a wooden board.

Using a small plate as a guide, cut a 3½-inch circle from center of cake, hollowing out a depression for the ice cream. Leave about a 1-inch layer of cake in the bottom of the depression.

Beat egg whites with cream of tartar until stiff. Beat in sugar a little at a time until meringue forms stiff, glossy peaks but is not dry.

Firmly pack the hollow with 1 quart ice cream; level off with top of cake.

Quickly spread meringue on sides and top of cake, covering completely.

Brown in very hot oven (450°F.) for 4 to 5 minutes, or until meringue is lightly browned. Slip the cake from board onto a serving platter and garnish with fresh flowers or fruit. Cut into wedge-shaped pieces and serve at once with extra ice cream, if desired. Serves 8.

Tricks with Ice Cream

SPONGE CAKE SUNDAE

    2 1-ounce squares unsweetened choc-
         olate
    1 cup light or dark corn syrup
    ¼ teaspoon vanilla
    4 sponge cake dessert shells
    1 pint peppermint ice cream
    Hot chocolate sauce

Melt chocolate in top of double boiler. Add syrup, stir only until blended, then add vanilla.

Place dessert shells on dessert plates. Top with pink peppermint ice cream. Pass hot chocolate sauce.

PINK AND LOVELY ICE CREAM

    ½ cup top milk
   12 fig cookies, crumbled
    1 quart strawberry ice cream
    3 bananas, mashed fine
    ½ cup very finely ground or chopped
         dried coconut
    3 tablespoons lemon juice
    1 cup heavy cream
    ⅓ cup confectioners' sugar
    1 teaspoon vanilla

In a saucepan, combine top milk and fig cookies that have been crumbled. Stir until cookies are almost blended with the milk. Cool.

Meanwhile, soften (but do not melt) the ice cream. Add the mashed bananas, coconut, lemon juice, and fig cookie mix. Stir together quickly.

Place in freezing tray or in an oiled mold. Cover tightly and freeze quickly.

Whip cream; add sugar and vanilla. Decorate the turned-out mold, then freeze before serving or cover the ice cream in the refrigerator tray and freeze before serving. For a birthday, add candles and flowers. Serves 8 to 10.

FRUIT SURPRISE

    4 oranges
    2 bananas
    ¼ cup sugar
    1 quart vanilla ice cream

Peel and section oranges. Peel and slice bananas. Combine fruits. Stir in sugar. Serve over ice cream.

ORANGE CHOCOLATE SWIRL

Soften 1 quart chocolate ice cream. Swirl one 3-ounce can frozen orange juice concentrate through ice cream. Turn into refrigerator tray and freeze until firm.

Fruit Surprise

Ice Cream Tarts

ICE CREAM TARTS

Fill baked tart shells with fresh, sliced, sweetened peaches or strawberries. Top with a scoop of vanilla ice cream.

Serve with additional fruit, if desired.

CRUNCHY CHOCOLATE SUNDAE

8 chocolate chip cookies
1 pint vanilla ice cream

Break chocolate chip cookies into coarse crumbs.

Scoop out ice cream in 4 balls; roll in crumbs.

Serve immediately, or store in freezer until needed. Top with chocolate sauce and serve with additional chocolate chip cookies.

Variations: Use other crumbled cookies such as coconut macaroons, vanilla wafers or use chocolate cake or baked meringue crumbs. Ice cream balls or squares may be prepared in advance by rolling in crumbs and stored in freezing compartment of refrigerator or freezer until time to serve.

CRUNCHY CHOCOLATE SUNDAE #2

$1\frac{1}{2}$ $6\frac{1}{2}$-ounce packages semisweet chocolate pieces
4 cups crisp cereal flakes
1 quart ice cream
Chocolate sauce

Melt chocolate over hot water. Stir in cereal flakes; toss with fork until flakes are well coated. Form in wreaths on waxed paper placed on cooky sheet. Chill until firm, about 15 minutes.

To serve, fill wreaths with ice cream and top with chocolate sauce. Makes 8 wreaths.

Note: Remove wreaths from refrigerator a few minutes before serving time.

ICE CREAM CHERRY TARTS

  6 individual pastry shells
  1 quart vanilla ice cream
  1 pint fresh or frozen cherries or
   2 cups canned sweet red cherries

Fill cooled individual pastry shells generously with vanilla ice cream. Top with red cherries and cherry sauce (below). Serves 6.

Cherry Sauce:

  1 cup cherry juice (sweetened juice from fresh, frozen, or canned sweet red cherries)
  1/4 cup sugar
  1 1/2 teaspoons cornstarch
  1 teaspoon lemon juice

Blend sugar, cornstarch, and lemon juice. Add to cherry juice and cook, stirring until slightly thickened. Cool and serve over the ice cream. If canned cherries are used, add more sugar to suit taste.

JIFFY CHOCOLATE PARFAIT

Alternate chocolate ice cream, whipped cream, and canned crushed pineapple.

JIFFY ORANGE PARFAIT

Alternate orange sections, vanilla ice cream, and strawberry jam.

STRAWBERRY PINEAPPLE SUNDAE

Cut 1 large pineapple in half lengthwise, through green tops. Remove meat with sharp knife, cutting to within 1/4 inch of edges. Remove core and cut in cubes.

Wash 1 pint strawberries and remove hulls. Slice and sweeten with 1/4 cup sugar. Combine with pineapple and chill until serving time.

Place pineapple shells on large serving tray. Fill each half with ice cream (use 1 quart in all). Serve with pineapple strawberry sauce. Serves 6.

*Strawberry
Pineapple Sundae*

Ribbon Cake

RIBBON CAKE

Cut baker's pound cake into 4 rectangular slices. Cut 1 pint strawberry ice cream into slices. Alternate cake and ice cream layers. Freeze until firm. Serve with thawed frozen strawberries or raspberries.

TRIPLE DELIGHT

1 quart pistachio ice cream
1 quart strawberry ice cream
1 quart vanilla ice cream
½ pint heavy cream
¼ cup sifted confectioners' sugar
Green food coloring
Whole strawberries

Pack pistachio ice cream, strawberry ice cream, and vanilla ice cream individually into three 9-inch layer cake pans. Freeze until firm.

Whip cream until stiff. Fold sugar into cream. Add enough food coloring to tint cream a delicate green.

Unmold ice cream layers on serving plate.

Frost sides of ice cream layers with cream. Garnish with strawberries and mint leaves.

BELMONT COUPE

1 No. 2 can pear halves
Cinnamon
1 pint vanilla ice cream
1 cup chocolate syrup

Drain pear halves well. Sprinkle each half lightly with cinnamon.

Alternate layers of pears, ice cream, and chocolate syrup in parfait glasses. Serves 6.

FLAMING MINCEMEAT

Spoon heated prepared mincemeat onto vanilla or coffee ice cream. Top with sugar cube dipped into lemon extract; light and serve.

ICE CREAM BUTTERFLIES

Buy or prepare 6 cupcakes from instant cake mix, or use own recipe; cool. Cut off tops of cupcakes; cut tops in half.

Using 1 quart ice cream, place a large scoop of it on each cupcake; insert halves of top of cupcake in ice cream to resemble butterfly wings. Serve plain or with sauce and whipped cream. Serves 6.

RED AND WHITE SWIRL

Soften 1 quart vanilla ice cream. Swirl ½ cup strawberry sundae topping through ice cream. Turn into refrigerator tray and freeze until firm.

PARTY CLOWNS

Place a scoop of ice cream in center of each cooky or cake round for clown's head. Then make his face, using raisins for eyes, nose, and mouth.

Place an ice cream cone on each scoop of ice cream for the hat. (If desired, cones may be decorated ahead of time with candy. Use a little confectioners' sugar mixed with water to hold candy decoration on cones.)

Party Clown

CHERRY CANTALOUPE SUNDAE

3   small cantaloupes
2   cups pitted Bing cherries
1   cup cherry juice or water
1½ cups sugar
Few grains of salt
2   tablespoons lemon juice
2   drops almond extract
1   quart vanilla ice cream

Wash cantaloupes and cut in halves crosswise. Remove seeds and cut out inside of each to within ¼ inch of edge; dice. Chill halves. Wash and pit cherries.

Combine remaining ingredients except ice cream. Heat to boiling and cook until syrup is thick. Add diced cantaloupe and cherries and chill.

Add a little sauce to each cantaloupe half. Top with ice cream and garnish with Bing cherries and diced cantaloupe. Serve with extra sauce. Serves 6.

APRICOT ICE CREAM PIE

¼   pound marshmallows
Apricot preserves
2   egg whites
⅛   teaspoon salt
¼   cup sugar
2   pints vanilla ice cream
1   9-inch baked pastry shell, chilled

Heat marshmallows and 2 tablespoons preserves in top part of double boiler over boiling water, until marshmallows are half melted. Remove from heat, and beat until smooth.

Beat egg whites with salt until foamy; gradually add sugar, and beat until stiff. Fold in marshmallow mixture.

Press ice cream quickly into chilled shell. Spread with ½ cup preserves. Cover with marshmallow meringue, spreading to cover ice cream completely.

Put under preheated broiler 1 or 2 minutes, or until lightly browned. (This meringue browns very quickly.) Cut in wedges, and garnish with spoonful of preserves.

*Cherry
Cantaloupe Sundae*

Cranberry Ice Cream Pie

CRANBERRY ICE CREAM PIE

1½ cups gingersnap crumbs
¼ cups sugar
¼ cup melted butter or margarine
1 quart vanilla ice cream
1 cup canned whole cranberry sauce

Combine gingersnap crumbs, sugar, and melted butter in bowl. Mix until thoroughly blended.

Cover bottom and sides of a buttered 8-inch pie pan with crumb mixture. Pack down firmly. Chill in refrigerator.

When crust is thoroughly chilled, fill with vanilla ice cream. Top with whole cranberry sauce. Place in freezing unit and freeze until serving time.

FRUIT COCKTAIL FREEZE

1 pint vanilla ice cream
1 No. 2 can fruit cocktail, drained
¾ cup vanilla wafer crumbs (15 wafers)

Spread ice cream in bottom of refrigerator tray. Top with fruit cocktail, then vanilla wafer crumbs. Turn refrigerator to coldest temperature. Keep in freezing compartment during dinner. Serves 5.

ICE CREAM SHADOW CAKE

1 bought large angel food cake ring
2 pints chocolate ice cream
1 pint heavy cream, whipped and sweetened
Chocolate sauce

Cut angel cake in 3 layers. Spread 1 pint ice cream (softened) between each layer. Spread whipped cream on top and sides of cake; freeze.

When ready to serve, remove from freezer, and dribble cooled chocolate sauce over top and sides of cake. Cut in wedges to serve. Serves 12.

Note: If freezer isn't available, chill cake and have cream whipped before filling cake. Fill with ice cream; spread with cream. Dribble sauce over top and sides, and serve at once.

JIFFY ICE CREAM SUNDAE SAUCES

Marshmallow Sauce: In saucepan, combine 1/4 pound (16) marshmallows with 1/3 cup honey, 1/3 cup heavy cream and pinch of salt.

Cook until marshmallows are almost melted, stirring occasionally. Remove from heat; stir until completely melted.

Chocolate Marshmallow Sauce: Add 1 1/2 squares unsweetened chocolate to marshmallows. Cook as in marshmallow sauce (above).

Maple Walnut Syrup: Heat some maple syrup and chopped walnuts over boiling water about 5 minutes. Good hot or cold.

Honey Almond Syrup: Heat honey and chopped toasted almonds over boiling water about 5 minutes. Good hot or cold.

Coffee Coconut Syrup: Heat 1 cup of light corn syrup with 1 tablespoon instant coffee and 1/2 cup coconut over boiling water about 5 minutes. Good hot or cold.

Pineapple or Grape Sauces: Slightly thaw frozen pineapple or grape juice concentrate.

Honey Sauce: Stir together 1/4 cup honey and 2 tablespoons melted butter or margarine.

Coffee Sauce: Mix 1 to 2 tablespoons instant coffee with 1 cup canned sweetened condensed milk.

DATE-NUT SUNDAE SAUCE

1/2 cup chopped pitted dates
1/2 cup dark corn syrup
1/4 cup brown sugar
1/4 cup water
1/4 teaspoon salt
1/2 teaspoon vanilla
1/4 cup chopped pecans

Combine dates, corn syrup, brown sugar, water, and salt in saucepan. Bring to a boil and cook 2 minutes over medium heat, stirring constantly.

Remove from heat and add vanilla and pecans. Cool and serve over vanilla ice cream. Makes 1 1/2 cups.

CHOCOLATE PEANUT BUTTER SUNDAE SAUCE

1 8-ounce package semisweet chocolate bits
1/4 cup peanut butter, cream or chunk style
1/4 cup light corn syrup
2 tablespoons cream

Melt chocolate in double boiler over hot water. Add peanut butter and stir until blended. Remove from heat and add corn syrup and cream.

Serve warm over vanilla ice cream.

This sauce may be stored in the refrigerator, but should be heated before using. If it becomes too thick, add a small amount of cream to thin it down. Makes 1 1/2 cups sauce.

HONEYDEW-RASPBERRY DELIGHT

1 medium honeydew melon
1 quart vanilla ice cream
2 cups sweetened raspberries

Cut honeydew melon into 8 crosswise slices 1/4- to 1/2-inch thick. Remove seeds and rind.

With a sharp knife, make diagonal slashes around edge of melon slices.

Place slices of melon on dessert plates and top each with a large scoop of ice cream. Circle scoop of ice cream with sweetened raspberries. Serves 8.

HOLIDAY PEANUT CRUNCHY LOAF

Roll 1 pint vanilla ice cream in 1 cup crushed peanut brittle. Serve with butterscotch sauce.

SUGAR-SPICED LOG

Roll 1 pint vanilla ice cream in 1 cup chopped salted peanuts, 1/4 teaspoon cinnamon, and 1/2 teaspoon allspice. Top with chocolate sauce.

*Ice Cream
Snowballs*

CHOCOLATE MERINGUES

Fill cooled meringue shells (see Index) with scoops of chocolate ice cream. Top with chocolate sauce.

STRAWBERRY ICE CREAM PIE

3   egg whites
1/4 teaspoon salt
1/4 teaspoon cream of tartar
3/4 cup sugar
3/4 teaspoon vanilla
1   quart vanilla ice cream
1   quart strawberries
4   tablespoons confectioners' sugar
1/2 cup heavy cream, whipped
1/2 teaspoon vanilla

Beat egg whites with salt and cream of tartar until stiff but not dry. Gradually add 3/4 cup sugar and 3/4 teaspoon vanilla and beat until it holds up in peaks.

Cut a circle of brown paper to fit bottom of 9-inch pie pan. Spread meringue on paper in pie pan and build up edges.

Bake in very slow oven (250°F.) 1 hour.

Turn off heat and allow to remain in oven 1 hour longer or until dry.

Fill cooled shell with ice cream. Top with sliced strawberries to which have been added 2 tablespoons confectioners' sugar. Top with whipped cream sweetened with 2 tablespoons confectioners' sugar and flavored with 1/2 teaspoon vanilla. Decorate with a few whole berries. Serves 8.

REFRIGERATOR TRAY PIE

1/4 cup butter or margarine
1/4 cup sugar
1 1/2 cups chocolate wafer crumbs
1 1/2 pints vanilla or coffee ice cream, softened

Cream butter and add crumbs and sugar. Blend together. Pack half the crumb mixture into a refrigerator tray. Chill.

Spoon ice cream over crumb mixture and pack down well. Press remaining crumbs on top of the ice cream. Spread with whipped cream, if desired. Return to refrigerator to freeze. Serves 6.

ICE CREAM SNOWBALLS

Make large snowballs of vanilla ice cream, using ice cream scoop or large spoon.

Quickly roll each ball in chopped pecans or walnuts. Serve plain or with a butterscotch sauce.

Cherry Mint Ice Cream

Homemade Ice Creams

CHERRY MINT ICE CREAM

½   cup sugar
1   tablespoon cornstarch
1½ cups milk
2   eggs, separated
⅛   teaspoon salt
Few drops mint extract
1   cup heavy cream, whipped
¾   cup coarsely chopped maraschino
       cherries (about 30)
Green food coloring

Combine sugar and cornstarch in top of double boiler; gradually stir in milk. Place over direct heat and cook, stirring constantly, until mixture thickens. Place over boiling water and cover; cook 10 minutes, stirring occasionally.

Beat egg yolks. Stir a little of hot mixture into beaten egg yolks; then stir into milk mixture. Cook over hot, not boiling, water, stirring constantly, for 3 minutes. Remove from hot water and cool.

Beat egg whites until stiff; add salt and fold into cooled custard. Add mint flavoring.

Pour into refrigerator tray and freeze until frozen about 1 inch from sides of tray.

Turn into mixing bowl. Beat with rotary or electric beater until light and fluffy.

Fold in whipped cream and maraschino cherries. Add enough food coloring to tint mixture a light green.

Pour into freezing tray or mold. Freeze until firm. Stir occasionally during freezing process.

Unmold and garnish with whipped cream and additional maraschino cherries, if desired. Makes 1½ pints.

MASTER REFRIGERATOR ICE CREAM
(Uncooked Base)

2 teaspoons (⅔ envelope) unflavored gelatin
½ cup cold water
1¾ cups evaporated milk
½ cup sugar
2 teaspoons vanilla
1½ cups heavy cream, whipped

Soften gelatin in cold water. Dissolve in hot milk. Add sugar and vanilla. Cool.

Turn into freezing tray and chill until slightly thickened. Fold in whipped cream.

Return to tray and freeze to mush-like consistency. Turn into chilled bowl and beat until smooth, but not melted.

Return to cold tray and freeze. Makes 1 quart.

MASTER REFRIGERATOR ICE CREAM
(Cooked Base)

⅔ cup sugar
1½ tablespoons cornstarch
1½ cups top milk
2 eggs, separated
2½ teaspoons vanilla
¼ teaspoon salt
1 cup cream, whipped

Combine sugar and cornstarch in top of double boiler. Gradually stir in milk. Cook over boiling water, stirring constantly, until mixture thickens. Cover and cook 10 minutes.

Stir a little of hot mixture into beaten egg yolks. Add yolks to remaining hot mixture. Cook over hot, not boiling, water, stirring constantly for 3 minutes.

Cool. Add vanilla and salt. Fold beaten egg whites into cooled custard. Pour into refrigerator tray and freeze until firm throughout.

Remove to chilled bowl. Quickly beat with rotary beater until smooth. Fold in whipped cream. Return to cold tray. Freeze. Makes 6 to 8 servings.

Variations of Refrigerator Ice Cream

Banana: Add 1 cup ripe mashed bananas and 1 teaspoon lemon juice with whipped cream.

Cherry: Add 1¼ cups chopped pitted cherries to chilled mixture just before folding in whipped cream.

Chocolate: Melt 2 squares (2 ounces) chocolate in milk; beat with rotary beater until blended. Increase sugar to ¾ cup. Use only 1 teaspoon vanilla.

Coffee: Substitute ½ cup strong coffee for ½ cup milk.

Frozen Pudding: Combine and add with the whipped cream, ½ teaspoon grated orange rind, ½ cup mixed chopped candied fruit, ¼ cup chopped maraschino cherries, and 3 tablespoons maraschino cherry juice.

Ginger: Add 2 tablespoons ginger syrup with vanilla. Add 3 tablespoons chopped preserved ginger with whipped cream.

Mint: Reduce vanilla to 1 teaspoon. Add oil of peppermint to taste (few drops) and green coloring.

Nut Brittle: Grind or crush ¼ pound nut brittle and fold in before final freezing.

Peach: Add 1¼ cups mashed peaches to chilled mixture just before folding in whipped cream.

Pistachio: Use only 1 teaspoon vanilla. Add ½ teaspoon almond extract. Add green food coloring. Add ½ cup chopped pistachio nuts with whipped cream.

Raspberry or Strawberry: Add 1¼ cups crushed berries to chilled mixture just before folding in whipped cream.

BLACK WALNUT ICE CREAM

- 2 cups milk
- ¾ cup sugar
- 1 tablespoon flour
- ¼ teaspoon salt
- 2 eggs, separated
- 2 teaspoons vanilla
- 2 cups light cream
- ¾ cup chopped black walnuts

Scald milk in top of double boiler. Mix sugar, flour, and salt. Gradually stir into scalded milk. Cook 5 minutes over simmering water, stirring constantly.

Beat egg yolks slightly. Add about ½ cup of hot milk mixture to egg yolks, blending well. Add to remaining milk and cook 2 minutes over simmering water, stirring constantly.

Chill. Add vanilla, cream, and nuts and blend well.

Beat egg whites until stiff but not dry and gently fold into mixture. Pour into 2 refrigerator trays. Freeze until nearly solid.

Turn into chilled bowl and beat until creamy. Return to trays and freeze firm. Makes 1½ quarts.

BUTTER PECAN ICE CREAM

- 1⅓ cups sweetened condensed milk (15 ounce can)
- ¼ cup melted butter or margarine
- 1 cup cold water
- 1 teaspoon vanilla
- 1 pint heavy cream
- 1 cup pecans, chopped

Combine condensed milk and melted butter thoroughly. Add water and vanilla. Mix well and chill.

Whip cream until fluffy but not stiff. Fold into chilled mixture.

Pour into freezer tray and freeze to consistency of mush. Do not allow to freeze too much or ice cream will be coarse.

Remove half-frozen mixture from refrigerator. Scrape into a chilled bowl and beat until smooth but not melted.

Add nuts and blend in well. Return to freezing tray and freeze until firm. Serves 10 to 12.

PEPPERMINT CANDY ICE CREAM

2 tablespoons cornstarch
1 cup sugar
1/8 teaspoon salt
2 cups light cream
3 well beaten egg yolks
3 egg whites, stiffly beaten
2 cups heavy cream, whipped
1 cup finely crushed peppermint sticks

Mix cornstarch, sugar, and salt in top of double boiler. Add cream and cook over boiling water 10 minutes, stirring constantly.

Add small amount of hot mixture to egg yolks and blend thoroughly. Return to double boiler and cook 5 minutes longer, stirring constantly.

Cool. Fold in stiffly beaten egg whites and pour into large refrigerator tray. Freeze until mushy.

Turn into large chilled bowl and beat with electric or rotary beater until smooth. Fold in whipped cream and crushed candy. Blend thoroughly.

Return to cold refrigerator tray and freeze firm. Stir well once during first hour of freezing. Makes 1 quart.

CARAMEL ICE CREAM

3 tablespoons granulated sugar
1 cup milk
1/2 cup confectioners' sugar
1/8 teaspoon salt
1 1/2 tablespoons flour
2 eggs, separated
1 pint coffee cream
1 teaspoon vanilla

Stir granulated sugar in heavy skillet over low heat until sugar is melted and becomes light brown in color. Remove from heat. Gently stir in milk. Cook until sugar is dissolved.

Mix confectioners' sugar, salt, and flour in top of double boiler.

Add sugar-milk mixture. Cook over hot water until thickened, stirring constantly, about 15 minutes.

Combine with beaten egg yolks and cook 5 minutes longer, stirring constantly. Add cream and blend well.

Freeze in refrigerator tray until firm. Remove to chilled bowl.

Add vanilla and beat until mixture is light and creamy. Fold in stiffly beaten egg whites. Return to freezing tray. Freeze firm. Serves 8.

Ice Cream Filled Éclairs

Ice Cream in Meringue Shells

BUTTERSCOTCH ICE CREAM

3 tablespoons butter or margarine
½ cup brown sugar
1 cup milk
1½ tablespoons cornstarch
2 tablespoons cold milk
Pinch of salt
¼ teaspoon vanilla
1 cup heavy cream, whipped

Heat butter and sugar in top of double boiler until butter is melted and well blended with sugar. Add 1 cup milk and heat to boiling.

Mix cornstarch with 2 tablespoons cold milk; stir into butter and sugar mixture.

Add salt and cook, stirring constantly, until thickened.

Cool and add vanilla. Fold in whipped cream.

Turn into refrigerator tray. Freeze to a mush.

Remove to chilled bowl and beat quickly but thoroughly with rotary beater until smooth and fluffy. Return to tray and freeze. Serves 6.

AVOCADO ICE CREAM
(Freezer)

2 cups milk
½ cup granulated sugar
¼ teaspoon salt
2 well beaten eggs
1 cup heavy cream
1 teaspoon lemon extract
1 cup sieved avocado

Combine milk, sugar, and salt; scald. Pour over eggs, stirring constantly. Add cream and lemon extract and cool.

Add fruit and mix thoroughly. Freeze in ice cream freezer. Makes about 1 quart.

Since the smooth texture of this ice cream is due to the emulsified avocado oil, it is best done in a freezer.

GELATIN ICE CREAM
(Freezer)

1 tablespoon (1 envelope) unflavored
    gelatin
2 tablespoons cold water
2 cups milk
3/4 cup sugar
1/8 teaspoon salt
2 cups light cream
2 teaspoons vanilla

Soften gelatin in cold water.

Scald milk; add gelatin, sugar, and salt. Stir until dissolved. Cool.

Add cream and vanilla. Freeze. Makes 1 1/2 quarts.

Pumpkin Tarts Á La Mode

CUSTARD ICE CREAM
(Freezer)

2 cups milk
1 tablespoon flour
3/4 cup sugar
1/4 teaspoon salt
2 slightly beaten egg yolks
2 cups heavy cream
1 tablespoon vanilla

Scald 1 1/2 cups milk. Mix flour, sugar, and salt. Add remaining cold milk. Add scalded milk slowly.

Cook over hot water 7 minutes, stirring constantly.

Stir hot mixture slowly into egg yolks. Cook and stir 2 minutes longer. Cool.

Add cream and vanilla. Freeze. Makes 1 1/2 quarts.

RENNET ICE CREAM
(Freezer)

1 rennet tablet
1 tablespoon cold water
3 cups lukewarm milk
3/4 cup sugar
1/8 teaspoon salt
1 cup heavy cream
2 teaspoons vanilla

Dissolve rennet tablet in cold water.

Mix remaining ingredients and heat until lukewarm. Add rennet and mix well.

Let stand until slightly thickened. Freeze. Makes 1 1/2 quarts.

FRENCH ICE CREAM
(Freezer)

1/2 cup sugar
1/8 teaspoon salt
5 slightly beaten egg yolks
2 cups scalded milk
2 cups heavy cream
2 to 3 vanilla beans, crushed or 2 teaspoons vanilla

Mix sugar, salt, and egg yolks. Add scalded milk slowly, mixing well. Cook over hot water until mixture coats spoon, 5 to 8 minutes. Cool.

Strain and add cream and vanilla. Freeze. Makes 1 1/2 quarts.

PHILADELPHIA ICE CREAM
(Freezer)

1 quart light cream
1 cup sugar
Dash of salt
2 teaspoons vanilla

Scald cream. Add sugar and stir until dissolved.

Add salt and vanilla. Cool and freeze. Makes 1 1/2 quarts.

FREEZER ICE CREAM VARIATIONS

(Use French, Gelatin, Custard, Philadelphia, or Rennet Recipes)

Bisque: In master recipe, substitute 2 tablespoons sherry for vanilla. Add ¾ cup chopped nuts just before freezing.

Butter Crunch: In master recipe, add ¾ pound finely crushed butter crunch to mixture just before freezing.

Caramel: In master recipe, add ¼ cup caramel flavoring with cream and vanilla.

Burnt Almond: Add 1 cup finely chopped, blanched, and toasted almonds to caramel ice cream mixture.

Chocolate: Melt 2 squares (2 ounces) unsweetened chocolate. Add ¼ cup hot water and blend thoroughly. Add to hot mixture in master recipe.

Coffee: Scald ⅓ cup ground coffee with milk or cream. Strain before adding other ingredients. Omit vanilla in master recipe.

Macaroon: In master recipe, add 1 cup crushed macaroons just before freezing. Reduce sugar to ½ cup.

Maple: In master recipe, substitute maple syrup or maple sugar for granulated sugar. If desired, stir in 1 cup chopped nuts when partially frozen.

Mint: In master recipe, substitute mint flavoring for vanilla; add green food coloring.

Peach: In master recipe, use only 1 teaspoon vanilla; add ½ teaspoon almond extract. Just before freezing, add 2 cups crushed peaches, sweetened with ½ cup sugar.

Peanut Brittle: In master recipe, add ¾ cup finely crushed peanut brittle to mixture just before freezing.

Peppermint: In master recipe, add ¾ cup finely crushed peppermint stick candy to mixture just before freezing.

Pineapple: In master recipe, substitute 1 tablespoon lemon juice for vanilla. Add 2 cups well drained, crushed pineapple just before freezing.

Pistachio: To master recipe, add 1 teaspoon almond extract and green food coloring. Add ¾ cup chopped pistachio nuts.

Strawberry or Raspberry: Combine 2 cups mashed berries with ½ cup sugar; add to master recipe just before freezing.

Tutti-Frutti: In master recipe, use only ½ teaspoon vanilla. Combine and add 4 teaspoons maraschino cherry juice, ½ cup chopped maraschino cherries, ½ cup drained crushed pineapple, and ½ cup chopped nuts just before freezing.

Santa Sundae

Marlows

FROZEN HAWAIIAN MARLOW

1½ cups milk
¼ pound marshmallows, cut in halves (about 16)
½ cup heavy cream, whipped with 1 teaspoon vanilla
1½ cups (No. 2 can) drained crushed pineapple
¼ cup maraschino cherry halves
¼ cup chopped pecans or other nuts

Measure milk and marshmallows into top part of a double boiler. Heat over boiling water until marshmallows melt. Remove from heat and cool.

Fold vanilla flavored whipped cream, fruit, and nuts into cooled mixture and pour into 1-quart refrigerator tray. Freeze. Makes about 1 quart or 6 to 8 servings.

VANILLA MARLOW
(Master Recipe)

30 marshmallows
¾ cup hot milk or water
2 teaspoons vanilla
1½ cups heavy cream, whipped

Melt marshmallows in hot milk or water.

Cool. Add flavoring. Chill.

When mixture begins to thicken, combine with whipped cream. Pour into tray and freeze without stirring. Serves 4 to 6.

Vanilla Marlow Variations

Banana Marlow: Omit vanilla in master recipe. Add 1 cup mashed ripe banana and 1 tablespoon lemon juice to hot milk.

Chocolate Marlow: Add 2 squares (2 ounces) melted chocolate to hot milk in master recipe.

Peach Marlow: Add 2 cups peach pulp and 1 tablespoon lemon juice to

hot milk in master recipe. Substitute 1 teaspoon almond extract for vanilla.

BANANA GRAPE MARLOW

10 marshmallows
⅓ cup grape juice
2 tablespoons lemon juice
1 cup mashed ripe bananas (2 to 3 bananas)
½ cup heavy cream

Combine marshmallows and 2 tablespoons grape juice. Heat slowly, folding over and over, until marshmallows are half melted.

Remove from heat and continue folding until mixture is smooth and fluffy. Fold in remaining grape juice, then fold in lemon juice and bananas.

Turn into freezing tray and chill until mixture begins to freeze. Turn into a bowl and beat well.

Whip cream until thickened. Fold into marshmallow-banana mixture. Return to tray and freeze firm.

Serves 4 to 6.

STRAWBERRY MARLOW

1 cup crushed sweetened strawberries
1 tablespoon orange juice
¼ pound marshmallows (16)
¼ cup water
1 cup whipping cream
½ teaspoon vanilla
Few grains salt

Combine strawberries and orange juice.

Combine marshmallows and water; cook over hot water, stirring occasionally, until melted. Fold into strawberry mixture. Cool.

Whip cream slightly stiff; add vanilla and salt. Fold into strawberry mixture.

Pour into freezing tray and freeze firm. Serves 4.

Miscellaneous Frozen Desserts

*Frozen Orange Balls
in Orange Cups*

FROZEN ORANGE BALLS IN ORANGE CUPS

2	teaspoons (2/3 envelope) unflavored gelatin
1/4	cup cold water
1	cup water
3/4	cup sugar
1	teaspoon grated lemon rind
1	teaspoon grated orange rind
1	can frozen orange juice concentrate, thawed, or 1 cup fresh orange juice
1/3	cup lemon juice
2	egg whites
1/8	teaspoon salt
8	orange shell halves

Soften gelatin in 1/4 cup cold water 5 minutes.

Boil 1 cup water with sugar 10 minutes. Dissolve gelatin in hot syrup. Cool.

Add lemon and orange rind and juices. Chill until it begins to thicken. Turn into chilled bowl and beat with rotary beater until fluffy.

Beat egg whites with salt until stiff. Fold gently into fruit mixture. Turn mixture into freezer tray and freeze firm.

Form balls with an ice cream scoop. Place balls in scalloped orange shells. Cut a thin slice off bottom side of shells to make them stand secure.

Serve on galax leaves in chilled serving dishes. Serves 8.

FROZEN LIME CREAM CUPS

2	eggs
1/2	cup sugar
1/2	cup light corn syrup
1	cup cream
1	cup milk
1/3	cup lime juice

The magic of modern food-freezing provides almost any combination of family favorites in-a-jiffy.

fruits

1 teaspoon grated lime rind
Green food coloring
Whipped cream

Beat eggs until lemon colored. Slowly add sugar to eggs, beating until mixture is thick and custard-like.

Add corn syrup, cream, milk, lime juice, and grated lime rind, blending well. Tint a delicate green with food coloring.

Turn into refrigerator tray and freeze. When frozen, remove to chilled bowl and beat with rotary beater until light and creamy.

Line muffin pans with pastel colored fluted paper cups or use standard ice cream cups. Spoon mixture into them, filling almost to top. Freeze firm.

To serve, pipe whipped cream over tops with pastry tube. Decorate with thin slivers of lime. Serves 12.

LEMON VELVET

2 cups sugar
2 cups rich milk
Grated rind of 2 lemons
1/2 cup lemon juice
2 cups heavy cream

Combine sugar and milk and let stand 1 hour. Add lemon rind and juice, stirring well. Mixture will thicken slightly.

Whip cream until fairly stiff. Fold into milk mixture.

Pour into 2 refrigerator trays and freeze rapidly, 3 or 4 hours. Stir twice during freezing process to avoid separation. Serves 6 to 8.

Variation: One tall can undiluted evaporated milk (12/3 cups) may be used in place of heavy cream. To prepare for whipping, pour into refrigerator tray and freeze until fine ice crystals form around edges. Scrape milk into chilled bowl and beat until stiff.

APRICOT VELVET CREAM

1 No. 2 1/2 can apricot halves
1/4 cup confectioners' sugar
1/8 teaspoon salt

1 cup evaporated milk, chilled for whipping

Mash apricots, reserving a few for garnish, and add sugar and salt.

Whip chilled milk until thick. Fold in apricot mixture.

Freeze in freezing tray for 2 hours. Serves 6.

FROZEN VANILLA CUSTARD

1 egg, separated
1/4 cup sugar
1/2 teaspoon vanilla
1 small can (2/3 cup) evaporated milk, chilled

Beat egg yolk. Add sugar and vanilla. Beat until sugar is dissolved.

Beat egg white stiff. Fold into yolk mixture.

Whip milk very stiff. Fold in egg mixture lightly. Pour at once into cold freezing tray. Freeze until firm. Makes 1 pint.

Variations of Vanilla Custard

Frozen Chocolate Chip Custard: In frozen vanilla custard, fold in 2 ounces (2 squares) semi-sweet chocolate, shaved or grated, after combining egg and sugar mixture with whipped milk.

Frozen Cocoa Custard: In frozen vanilla custard, omit sugar. Use in its place a syrup made by blending 1/4 cup sugar, 1/4 cup cocoa, and 1/2 cup water and boiling until thick. Chill syrup, then add to the beaten egg yolk.

Frozen Lemon Custard: Follow recipe for frozen vanilla custard and omit vanilla. Fold 3 tablespoons lemon juice and 1/2 teaspoon grated lemon rind into whipped milk before adding egg and sugar mixture.

Frozen Peanut Brittle Custard: In frozen vanilla custard, fold 2/3 cup crushed peanut brittle into egg and sugar mixture, then add to whipped milk.

STRAWBERRY BOMBE
Graham Cracker Crust:

  1/4 cup (1/2 stick) butter or margarine
  1/4 cup sugar
20 graham crackers, finely rolled

Let butter or margarine stand at room temperature until softened. Blend all ingredients well with pastry blender or hands.

Pour crumb mixture into 1 1/4-quart mixing bowl. Set a smaller bowl on top of crumbs, and press them firmly into an even layer against bottom and sides of bowl.

Strawberry Bombe Filling:

2 eggs, separated
1 15-ounce can sweetened condensed
    milk

1/4 cup lemon juice
1 pint strawberries, sliced
Few drops red food coloring

Beat egg yolks until thick and lemon colored; mix in condensed milk. Add lemon juice; mix until thick. Beat in half the berries.

Beat egg whites stiff; fold in egg yolk mixture and remaining berries. Tint pink with a few drops of red coloring.

Pour into graham cracker crumb crust in bowl. Freeze for at least 6 hours.

To unmold, run a spatula around sides of bowl. Put serving plate upside down on bowl and invert. Serve garnished with whipped cream and strawberry halves. Serves 8.

Strawberry Bombe

FROZEN MINT PUDDING

1½ teaspoons (½ envelope) unfla-
      vored gelatin
2   tablespoons water
½   cup crushed white peppermint
      candy (2 ounces)
¼   cup milk
2   eggs, separated
6   drops green food coloring
¼   teaspoon salt
6   tablespoons sugar
1   cup heavy cream
12 plain chocolate cookies, crushed
      (¾ cup)

Sprinkle gelatin on the water and soak a few minutes.

Dissolve candy in milk over boiling water.

Beat egg yolks well. Pour a little of the hot liquid into them. Add to the rest of the hot mixture, and cook until thick, stirring constantly. Stir in the coloring.

Add gelatin to the cooked mixture and stir until dissolved. Cool until thick but not set.

Add salt to egg whites, beat until stiff but not dry. Gradually add sugar, beating constantly. Combine the beaten egg whites and gelatin mixture.

Whip the cream and fold it in.

Put half the crumbs into two freezing trays. Pour in prepared mixture, and cover with rest of crumbs.

Freeze without stirring, at the coldest refrigerator temperature, 3 to 4 hours. Serves 8.

FROZEN PLUM PUDDING

½   cup sugar
2   ounces (2 squares) chocolate
½   cup milk
2   cups heavy cream
1   teaspoon vanilla
½   cup chopped nuts
¼   cup chopped maraschino cherries
1   cup chopped raisins
¼   cup chopped dates

Add sugar and grated chocolate to milk in a saucepan and cook until chocolate is melted and mixture is slightly thick. Chill.

Whip the cream until thick but not stiff; add chocolate mixture, vanilla, nuts, cherries, and the raisins and dates which have been "plumped" by cooking in a small amount of water which is allowed to evaporate.

Freeze at coldest temperature for 1½ hours, then reduce cold for remainder of freezing period. Serves 8.

BRAZILIAN FROZEN COCONUT CUSTARD

2   ripe coconuts
1½ quarts milk
2   tablespoons flour
½   teaspoon salt
1½ cups sugar
6   egg yolks
6   egg whites
1½ cups heavy cream, whipped

Crack coconuts; reserve the liquid inside. Pare brown part of meat; grate or grind kernels in food chopper. Put these gratings in double boiler over hot water with milk. Cook 5 minutes.

Cool until it can be handled. Strain the coconut milk into a bowl through a fresh dish towel, wringing to extract each creamy drop. Discard grated kernels.

Return milk to double boiler along with reserved coconut liquid. Mix together flour, salt, and sugar. Sift this mixture into cooking milk and mix well. Cook about 2 minutes longer, stirring diligently.

Beat egg yolks lightly. Stir into the coconut milk. Flavor to taste; cook 2 minutes longer.

If it is to be frozen in refrigerator, first let mix cool. Put into trays; freeze for 2 hours, then mix in the egg whites, beaten stiff, and the whipped cream. Return to the refrigerator freezing tray.

If an ice cream freezer is used, open it when the mix starts to harden, and add the stiff egg whites and whipped cream. Freeze well. Serves 8 to 10.

BISCUIT TORTONI

2 teaspoons (2/3 envelope) unflavored gelatin
1/4 cup cold water
1/3 cup light corn syrup
1/4 cup sugar
2 egg yolks
1/4 teaspoon salt
1 teaspoon vanilla
1/2 teaspoon almond extract
1 cup heavy cream or evaporated milk, whipped
1/4 cup chopped pistachio nuts (optional)
1/2 cup vanilla wafer or macaroon crumbs

Soften gelatin in cold water. Heat corn syrup and sugar to boiling, stir until sugar is dissolved and stir into gelatin.

Beat egg yolks until very light and add syrup mixture gradually, beating constantly.

Cool thoroughly; add salt and flavorings, and fold in whipped cream or milk.

Add pistachio nuts and pour into small fluted paper cups (the kind in which biscuit tortoni is served generally) or into a tray of refrigerator. Dust top thickly with crumbs.

Freeze without stirring until firm. Makes enough for about 14 small cups or 6 to 8 servings.

FROZEN LEMON CHIFFON PIE

10 vanilla wafers, 2 inches in diameter
2 eggs, separated
1/3 cup light corn syrup
Dash of salt
1/2 teaspoon grated lemon rind
1/4 cup lemon juice
1/4 cup sugar
3/4 cup cream or evaporated milk, whipped

Roll wafers into fine crumbs. Grease a refrigerator tray with butter or margarine and coat well with crumbs. Place in freezing compartment.

Mix well in the top of a double boiler the egg yolks, syrup, salt, lemon rind and juice. Cook over boiling water, stirring constantly until mixture is slightly thickened, and cool.

Beat egg whites until stiff, add sugar and whip until mixture stiffens again.

Whip lemon juice–egg yolk mixture into whipped cream or milk, then fold in the blend of egg whites and sweetening.

Pour into the prepared tray and freeze quickly. To serve, cut into slices or pie-shaped wedges. To make the latter, cut across the tray diagonally from corner to corner, and then crosswise through center. Serves 6.

GRAHAM CRACKER FREEZE (Master Recipe)

2 cups graham cracker crumbs
10 marshmallows, quartered
1 cup walnuts, chopped
1/2 cup confectioners' sugar
1 teaspoon vanilla
1 cup shredded coconut
1/2 cup cream
1/2 cup heavy cream, whipped

Mix crumbs, marshmallows, walnuts, sugar, vanilla, coconut, and cream.

Pack into refrigerator tray lined with waxed paper. Freeze until firm.

To serve, slice with knife dipped in hot water. Top with whipped cream. Serves 8 to 10.

Graham Cracker Freeze Variations

Macaroon Crumb Freeze: Substitute 2 cups macaroon crumbs for graham crackers.

Pineapple Crumb Freeze: In master recipe, substitute 1/2 cup crushed pineapple for coconut and 1/2 cup pineapple juice for 1/2 cup cream.

Prune Crumb Freeze: In master recipe, substitute 1 cup cooked prune pulp for 1/2 cup cream.

Vanilla or Chocolate Crumb Freeze: In master recipe, substitute 2 cups vanilla or chocolate crumbs for graham crackers.

FROZEN BRÛLÉ

2 cups sugar
1/2 cup boiling water
2 tablespoons cornstarch
1 1/2 cups milk
2 slightly beaten egg yolks
1 1/4 cups heavy cream, whipped

Cook sugar in heavy frying pan over moderate heat until melted and pale yellow in color; stir in water and cook until dissolved.

Mix cornstarch to a smooth paste with 1/2 cup milk in top of double boiler, then add remaining milk; add syrup and cook over hot water 15 minutes, stirring until mixture is thickened.

Stir small amount into egg yolks, then return to remaining hot mixture and cook 2 minutes longer.

Cool, then fold in cream and turn into freezing trays. Freeze until firm. Makes 1 quart.

FROZEN FIG SHORTCAKE

1 cup dried figs, chopped
1 cup water
1/4 cup sugar
1 teaspoon lemon juice
1 tablespoon (1 envelope) unflavored gelatin
1 tablespoon water
1 egg
4 tablespoons sugar
1 teaspoon vanilla
1/2 cup heavy cream, whipped
Sponge, angel cake, or jelly roll, 1 inch
   thick, or fig newtons

Simmer chopped figs and water with 1/4 cup sugar 15 minutes; add lemon juice. Dissolve gelatin in cold water, then dissolve in the fig mixture. Cool.

Beat egg with 4 tablespoons sugar until light; add vanilla and fold in whipped cream.

Line deep refrigerator tray with waxed paper; place inch-thick slice or layer of cake on bottom. Spread cooled fig mixture over cake, then top off with the cream.

Freeze several hours or overnight. Garnish with fig flowers and whipped cream. Serves 6 to 8.

Frozen Fig Shortcake

Peach Velvet Sherbet

PEACH VELVET SHERBET

8 to 10 canned cling peach halves
1/4 cup lemon juice
1/4 cup orange juice
1 teaspoon grated lemon rind
1 cup sugar
1/8 teaspoon salt
1/2 teaspoon unflavored gelatin
1 tablespoon cold water

Press peaches through sieve and measure 2 cups pulp. Blend in juices, lemon rind, sugar, and salt.

Soften gelatin in cold water and dissolve over hot water. Add peach mixture to gelatin slowly, stirring constantly until well mixed.

Pour into refrigerator tray and freeze firm without stirring.

Place in chilled bowl and beat with rotary beater until light and fluffy. Return to tray and freeze firm. Serve garnished with sliced peaches, if desired. Serves 6.

CRANBERRY ORANGE SHERBET

1 pound (4 cups) cranberries
2 cups water
2 cups sugar
2 teaspoons (2/3 envelope) unflavored
     gelatin
1 cup orange juice

2 teaspoons grated orange rind
1/3 cup lemon juice

Cook cranberries with water until skins pop open.

Strain and add sugar and gelatin which has been softened in orange juice. Add grated rind and lemon juice.

Turn into refrigerator tray. Freeze until firm, stirring once or twice during freezing. Serves 6 to 8.

WATERMELON SHERBET

About 2 cups diced watermelon
24 marshmallows
1/4 cup lemon juice
2 stiffly beaten egg whites

Press diced watermelon through sieve to extract 1 cup juice.

Heat marshmallows and watermelon juice over hot water, stirring until marshmallows are melted and smooth.

Cool. Add lemon juice.

Combine marshmallow mixture with stiffly beaten egg whites. Fold gently until blended.

Pour into small refrigerator tray and freeze. When partially frozen, turn into chilled bowl. Beat quickly with rotary beater. Return to tray and freeze. Serves 5.

ORANGE CREAM SHERBET

¾ cup sugar
¾ cup water
Grated rind of 1 orange
1½ cups orange juice
1 tablespoon lemon juice
½ cup light cream
2 egg whites
Few grains salt

Cook sugar and water together slowly 10 minutes. Add grated rind, cooking 2 minutes longer. Strain. Add syrup to fruit juices. Cool.

Pour into freezing tray. Freeze until firm.

Remove to a chilled bowl; beat quickly until light. Add cream. Fold in stiffly beaten egg whites to which the salt has been added.

Turn into tray and freeze. If mixture separates, stir occasionally. Serves 6 to 8.

MINT SHERBET

1 cup sugar
2 cups boiling water
¼ cup chopped fresh mint
1 tablespoon (1 envelope) unflavored gelatin
½ cup cold water
1 cup lemon juice
Few drops green food coloring
2 egg whites

Add sugar to boiling water. Bring to boil again, stirring to dissolve sugar.

Add mint. Remove from heat. Cover pan and let steep 1 hour.

Soften gelatin in cold water 5 minutes and dissolve over boiling water. Stir into steeped mixture, mixing well.

Add lemon juice. Tint a pale green with food coloring.

Pour into refrigerator tray. Freeze to mush.

Beat egg whites stiff. Turn sherbet into chilled bowl. Beat quickly and fold in egg whites. Return to tray. Freeze firm.

To serve, garnish scoops of sherbet with sprigs of fresh mint. Serves 6.

FRESH PINEAPPLE SHERBET

1 medium pineapple
1 cup sugar
2 cups water
3 tablespoons lemon juice
1 egg white
Few grains salt

Slice pineapple and pare it. Cut out eyes and core. Grind the fruit, saving all juice which is thus extracted. Drain juice from pulp.

Boil sugar and water together 5 minutes and pour, while hot, over pineapple pulp to absorb pineapple flavor.

Allow to stand for a few minutes. Strain, pressing pulp well to extract as much more of juice as possible.

Cool syrup and combine with pineapple juice and lemon juice. Freeze to a mush.

Whip until light and fold in beaten egg white and salt. Return at once to freezing tray and freeze until firm. Serves 6.

ORANGE FREEZER SHERBET
(Master Recipe)

2 cups milk and 1 cup cream or 3 cups rich milk
1¼ cups sugar
1½ cups orange juice
2 tablespoons lemon juice
¼ teaspoon salt

Heat 1 cup milk. Add sugar and stir until dissolved. Add other ingredients.

Use freezing mixture of 1 part salt to 4 to 6 parts ice. Turn crank freezer slowly.

After freezing, remove dasher. Pack freezer with more ice and salt. Let sherbet stand an hour or more to ripen. Makes about 3 pints.

Variations:

Lemon Sherbet: In master recipe, omit orange juice. Use 1 cup lemon juice and ½ cup water.

Pineapple Sherbet: In master recipe, substitute 1 cup drained crushed pineapple for ½ cup orange juice.

MINTED CREAM SHERBET

2   tablespoons butter or margarine
2   tablespoons flour
1/8   teaspoon salt
3 1/3 cups milk
1   cup sugar
1   tablespoon (1 envelope) unfla-
      vored gelatin
1/4   cup cold water
1/2   cup lemon juice
1/4   cup grated lemon rind
1/8   teaspoon mint extract
Sprigs of fresh mint

Melt butter or margarine in saucepan; stir in flour and salt; blend until smooth.

Add 1 1/3 cups milk gradually. Cook over low heat, stirring constantly until thickened. Cook 3 minutes longer.

Add remaining milk, sugar, gelatin (which has been softened in cold water), lemon juice, rind, and mint flavoring.

Lemon Cream Sherbet

Beat mixture with egg beater until curdled particles are very tiny. Pour into refrigerator tray and freeze until fairly firm.

To make a creamy mixture, remove from tray at this point, beat well with a wire whisk or beater. Put back into tray and freeze until firm.

Serve in sherbet glasses with a sprig of fresh mint. Serves 6.

LEMON CREAM SHERBET

1 1/3 cups sugar
1 2/3 cups milk
Juice and grated rind of 2 lemons
1   cup heavy cream

Combine sugar and milk and mix well. Add lemon juice and rind.

Whip cream until stiff and fold into lemon mixture.

Pour into freezer tray. Freeze until firm. Stir once or twice while freezing. Serves 6.

REFRIGERATOR SHERBET
(Master Recipe)

2   teaspoons (2/3 envelope) unfla-
      vored gelatin
2 1/4 cups cold water
1   cup sugar
Pinch of salt
Fruit and juice as desired (see below)
2   egg whites

Soften gelatin in 1/4 cup cold water. Cook sugar and 2 cups water together 2 to 3 minutes. Add softened gelatin and dissolve thoroughly. Add salt and fruit juice.

Freeze in refrigerator tray to mush-like consistency.

Remove mixture to a chilled bowl and break into small pieces. Add unbeaten egg whites and beat until fluffy (1 minute).

Turn into chilled trays and freeze until firm. Serves 6.

Refrigerator Sherbet Variations

Apricot Sherbet: Use 2 cups apricot pulp and 2 tablespoons lemon juice.

Lemon or Lime Sherbet: Use ½ cup lemon or lime juice and grated rind of ½ lemon.

Orange Sherbet: Omit 1 cup of water. Use 1½ cups orange juice, grated rind of ½ orange, and ¼ cup lemon juice.

Peach and Cherry Sherbet: Use 1½ cups peach pulp, 2 tablespoons orange juice, and ¼ cup maraschino cherries, diced fine.

Pineapple Sherbet: Use 1 cup crushed pineapple and 1 tablespoon lemon juice.

Raspberry Sherbet: Use 1½ cups crushed fresh or canned raspberries and 2 tablespoons lemon juice.

Homemade Ices

PINEAPPLE MINT ICE

1   teaspoon (⅓ envelope) unfla-
         vored gelatin
2   tablespoons cold water
1½ cups pineapple juice
½   cup sugar
⅛   teaspoon salt
1   tablespoon chopped fresh mint
1   cup crushed pineapple
2   tablespoons lemon juice
Grated rind of 1 lemon
2   egg whites

Soften gelatin in cold water 5 minutes.

Heat pineapple juice to boiling point and add softened gelatin, sugar, and salt. Stir until dissolved.

Cool. Add mint, crushed pineapple, lemon juice, and rind. Freeze to mush.

Turn into large chilled bowl. Add unbeaten egg whites and beat until light and fluffy. Return to tray and freeze, stirring several times. Serves 8.

REFRIGERATOR ICE
(Master Recipe)

⅔   cup sugar
Pinch of salt
1½ cups water
1½ teaspoons (½ envelope) unfla-
         vored gelatin
3   tablespoons cold water
Fruit juice, as desired (see below)

Boil sugar, salt, and water 5 minutes.

Soften gelatin in 3 tablespoons cold water. Dissolve in hot syrup. Cool and add fruit juices.

Freeze in refrigerator tray to a mush-like consistency.

Remove to a chilled bowl; break into small pieces. Beat with rotary beater until fluffy (1 to 2 minutes). Return to freezing tray and freeze until firm. Serves 6.

Variations of Refrigerator Ice

Berry Ice: Follow master recipe. Use 2 cups red raspberries or strawberries crushed and sieved and 1 tablespoon lemon juice.

Cherry Ice: Follow master recipe. Use 2 cups ground cherries and juice, 1 tablespoon lemon juice, and few grains nutmeg. Omit ½ cup water.

Cranberry Ice: Follow master recipe. Use 2 cups cooked strained cranberries.

Lemon or Lime Ice: Follow master recipe. Use ⅓ cup of lemon or lime juice.

Mint Ice: To lemon ice, add ¼ teaspoon peppermint flavoring and 2 tablespoons finely minced mint leaves.

Orange Ice: Follow master recipe. Add 1 tablespoon grated orange rind to hot syrup and cool. Use 1½ cups orange juice and 2 tablespoons lemon juice.

CRANBERRY MINT ICE

1 1-pound can jellied cranberry
    sauce
1 cup pineapple juice
1/4 teaspoon peppermint extract

Crush cranberry sauce with a fork. Add pineapple juice and peppermint extract.

Pour into freezing tray of refrigerator. Freeze.

Serve immediately. Use to top fresh fruit cup.

FREEZER LEMON ICE
(Master Recipe)

1   quart water
1 1/4 to 1 1/2 cups sugar
1   cup strained lemon juice
1/4   teaspoon salt
1   egg white

Boil water and sugar together 2 minutes, then put aside.

When cold, add lemon juice, salt, and unbeaten egg white. Freeze with a mixture of 1 part salt to 4 to 6 parts ice.

Turn crank slowly until ice is firm. Remove dasher and pack freezer with more ice and salt. Let ice stand 1 hour or more to ripen.

Lemon Ice Variations

Lime Ice: In master recipe, substitute lime juice for lemon juice. Add green food coloring.

Mint Ice: To lemon ice, add 1/4 teaspoon mint flavoring and 2 tablespoons finely minced mint leaves.

Berry Ice: Make syrup of 1 cup sugar and 2 cups water. Mash 1 quart berries and press through sieve. Add to syrup. Cool and freeze. Raspberries, blackberries, or strawberries may be used.

Cherry Ice: Make syrup of 1 cup sugar and 2 cups water. Grind 1 quart pitted cherries and press through sieve. Add to syrup Cool and freeze.

Grape Ice: Make syrup of 1 cup sugar and 2 cups water. Add 2 cups grape juice, 1/4 cup orange juice, and 1/4 cup lemon juice. Cool, strain, and freeze.

Orange Ice: Make syrup of 1 cup sugar and 2 cups water. Add 2 cups orange juice and 4 tablespoons lemon juice. Cool, strain, and freeze.

*Cranberry
Mint Ice*

GRAPEFRUIT MINT ICE

2 teaspoons (2/3 envelope) unfla-
    vored gelatin
2 1/2 cups grapefruit juice, fresh or
    canned unsweetened
3/4 cup sugar
1/2 cup water
Few drops peppermint extract
Green food coloring
2 egg whites, stiffly beaten

Soften gelatin in 1/4 cup cold grapefruit juice.

Boil sugar and water together 5 minutes and dissolve softened gelatin in it
while hot.

Cool. Combine with remaining fruit
juice. Add peppermint flavoring and a
few drops of food coloring to tint pale
green.

Turn into refrigerator tray. Freeze to
mush.

Turn partially frozen ice into chilled
bowl. Beat until smooth. Fold in stiffly
beaten egg whites. Freeze firm, stirring
several times. Serves 6.

Variation: Mint flavoring and coloring may be omitted if plain grapefruit
sherbet is desired.

AVOCADO GRAPEFRUIT ICE

2/3 cup sieved avocado
2 cups grapefruit juice
1/2 cup sugar
1/4 teaspoon salt

Cut a large avocado in halves lengthwise. Remove seed and skin, and force
pulp through sieve.

Blend in grapefruit juice, sugar, and
salt. Pour into refrigerator tray. Freeze
firm.

Turn into chilled bowl. Beat with
rotary beater until smooth and fluffy.

Return to tray and freeze to desired
consistency. Makes 1 1/2 pints.

CRÈME DE MENTHE ICE

1 2/3 cups sugar
3 cups water
1/2 cup lemon juice
1/4 cup crème de menthe

Cook sugar and water together 5
minutes.

Cool and add lemon juice and crème
de menthe. Pour into small refrigerator tray.

Freeze, stirring several times during
freezing. Serves 6 to 8.

Parfaits

BLUEBERRY AND PEACH PARFAIT

2 cups blueberries
1 cup heavy cream, whipped
2 fresh peaches, pared
1/3 cup sugar

Fold washed blueberries into whipped
cream.

Mash peaches; add sugar and fold
into blueberry mixture.

Chill, but do not freeze, in refrigerator tray. Serve in parfait glasses. Serves 6.

PISTACHIO PARFAIT

1 cup sugar
1/4 cup water

2 egg whites
Green food coloring
1/2 cup chopped pistachio nuts
1 teaspoon almond extract
Few grains salt
2 cups heavy cream

Combine sugar and water; boil to
238°F. (or when small amount dropped
from tip of spoon spins long thread).

Beat egg whites stiff; gradually add
syrup, beating constantly. Tint light
green. Cool. Add nuts, almond extract,
and salt.

Whip cream; fold in. Pour into freezing tray and freeze firm. Serves 4 to 6.

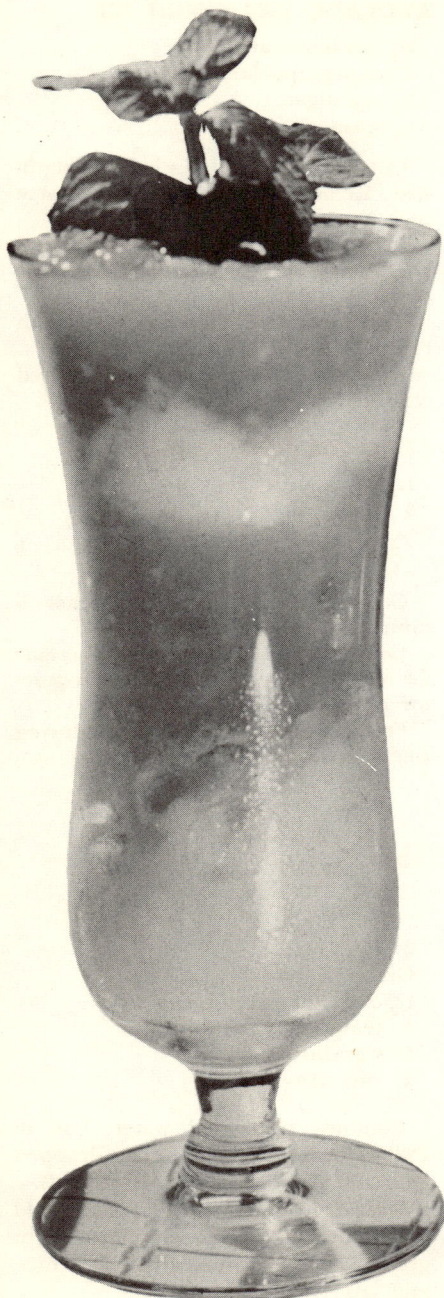

APPLE-LIME PARFAIT

1½ teaspoons (½ envelope) unfla-
    vored gelatin
2   tablespoons cold water
1½ cups cold water
¾   cup sugar
¼   cup lime juice
⅓   cup orange juice
2   tablespoons lemon juice
Few grains salt
Green food coloring
2   egg whites
Cinnamon apple sauce (below)

Soften gelatin in 2 tablespoons cold water for 5 minutes.

Combine remaining water and sugar; boil for 2 minutes. Add gelatin; stir until dissolved. Add lime, orange, lemon juices and salt; cool. Tint light green.

Pour into freezing tray and freeze to mush.

Place in chilled bowl. Beat with rotary beater until smooth. Beat egg whites stiff and fold in. Return to tray and freeze firm. Stir several times.

Just before serving, spoon alternate layers of applesauce and lime sherbet into parfait glasses. If desired, garnish with green maraschino cherry and sprig of mint. Serves 4 to 6.

Cinnamon Applesauce:

2   cups canned applesauce
¼   cup light brown sugar
¼   teaspoon cinnamon
½   teaspoon grated lemon rind

Combine applesauce, sugar, cinnamon, and lemon rind. Chill.

PEPPERMINT STICK PARFAIT

½ cup sugar
½ cup water
Few grains salt
2   egg whites
1   tall can evaporated milk (1⅔
    cups), chilled icy cold
½ cup finely crushed peppermint
    stick candy

Combine sugar and water and bring slowly to a boil. Boil rapidly until

Apple-Lime Parfait

syrup spins a thread (230°F.).

Add salt to egg whites and beat until stiff but not dry.

Pour syrup slowly into egg whites, beating constantly.

Chill. Beat milk until very stiff. Fold in egg white mixture and candy. Pour at once into freezing trays. Freeze. Makes 1½ quarts.

GOLDEN PARFAIT

½ cup sugar
¼ cup water
4 egg yolks
Few grains salt
1½ teaspoons vanilla
1½ cups heavy cream, whipped

Boil sugar and water together. Pour slowly over well beaten egg yolks. Cook until mixture coats spoon.

Cool. Add salt and vanilla. Fold in whipped cream.

Turn into chilled tray. Freeze until firm. Serve with additional whipped cream, if desired. Serves 6.

Golden Parfait Variations

Butterscotch Parfait: In golden parfait, substitute ⅔ cup brown sugar for the granulated sugar and add 2 tablespoons butter.

Maple Nut Parfait: In golden parfait, substitute ½ cup maple syrup for sugar and water. Heat syrup over low heat and proceed as directed. Add ½ cup chopped nuts.

VANILLA PARFAIT
(Master Recipe)

1 cup sugar
¾ cup water
2 egg whites
¼ teaspoon salt
3 teaspoons vanilla
1½ cups whipping cream, whipped

Boil sugar and water to 230°F. or until it forms a thread.

Beat egg whites until frothy. Add salt and beat until stiff but not dry.

Slowly pour hot syrup over egg whites, beating constantly. Continue beating until mixture is cool and holds shape. Add vanilla and fold in whipped cream.

Turn into chilled trays and freeze until firm. Serve with additional whipped cream, fruits, and nuts. Serves 8.

Vanilla Parfait Variations

Banana Parfait: Omit vanilla in master recipe. Add 1 teaspoon lemon juice. Fold in 1 cup mashed ripe banana with whipped cream.

Chocolate Parfait: In master recipe, add 2 squares (2 ounces) unsweetened shaved chocolate to hot syrup. Beat with rotary beater until blended before adding other ingredients.

Coffee Parfait: In master recipe, substitute ¾ cup strong coffee for water.

Maple Parfait: In master recipe, substitute 1 cup hot maple syrup for sugar syrup.

Maraschino Cherry Parfait: In master recipe, substitute ¼ cup maraschino cherry juice for equal amount of water in making syrup. Add ⅓ cup or more diced maraschino cherries with whipped cream.

Pineapple Parfait: Omit vanilla in master recipe. Add 1 cup crushed well drained pineapple and 1½ tablespoons lemon juice with whipped cream.

Strawberry or Raspberry Parfait: Omit vanilla in master recipe. Add 2 cups crushed berries and 1¼ tablespoons lemon juice with whipped cream.

Toasted Coconut Parfait: In master recipe, add ½ cup toasted shredded coconut with whipped cream.

Molasses Mousse

Mousses

MOLASSES MOUSSE

4 eggs
½ cup molasses
2 tablespoons orange juice
½ teaspoon cinnamon
Few grains salt
2 cups heavy cream

Beat eggs; add molasses. Cook over hot water, stirring constantly until slightly thickened.

Cool quickly by setting pan in ice water, stirring occasionally. Add orange juice, cinnamon, and salt.

Beat cream until slightly stiff, fold in molasses mixture.

Pour into refrigerator tray and freeze firm.

Or pour into 1½-quart mold with cover. Seal tight. Pack in equal parts crushed ice and ice cream salt. Freeze 4 hours. Makes about 1½ quarts.

SHERRY PEACH DELIGHT

1 cup light cream or 1 cup evaporated milk, chilled
4 peaches, sliced fine
½ cup sherry
1 teaspoon unflavored gelatin
2 tablespoons cold water
2 eggs
⅓ cup sugar
½ teaspoon salt
2 cups milk
1 teaspoon almond extract

Pour light cream into freezing tray, allowing about 1 hour for the cream to begin to freeze. When crystals have formed throughout, it is ready to whip.

Slice peaches and marinate in sherry. Soften gelatin in cold water.

Beat eggs with sugar and salt; stir in milk. Cook over boiling water, stirring constantly, until mixture coats the spoon. Do not overcook. Remove from heat. Stir in softened gelatin. Cool.

Add peaches and sherry. Add almond extract.

Whip the frozen cream (or evaporated milk) and fold into peach-custard. Turn into tray and freeze partially. Whip with rotary beater. Freeze until firm. Makes 1 quart.

PERSIMMON MOUSSE

1½ cups ripe persimmon pulp
¼ cup diced orange
½ cup diced canned pineapple
About ¼ cup sugar
Dash of salt
1   tablespoon lemon juice
1   cup evaporated milk, whipped

Select 4 to 6 very ripe persimmons. Wash, dry, cut away from stem. Carefully strip off thin skin, quarter, discarding pit and any black specks. Put pulp through a sieve and measure.

Combine persimmon pulp, orange, pineapple, sugar, salt, and lemon juice; gently blend, not to destroy the delicate persimmon flavor. Fold in whipped milk.

Pour into a refrigerator tray and freeze. Serves 6.

RASPBERRY MOUSSE DELUXE

1   quart raspberries
1⅓ cups confectioners' sugar
Few grains salt
2   cups heavy cream

Mix raspberries, sugar, and salt. Let stand 1 hour. Press through sieve.

Whip cream slightly stiff; fold in sieved berries. Pour into freezing tray and freeze firm.

Or pour into mold; cover. Pack in equal parts crushed ice and ice cream salt. Freeze 4 hours. Serves 8.

MAPLE NUT MOUSSE

4   beaten egg yolks
1   cup maple syrup
⅛ teaspoon salt
1   teaspoon vanilla
½ cup chopped black walnuts
1   pint heavy cream, whipped

Combine beaten egg yolks, maple syrup, and salt in top of double boiler. Cook over hot water, stirring constantly, until mixture coats spoon.

Remove immediately from heat and stir over ice cubes until cool. Add vanilla and walnuts.

Gently fold whipped cream into custard. Pour into 2 refrigerator trays. Freeze without stirring.

To serve, pile into parfait glasses. Top with additional whipped cream. Garnish with chopped walnuts. Makes about 1 quart.

CRANBERRY MOUSSE

1   cup evaporated milk, undiluted
2   tablespoons lemon juice
1½ cups or 1 can jellied cranberry
       sauce, mashed
¼ cup orange juice

Chill evaporated milk thoroughly. Whip until stiff.

Add lemon juice and continue whipping until very stiff.

Cut and fold in cold cranberry sauce and orange juice, lightly but thoroughly.

Pour into cold freezing tray of refrigerator and freeze, or pour into a mold and pack in a 1- to 3-part salt-ice mixture. Makes 1 quart.

BISQUE MOUSSE

3   well beaten egg yolks
1   cup sugar
3   egg whites, stiffly beaten
2   cups heavy cream, whipped
½ pound dry macaroons, crumbled
2   teaspoons vanilla or brandy flavoring

Beat egg yolks and sugar until thick and lemon colored. Fold in remaining ingredients.

Pour into large refrigerator tray. Freeze firm. Serves 12.

GOLDEN MOUSSE

1   cup mashed ripe bananas
2   tablespoons orange juice
¼ cup shredded coconut
3   tablespoons brown sugar
Few grains salt
⅛ teaspoon grated orange rind
1   cup heavy cream, whipped

Combine and mix first 6 ingredients. Fold in stiffly whipped cream.

Turn into freezing tray. Freeze rapidly, without stirring, until firm. Serves 6 to 8.

VANILLA MOUSSE
(Master Recipe)

1   teaspoon (1/3 envelope) unfla-
      vored gelatin
1   cup light cream or rich milk
6   tablespoons sugar
1/16 teaspoon salt
1/2 teaspoon vanilla
1   cup heavy cream, whipped
2   egg whites

Soften gelatin in a little light cream or milk.

Heat remainder of light cream or milk and pour over gelatin. Add sugar and salt; stir until dissolved. Chill.

When gelatin mixture has thickened slightly, beat to incorporate air. Add vanilla. Fold in whipped cream and well beaten egg whites.

Mold, pack into ice and salt and freeze or turn into freezing trays and freeze until firm. Makes about 1 quart.

Vanilla Mousse Variations

Applesauce Mousse: In master recipe, omit vanilla. Add 2 cups cinnamon-flavored applesauce and 2 tablespoons lemon juice with the cream.

Banana Mousse: In master recipe, add 1 cup mashed ripe banana and 2 teaspoons lemon juice with whipped cream.

Burnt Almond Mousse: Melt 8 teaspoons sugar carefully and stir in 1/2 cup ground almonds. Heat until almonds are browned. Add to milk or light cream in master recipe. Add 1/4 teaspoon almond extract. Omit vanilla.

Chocolate Mousse: Add 2 squares (2 ounces) unsweetened chocolate to milk or light cream in master recipe. Add 1/2 cup sugar. Heat in top of double boiler, beating with rotary beater until blended.

Coffee Mousse: In master recipe, substitute 1/2 cup strong coffee for 1/2 cup light cream.

Maple Mousse: In master recipe, substitute 1/3 cup maple syrup for sugar.

Peach Mousse: Omit vanilla in master recipe. Add 1/4 teaspoon almond extract. Add 2 cups peach pulp and 1/4 cup sugar.

Peanut Brittle Mousse: In master recipe, substitute 1/4 pound finely ground peanut brittle candy for sugar.

Peppermint Mousse: In master recipe, substitute 1/4 crushed peppermint stick candy for sugar. Add green food coloring.

Strawberry or Raspberry Mousse: Omit vanilla in master recipe. Add 1 to 2 cups crushed berries and 1 to 2 tablespoons lemon juice with whipped cream.

SPUMONE

1/2 cup sugar
1/2 cup maraschino cherries, drained
     and cut into quarters
3   tablespoons candied orange peel,
     cut into thin strips
1   teaspoon lemon juice
1 1/2 cups heavy cream, whipped
1/2 cup chopped blanched almonds
1 1/2 quarts vanilla ice cream
1/4 teaspoon almond extract

Fold sugar, cherries, orange peel, and lemon juice into whipped cream. Put into refrigerator tray to harden.

Add chopped nuts to ice cream, then flavor with almond extract. If ice cream becomes soft, put in freezer to harden.

To Pack Mold: Line a chilled 1-quart melon mold with ice cream to depth of 1 inch. Leave hollow in center but bring ice cream well up on sides of mold.

Fill mold with whipped cream mixture. Cover with waxed paper; fit lid on tightly. Put in freezing compartment for 24 hours.

Unmold onto chilled plate. To serve, cut into 1-inch slices. Serves 10 to 12.

Note: If desired, use a mixture of chopped candied angelica, citron, apricot, and lemon and orange peel instead of 3 tablespoons candied orange peel.

FRUIT AND FRUIT DESSERT COOKBOOK

Whether you choose fresh fruits in season or rely on canned, frozen, or dried ones, the choice is wide. For a light dessert to top a heavy meal, fresh fruit, raw or cooked, is most welcome. Fruits are not only high in essential nutrients but they also have a general appeal and are simple to prepare.

Wash All Fruit: All fruit should be washed carefully before using, because the sprays used on some fruit trees may be harmful. This also applies to wrapped fruit because there is always a possibility of traces of the spray lingering on the fruit even though it is usually washed before packaging.

To Prevent Darkening of Peeled Fruit: Many fruits darken when peeled. This is harmless but detracts from the appearance, and can be avoided if the fruit is dipped immediately into citrus or pineapple juice.

Dried Fruits: The dried fruits (prunes, apricots, dates, raisins, peaches, apples, currants, figs, and pears) are among the magic fruits of the kitchen. They are popular either stewed as a breakfast fruit or in preparing tempting, tasty desserts.

To Stew Dried Fruits: Modern processing methods have removed the necessity of long soaking of most types of dried fruits. Always check the package directions. Or use the directions given below.

Wash fruit quickly in several waters or until the water is clear. Drain, cover with water, bring to a boil, then simmer until tender. Add more water if needed. Unless otherwise specified, add sugar to taste 5 minutes before removing from heat. Specific recipes for various dried fruits are given throughout this book.

HOW TO GLAZE CANNED FRUITS FOR SALADS AND DESSERTS

Soften 1½ tablespoons (1½ envelopes) unflavored gelatin in ⅓ cup cold water 5 minutes. Add 1½ cups boiling water and stir to dissolve gelatin. Tint a delicate yellow with a drop or two of yellow food coloring.

Arrange chilled canned fruit on a cake rack which has been placed over a cooky sheet. When glaze is slightly congealed, pour small amounts over fruit. The excess that falls into cooky sheet may be spooned up, stirred, and used over again.

If glaze becomes too thick while being used, place over lukewarm water, stir until smooth, and chill over ice water to proper consistency.

Glazing may be done a day before fruit is to be served. Remove fruit from cake rack with spatula and store in refrigerator.

To add color to a pale fruit such as pears before glazing, add a few drops of yellow food coloring to the syrup of the canned fruit and let the fruit remain in the syrup until delicately colored.

To add a "blush" to fruits after glazing, brush lightly with red food coloring.

HOT SPICED LEMONADE FRUIT COMPOTE

    2 6-ounce cans concentrate for lem-
          onade
       Water (fill lemonade can twice)
    4 sticks cinnamon
   12 whole cloves
    4 peach halves
    4 pear halves
    8 cooked prunes
    2 bananas, cut in 2-inch chunks

Mix concentrate for lemonade with water and spices.

Arrange well drained fruit in deep baking dish and pour the lemonade mixture over fruit.

Bake in moderate oven (350°F.) about 20 minutes. Serves 4 to 6.

STEWED PARED FRUIT

    2 cups water
   ½ to 1 cup sugar
   ⅛ teaspoon salt
    1 quart prepared fruit

Boil water, sugar, and salt 3 minutes.

Drop prepared fruit into boiling syrup. Cook gently until tender.

*El Patio
Fruit Platter*

EL PATIO FRUIT PLATTER

1 No. 2½ can cling peach halves
1 cup strawberries
Salad greens
1 avocado
Lemon juice
Salt
1 large grapefruit
10 large cooked prunes
1 3-ounce package cream cheese
2 tablespoons peach syrup or prune liquid
1 banana
Mint sprigs

Drain peaches and arrange in ring around strawberries on crisp greens.

Cut avocado into halves and remove seed and skin. Cut crosswise in slices and sprinkle with lemon juice and salt.

Pare and section grapefruit. Drain and pit prunes.

Soften cheese with a fork and blend in peach syrup. Fill pitted prunes with cheese. Cut banana into thick slices.

Alternate grapefruit sections and avocado slices between peaches. Circle with banana slices and stuffed prunes.

Decorate with mint sprigs. Serve with lemon-honey dressing. Serves 5 to 7.

FRUITS BAKED IN WINE

4 pears, apples, or peaches or 12 plums
2 tablespoons lemon juice (optional)
½ cup Marsala, Madeira, or Port
About ¼ cup water
1 tablespoon or more brandy (optional)

Peel pears, apples, or peaches. Cut fruit in half and remove seeds. Arrange in covered baking dish with cut sides up.

Fill cavities with sugar and add lemon juice and wine. Pour water around fruit.

Cover and bake in moderate oven (350°F.) until fruit is tender, basting several times with juice in pan.

Soft fruits will require 20 to 30 minutes, hard pears about 1 hour. Add water as needed. Add brandy to juice in pan and pour over fruit. Serve warm or cold, plain or with cream. Serves 4.

Chocolate Minted Pears: Bake pears as above but omit lemon juice and wine. When tender, place a plain or chocolate mint patty or 2 in each cavity. Reheat uncovered until chocolate melts to form a sauce.

FRUITS STEWED IN RED WINE

½ cup to 1 cup sugar
1 cup water
3 cups assorted fresh fruits
1 cup red Burgundy
1 stick cinnamon
Rind of ½ lemon

Mix sugar and water and cook, stirring, until sugar is dissolved. Add fruit and cook, turning fruit carefully once or twice until tender. Strain and set fruit aside.

To juice, add Burgundy, cinnamon, and lemon peel. Boil until reduced to about 1½ cups.

Replace fruit in juice and simmer 10 minutes. Serve very cold with lady fingers. Serves 4.

OLD-FASHIONED GLAZED FRUITS

1 tablespoon lemon juice
¼ cup molasses
1 tablespoon butter or margarine
4 servings canned or cooked peaches, pears, apricots, or pineapple

Combine lemon juice and molasses. Bring slowly to boil and boil 3 minutes, stirring constantly.

Arrange fruit in well greased baking dish. Pour molasses mixture over fruit. Dot with butter.

Place in broiler or bake in moderate oven (375°F.) about 10 minutes, basting occasionally. Serves 4.

STEWED MIXED DRIED FRUIT

Wash fruit; remove cores from apples and pears. Cover generously with water; boil 35 to 45 minutes. Add ¼ cup sugar for each cup of fruit about 5 minutes before removing from heat.

STEWED UNPARED FRUIT

1 quart unpared fruit
2 cups boiling water
½ to 1 cup sugar

Add unpared fruit to boiling water. Simmer until nearly tender.

Add sugar; cook until fruit is tender. This method keeps the skin soft.

FRUIT WHIP OR SNOW

1 cup fruit, dried or sliced
Sugar to taste
1 teaspoon lemon juice
2 egg whites

Use soft, fresh fruit or any stewed fruit (apples, prunes, bananas, peaches, or apricots). If very juicy fruits are used, the juice should be drained thoroughly before rubbing through a sieve. Sour, raw apples may be grated.

Sweeten fruit pulp to taste and add lemon juice.

Beat egg whites until stiff, then beat in sweetened fruit pulp and continue beating until the mixture is very fluffy.

Pile lightly in individual serving dishes and chill thoroughly. Serve with cream or soft custard. Garnish with jelly. Serves 4 to 6.

SPICY DRIED FRUIT COMPOTE

1 11-ounce package mixed dried fruits
⅔ cup brown sugar
2 tablespoons lemon juice
1 teaspoon whole cloves
1 1-inch stick cinnamon

Combine ingredients in 1½-quart casserole. Add water to cover, about 2 cups.

Cover and bake in moderate oven (350°F.) 1½ hours. Serves 6.

DRIED FRUIT WHIP

¾ cup chilled evaporated milk
2 tablespoons chilled lemon juice
1½ cups dried fruit purée
½ cup sugar
¼ cup heavy cream or evaporated milk, whipped
½ teaspoon almond extract

Whip evaporated milk in a chilled bowl, gradually adding chilled lemon juice.

Blend the fruit purée with sugar, and fold into whipped evaporated milk.

Whip heavy cream; flavor with almond extract and use as topping. Serves 4.

DRIED FRUIT PURÉES

Cook the fruit slightly longer than when it is to be served whole. Put the cooked fruit through a sieve, colander, or ricer. If a ricer is used, remove the pits from prunes before ricing.

For some recipes such as whips and sauces, the cooked fruit may be beaten to a pulp instead of being puréed. One cup of uncooked fruit yields about 1 cup of purée.

BAKED FRESH FRUIT COMPOTE

Combine several varieties of fresh fruits in a baking dish. Add syrup made of 1 part water to 1 part sugar.

Cover and bake in a moderate oven (350°F.) until tender, 15 to 20 minutes.

JIFFY HOT FRUIT COMPOTE

Combine a variety of canned or cooked fruits. Heat with a small amount of juice. Flavor with brandy, sherry, or rum.

BAKED CANNED FRUIT

1 No. 2½ can fruit salad
½ cup ground macaroons, ground
     pine nuts, or other nuts
Juice of 1 lemon
3 or 4 tablespoons maraschino, bran-
     dy, or fruit juice
2 tablespoons butter or margarine

Drain the fruit salad and place the fruit in rows in a baking dish.

Sprinkle with ground macaroons, pine nuts or other nuts, lemon juice, maraschino, brandy, or fruit juice. Dot with butter.

Bake in moderate oven (350°F.) about 30 minutes. Serve hot. Serves 4.

FRESH FRUIT FRITTERS

1 cup sifted enriched flour
¼ teaspoon salt
2 eggs
⅔ cup milk
1 teaspoon salad oil
Salad oil or shortening for deep fry-
     ing
Apples, peaches, or bananas

Sift flour with salt into bowl.

Beat eggs, stir in milk and teaspoon of salad oil. Add dry ingredients and beat to a smooth batter. Cover and chill several hours.

To Prepare Fruit: Apples: core, pare and slice in rings ½ inch thick. Peaches: pare, and quarter. Bananas: peel, slice once lengthwise, and once crosswise.

Dip into batter and drain off excess batter. Deep-fry in oil or shortening heated to 370°F. until golden brown, 3 to 4 minutes. Drain on absorbent paper.

Serve with meat, or sprinkle with confectioners' sugar and serve with lemon sauce as a dessert. Serves 6 to 8.

Fruit Compote

Apples

Stuffed Baked Apples

BAKED APPLES
(Master Recipe)

Wash baking apples. Core ⅔ of the way down from top of apples. Do not break through blossom end of skins. Put in baking dish.

Fill each cavity with sugar, cinnamon, and nutmeg. Allow ¼ teaspoon cinnamon or nutmeg to 8 apples. If nutmeg is used, add to each apple a few drops of lemon juice and a few gratings of lemon rind.

Cover dish with boiling water ¼ inch in depth. Cover and bake in moderate oven (375°F.) about 40 minutes, or until apples are soft.

Remove cover, bake 10 minutes longer. If baked uncovered, baste occasionally with syrup in pan.

Remove apples. Boil syrup until thick and pour over apples. Serve hot or cold with cream.

Baked Apple Variations

Honey Baked Apples: In master recipe, substitute honey for sugar.

Maple or Brown Sugar Baked Apples: In master recipe, substitute maple or brown sugar for granulated.

Rosy Cinnamon Apples: In master recipe, add red cinnamon candies to water before baking.

Baked Apple Rings: Cut apples crosswise in rings and place in casserole. Add sugar, water, and lemon juice as for baked apples. Bake until tender.

Praline Apples: Bake apples as in master recipe, adding only the sugar and cinnamon.

Cool them and place in sherbet or dessert dishes.

Place ⅔ cup granulated sugar and ½ cup blanched and shredded almonds in a saucepan over medium heat. Heat until sugar is caramelized golden brown. Spoon quickly over apples. Cool. Serve with whipped cream.

Stuffed Baked Apples: Follow master recipe. Before baking, stuff cavities with mincemeat, chopped dates and nuts, sliced bananas, or bananas and cranberries combined, marmalade, jelly, crushed pineapple, etc.

Marshmallow Baked Apples: Follow master recipe. Stuff cavities with any suggested stuffings. When baked, top with marshmallow and return to oven to brown, about 5 minutes.

Cranberries in Baked Stuffed Apples: Fill the cavity in the center of each apple with cranberry sauce or jelly. Add sugar to water in pan if filling is not sufficiently sweet. Bake.

OB'L PUFFERS
(Pennsylvania-Dutch Apple Fritters)

1   cup sifted enriched flour
2   tablespoons sugar
1½ teaspoons baking powder
¼   teaspoon salt
1   beaten egg
½   cup milk
2   medium apples, pared, cut in ⅛ inch rings or wedges

Sift together dry ingredients.

Add milk to egg and blend with dry ingredients. Add the cut apples to batter.

Dip a long-handled spoon or tongs in the hot fat, then lift a batter-covered piece of apple with it and slide into deep hot fat (375°F.).

Re-dip the spoon about every fourth or fifth "puffer." (This process makes it easier and less messy in handling the food in the batter stage.)

Brown completely on one side and then turn for cooking the other side. Drain on absorbent paper and sprinkle with confectioners' sugar.

Serve piping hot. Makes 12 to 16 "puffers."

BROILED APPLES

Core and slice firm apples about ½ inch thick. Arrange in pan. Sprinkle with brown sugar and butter if tart.

Bake in broiling oven until brown and tender.

APPLES BAKED IN LEMON CUSTARD

4   small baking apples
1   egg, separated
½   cup sugar
¼   cup milk
Grated rind of 1 lemon
1   tablespoon lemon juice
¼   cup melted butter or margarine

Wash and core apples. Place in small baking dish. Bake in moderate oven (350°F.) 20 minutes.

Beat egg white until stiff. Add egg yolk and beat well. Add sugar, milk, lemon rind, and juice and beat well. Add butter.

Pour over apples and continue baking until apples are tender, about 10 minutes longer. Serve hot. Serves 4.

SPICED APPLES TO SERVE WITH MEAT

4   pounds sweet apples (12)
Whole cloves
1   cup cider vinegar
¼   cup water
1½ cups brown sugar
1   tablespoon ginger root
2   tablespoons mixed pickling spice
1   tablespoon lemon juice
1   teaspoon grated lemon rind

Wash apples; stick each apple with 4 whole cloves.

Make a syrup of vinegar, water, and brown sugar. Add spices, tied in a bag, lemon juice, and rind. Simmer 5 minutes.

Add apples; cook slowly until tender, spooning liquid over them occasionally.

Lift out on a platter and chill. Serve around the meat. Makes 12 apples.

GLAZED BAKED APPLES

6 firm, tart apples
½ cup sugar
¾ cup water
1 tablespoon sugar

Core apples; peel about ⅓ of way down; place in baking dish.

Boil together for 5 minutes the ½ cup sugar and the water; pour syrup over apples.

Bake, uncovered, in moderate oven (375°F.) about 30 minutes, until the apples are almost tender, basting frequently.

Take from oven; drain off syrup. Sprinkle each apple with a little sugar and put back on top rack of oven until sugar melts. Pour a little syrup over apples and return to oven.

Repeat 2 or 3 times until apples are glazed.

Chill and serve with the rich syrup plus a little cream. Serves 6.

BAKED APPLES IN CREAM

Peel and core 12 medium-sized sour apples. Roll in 3 tablespoons melted butter, then in sugar and cinnamon, and lastly in buttered breadcrumbs.

Place apples in a shallow baking dish. Fill centers with sugar and cinnamon. Add bits of butter. Bake in 400°F. oven.

When apples have baked about 20 minutes, add ½ cup cream. Continue baking until well done. Serves 6.

BRANDIED FRIED APPLES

Peel and core small, soft, sweet apples. Cut in thin rounds.

Soak in a mixture of equal parts brandy, lemon juice, and sugar. Drain and dust with flour.

Sauté in butter until light brown, turning carefully.

Sprinkle with powdered sugar and cinnamon mixture. Serve very hot.

*Glazed Apples
with Ice Cream*

APPLE COMPOTE
(Master Recipe)

1½ to 2 pounds cooking apples
1½ cups water
¾ cup sugar
Few grains salt
Slice of lemon (optional)
Candied orange peel (optional)

Wash, pare, and quarter ripe apples. Drop into cold water to prevent discoloration.

Bring to a boil the water, sugar, salt, lemon, and orange peel. Drop apple quarters, a few sections at a time, into syrup.

Cover and simmer gently until fruit is transparent and tender, turning apples when half done.

Serve hot or cold. If fruit is very hard, pre-cook before adding to syrup. Serves 6.

Apple Compote Variations

Apple Raisin Compote: In master recipe, add ¾ cup seedless raisins. Cook with apples.

Apple Slices: Follow master recipe. Cut apples crosswise into circles. Add to syrup and simmer until tender.

Cinnamon Apple Rings: Cut apples in rings. Add ½ cup red cinnamon candies to sugar and water in master recipe.

Glazed Apples: Core apples. Cook whole, unpeeled, in colored syrup. Score the skin in small squares before cooking to keep fruit from bursting.

Minted Apples: Color syrup pale green. When apples are done, flavor syrup with oil of peppermint.

STEWED DRIED APPLES

Rings or Quarters: Remove any remaining parts of core. Wash, drain, cover with boiling water and boil gently until tender, about 40 minutes.

Add ¼ cup sugar for each cup of fruit and cook 5 minutes longer. A few grains of salt may be added to round out flavor. Sugar may be omitted, giving a fresh apple flavor.

Whole: The whole fruit should be covered with cold water, brought slowly to a boil, then simmered until tender, about 60 minutes.

APPLESAUCE
(Master Recipe)

Wash, pare, and core 8 cooking apples. Add about ½ cup water and ⅛ teaspoon salt. Cook in covered pot until soft.

Add about ½ cup sugar while hot. Simmer just long enough to melt sugar. Amount of sugar and water varies with sweetness and juiciness of apples.

For additional flavoring, add with sugar, nutmeg, cinnamon, grated lemon rind or juice, or a combination of spices. Serves 8.

Applesauce Variations

Honey Applesauce: In master recipe, substitute ½ cup honey for sugar. Add 1 to 2 teaspoons grated lemon rind.

Minted Applesauce: In master recipe, add ¼ cup chopped mint with sugar.

Orange Applesauce: In master recipe, add 2 to 3 teaspoons grated orange rind with sugar.

Rosy Cinnamon Applesauce: In master recipe, cook ⅓ cup red cinnamon candies with apples.

Spiced Applesauce: In master recipe, substitute ⅓ cup firmly packed brown sugar for granulated sugar. Add ¼ teaspoon cinnamon and 1 teaspoon grated lemon rind.

Strained Applesauce: Do not pare apples. Remove any bruised spots. Cut into quarters and cook until soft. Force through a coarse sieve. Add sugar and flavoring. Simmer to dissolve sugar.

BAKED APPLESAUCE
(Master Recipe)

6 to 8 tart apples
Cinnamon to taste, or 2 thin slices
  lemon
2/3 cup water
About 3/4 cup sugar

Wash apples (do not peel), remove bruised spots, and cut in quarters.

Place in a baking dish. Add cinnamon or lemon and water.

Cover and bake in moderate oven (375°F.) until tender, 20 to 30 minutes.

Put through a strainer. Add sugar and mix. Serve hot or cold.

Serves 6 to 8.

Baked Applesauce Variations

Creamed Applesauce: Substitute 2/3 cup light cream for water. Add 1/2 teaspoon cinnamon and 1/4 teaspoon nutmeg with sugar.

Honey Applesauce: Substitute honey for sugar. Add 1 tablespoon grated lemon rind.

Maple Applesauce: Substitute 1 cup maple syrup for sugar and water.

Orange Applesauce: Add 2 tablespoons grated orange rind while cooking.

SPICED APPLESAUCE

6 tart apples
1 cup boiling water
3 whole cloves
1 1/2 tablespoons cider vinegar
1/3 cup sugar
1 tablespoon butter or margarine

Core and quarter apples; do not peel.

Put in saucepan with water and cloves. Simmer, tightly covered, until apples are tender; press through a sieve.

Return to heat; add vinegar and sugar; simmer 10 minutes.

Remove from heat; beat in butter. Serve either hot or cold with roast fowl or roast pork. Makes 1 1/2 cups.

FRIED APPLES

Wash, quarter, and core firm apples. Slice in medium thin pieces. Sauté in small amount of hot fat until brown. If tart, sprinkle with a little brown sugar or honey while cooking.

Apricots

Fresh apricots may be used in most dishes calling for peaches, or cooked and puréed in any dishes calling for applesauce.

To Peel Apricots: Drop raw apricots into boiling water. Remove from heat and let stand 1/2 minute. Remove apricots and plunge into cold water. The skin will pull off easily.

STEWED DRIED APRICOTS

Wash and drain apricots. Cover with water; boil until tender, 30 to 40 minutes. Add 1/4 to 1/2 cup sugar for each cup of fruit for the last 5 minutes of cooking.

ARMENIAN APRICOT DESSERT

1 pound dried apricots
1/4 pound prunes
1/4 pound seedless raisins
Sugar to taste
Almonds

Cover apricots and prunes with cold water and soak 4 hours. Put fruits in a saucepan with the same water.

Add raisins and additional water to cover. Let boil gently, adding sugar to taste.

When tender, remove from heat and cool. Serve cold with 6 or 7 blanched, skinned almonds on each portion. Serves 6 to 8.

APRICOT CREAM

¼ cup butter or margarine
1 cup confectioners' sugar
1 teaspoon vanilla
½ cup sieved cooked dried apricots
1 cup heavy cream, whipped
12 ladyfingers

Cream butter or margarine and sugar. Add vanilla and apricots. Fold in whipped cream.

Split ladyfingers; line sherbet glasses. Top with apricot mixture. Serves 4 to 6.

PICKLED CANNED APRICOTS

1 No. 2½ can whole peeled apricots
⅓ cup vinegar
2 sticks cinnamon
2 or 3 pieces ginger root
2 whole cloves

Drain apricots. Combine juice, vinegar, cinnamon, ginger root, and cloves; simmer 10 minutes.

Add apricots; simmer 10 minutes longer. Chill before serving.

Serves 4 to 6.

APRICOT SAUCE

Follow method in master recipe for applesauce or any of its variations.

DRIED APRICOT PURÉE

½ pound dried apricots
2 cups cold water
⅓ cup sugar (optional)

Wash apricots in lukewarm water. Drain, cover with cold water and soak 4 hours. Simmer 20 minutes in the soaking water.

Put through a sieve. If sugar is used, add it to the purée while it is hot. Stir to mix thoroughly. Makes 2 to 2½ cups purée. Serves 4.

Apricot Whip: Use apricot purée and follow method for Fruit Whip.

APRICOTS SUPREME

1 teaspoon cinnamon
½ teaspoon cloves
¼ cup mayonnaise
16 peeled apricots

Combine cinnamon and cloves. Sprinkle in centers of apricots. Spoon mayonnaise in centers of half the apricots. Top with remaining half.

Place on cooky sheet or broiler pan and broil about 5 minutes or until apricots begin to brown. Serve with baked ham.

Apricots Supreme with Baked Ham

For a buffet luncheon: avocado half-shells with creamed chicken or Creole shrimp for filling.

This rich, mild-flavored fruit should be completely ripe to be enjoyed. The flesh of the ripe avocado will yield slightly when pressed gently with the hand. Or if you shake it, the seed will move slightly if the pear is ripe. Because of its mild flavor, the fruit mixes well with other fruits or vegetables for salads or first-course cocktails. It is also used in fish, shellfish, and poultry salads and a variety of other dishes where its richness and mild flavor combine well.

Allow ½ medium-sized avocado per serving for a main dish luncheon salad. If it is puréed, seasoned with a French or other dressing and used as topping for salads, allow 3 to 4 servings per avocado.

Note: The term Calavo, widely known in the United States, is a trade name for California-grown avocados.

FRUIT FILLED AVOCADO

2 medium-sized avocados
Salt
2 cups grapefruit sections
1½ dozen stuffed olives
French dressing

Cut avocados in half and remove pits. Scoop out flesh, leaving a thin layer to hold shells in form. Cut portion removed into cubes and sprinkle with salt.

Cut grapefruit sections into cubes. Cut olives into rounds.

Toss fruit together lightly and refill shells. Add dressing and chill. Serves 4.

Avocados

AVOCADOS STUFFED WITH CHEESE (NICARAGUAN)

Peel medium-sized avocados. Cut lengthwise and remove pits. Stuff halves with any fresh cream cheese. (Nicaraguans use their own special curd cheese.)

Dip in beaten egg, then in crumbs. Sauté in butter until brown or fry in deep hot fat in basket.

Cover with any desired tomato sauce and heat through in oven. Serve as a vegetable.

BAKED AVOCADO

3 ripe avocados (4 cups mashed)
3 tablespoons lemon juice
¼ teaspoon salt
1 cup confectioners' sugar

Scoop avocado pulp from shells. Mash and put through a sieve. Combine with lemon juice, salt, and sugar in a buttered baking dish.

Bake in moderate oven (350°F.) 30 minutes, or until brown crust forms on top. Serves 6.

AVOCADO AND BACON

Mash the pulp of 1 avocado with a fork. Season with lemon juice, salt, and onion juice. Heap in small mounds on 2 plates.

Garnish with strips of fried bacon, chopped parsley, and paprika. Serves 2.

AVOCADO DESSERT

Pare ripe avocados and put the pulp through a fine sieve. Flavor with lemon juice, powdered sugar, and, if desired, a dash of cloves.

Beat mixture with a rotary beater until fluffy. Chill thoroughly.

Bananas

Banana Coconut Rolls

For immediate use, select bananas which are deep yellow in color and flecked with brown spots.

For proper ripening and best flavor, let bananas ripen at comfortable room temperature.

Don't keep bananas in refrigerator—except ones already fully ripe and flecked with brown.

To whip or mash 3 or more bananas: Break in pieces; beat with electric mixer or blender. For 1 or 2 bananas: Slice into bowl and mash with fork, or use mixer or blender.

BANANA COCONUT ROLLS

    4 firm ripe bananas
    2 tablespoons butter or margarine,
         melted
    2 tablespoons lemon or lime juice
    ½ cup shredded coconut

Peel bananas and cut crosswise into halves. Place into a well greased baking dish.

Brush thoroughly with butter or margarine, then with lemon or lime juice. Sprinkle bananas with coconut.

Bake in moderate oven (375°F.) 15 to 20 minutes, or until coconut is browned and bananas are tender, easily pierced with a fork.

Garnish with sliced pineapple, fluted orange slices, and cherries, if desired. Serve hot with hot orange sauce or pineapple sauce. Serves 4.

FRIED BANANAS

Peel and cut firm bananas in half lengthwise. Fry bananas slowly in butter until tender and golden brown, turning them to brown evenly. Serve hot as a vegetable.

Fried Banana Variations

Glazed for Dessert: Brush well with lemon juice before frying and sprinkle with brown sugar while frying.

Banana Newburg: Sprinkle fried bananas with brown sugar while cooking. Add a little sherry and let them simmer a few minutes.

Fried Bananas with Rum: Pour some rum into the pan when fried bananas are done. Light it. Baste bananas with flaming syrup. Serve immediately.

BANANAS IN BLANKETS

Peel and cut firm ripe bananas into quarters crosswise. Dip in lemon juice and sprinkle very lightly with sugar.

Roll in very thin slices of bacon or boiled ham.

Secure the bacon with toothpicks. Sauté bananas in a skillet or bake in moderate oven (350°F.) until bacon is crisp. When using ham, grease the skillet lightly.

BANANA CREAM WHIP

    1 cup mashed ripe bananas
    1 tablespoon lemon juice
    ¼ cup sugar
    ⅛ teaspoon salt
    ½ cup whipping cream, whipped

Mix together bananas, lemon juice, sugar, and salt. Fold in whipped cream. Chill.

Serve within 1 hour. Garnish with sliced bananas. Serves 4 to 6.

BAKED BANANAS

6 firm bananas
2 tablespoons melted butter or margarine
Salt

Peel bananas. Place into a well buttered baking pan. Brush well with butter and sprinkle with salt.

Bake in moderate oven (375°F.) 15 to 18 minutes, or until bananas are tender, easily pierced with a fork.

If desired, bake until almost done; then place under broiler heat until tender and browned. Serves 6.

Serve hot as a vegetable or as a dessert with cream or a hot fruit sauce.

Baked Banana Variations

Bananas Baked with Molasses: Just before baking, brush bananas with lemon juice. Pour 3/4 to 1 cup of molasses over bananas. Bake as above.

Serve hot as a sweet entrée with beef or ham, or garnish with chopped toasted almonds and serve as a hot dessert. Maple syrup may be substituted.

Bananas Baked with Brown Sugar: Just before baking, sprinkle bananas lightly with brown sugar. Bake as above.

Serve hot as a sweet entrée with beef, ham, lamb, or chicken.

Bananas Baked with Curry Sauce: Pour 2 cups of your favorite curry sauce over bananas. Bake as above.

Serve hot with rice, pork, lamb, chicken, duck, or shrimp.

Baked Bananas Served with Sour Cream: To serve as a vegetable, top each hot banana with 1/4 cup sour cream. Sprinkle with paprika, if desired.

To serve as a hot dessert, top each banana with 1/4 cup sour cream. Sprinkle with sugar, nutmeg, or cinnamon, if desired.

Bananas Baked with Cranberries: Pour 1 cup hot cranberry sauce over bananas. Bake as above. Serve hot with beef, chicken, or turkey. Tart jams, jellies or marmalades may be used in place of cranberry sauce.

Baked Bananas with Applesauce or Apple Butter: Spread bananas evenly from tip to tip with applesauce or apple butter. Use 1/4 cup for each banana. Bake as above. Serve as a hot dessert.

Honey Baked Bananas: Sprinkle honey over bananas with the butter. Add a sprinkling of lemon juice, if desired.

Baked Bananas with Sherry or Rum: Pour a little sherry or rum over bananas while baking.

BROILED BANANAS

Peel firm, ripe bananas. Place on broiler rack or into pan containing rack. Brush bananas well with melted butter or margarine and sprinkle lightly with salt.

Broil 3 to 4 inches from heat about 5 minutes on each side or until bananas are browned and tender and easily pierced with fork. Serve hot as vegetable.

Broiled Banana Variations

Broiled Bananas with Curry Sauce: To serve as hot vegetable, top broiled bananas with hot curry sauce.

Broiled Bananas with Applesauce: For a delicious new flavor, cover each banana with about 1/4 cup applesauce or apple butter. Top with plain, whipped or sour cream.

Broiled Bananas with Cream: To serve as vegetable, top each banana with about 1/4 cup sour cream. Sprinkle with paprika, if desired. To serve as hot dessert, top each banana with plain, whipped or sour cream. Sprinkle with sugar, nutmeg, or cinnamon, if desired.

Strawberry Meringue

Berries and Cherries

TO SERVE FRESH BERRIES

Spread berries on a tray; remove soft or moldy berries. Chill until ready to serve. Then wash in a colander; drain thoroughly. Remove caps of stems.

Sprinkle with sugar if desired and chill a little longer. If fruit is too tart, sprinkle with sugar and let stand 1 to 2 hours. A sprinkling of lemon juice will neutralize excess tartness.

STRAWBERRY MERINGUE FOR SPONGE CAKE

2   egg whites
1/8 teaspoon salt
1/2 cup sugar
1   teaspoon lemon juice
1 1/2 cups sliced strawberries

Beat egg whites until stiff, but not dry. Blend in salt, sugar, and lemon juice. Continue beating until meringue stands in peaks and is well blended. Fold in strawberries.

Serve over sponge or angel food cake. Makes strawberry meringue for one 13 1/2-ounce sponge cake.

DEVONSHIRE CREAM WITH BERRIES

Place milk in an oven-proof dish for 12 hours. Move it very gently onto the range and heat it very slowly until bubbles appear around the edges. Do not let the milk boil.

Remove it from the heat and let it stand for 24 hours in a cool place. Skim the cream. It will be thick and clotted. Serve very cold with berries.

BERRY AND COTTAGE CHEESE PARFAIT

1   cup cottage cheese
1   egg white
2   tablespoons sugar
1/2 teaspoon salt
1   cup heavy cream
1/2 teaspoon almond extract
1   box frozen strawberries, defrosted, or fresh strawberries, crushed and sweetened

Beat cottage cheese until smooth.

Beat egg white until frothy, then beat until stiff, adding sugar and salt. Fold into cottage cheese.

Whip cream, adding almond extract. Fold into mixture. Alternate spoonfuls of cottage cheese mixture and fruit into individual serving dishes. Serves 6.

BLACKBERRY WHIP

2   egg whites
Dash of salt
1/4 cup sugar
1   tablespoon lemon juice
Grated rind of 1 lemon
1   pint fresh blackberries

Beat egg whites with salt until stiff, then gradually beat in sugar, 1 tablespoon at a time.

Fold in lemon juice, rind, and washed, well drained blackberries. Chill. Serve plain or with custard sauce. Serves 4.

STEWED BLUEBERRIES

Cook blueberries in very little water. When they are nearly tender, add a few grains salt and sugar to taste. Cook a minute longer.

BLUEBERRY FLUMMERY

1   pint blueberries
2   cups water
1/2 cup sugar
3 1/2 tablespoons cornstarch
1/4 cup cold water
Dash of salt
Juice of 1 lemon

Simmer berries in 2 cups water until very tender. Put through sieve, pressing through as much pulp and skin as possible.

Add sugar to juice and sieved pulp; bring to boil.

Dissolve cornstarch in 1/4 cup cold water, and add with salt to hot mixture. Cook, stirring constantly, until mixture thickens.

Remove from heat; stir in lemon juice. Cool, then pour into serving dish, and chill. Serve with sugar and cream, if desired. Serves 4.

BLUEBERRY SLUMP

1   quart blueberries
1   cup sugar
4   tablespoons arrowroot or cornstarch
Juice of 1 lemon
4   tablespoons butter or margarine
1/2 cup sugar
1/4 teaspoon salt
1   egg
1/2 cup milk
1 1/2 cups sifted cake flour
2   teaspoons baking powder

Wash berries and drain. Mix sugar and arrowroot; add to berries. Place in greased casserole; sprinkle with lemon juice.

Cream together butter and sugar. Add salt. Beat egg and add to creamed mixture. Add milk and mix well. Stir in flour and baking powder briskly and spoon over berries.

Bake in hot oven (425°F.) 20 to 25 minutes. Serve warm with vanilla ice cream. Serves 8.

Note: If fresh blueberries are not available, frozen ones may be used. In that case, use two packages and let defrost slightly.

STEWED SOUR CHERRIES

1   quart sour cherries
1   cup water
1   cup sugar

Pick over the cherries, wash and remove pits and stems.

Combine water and sugar; stir over low heat until sugar is dissolved. Bring to a boil and boil for 5 minutes.

Add cherries and boil gently 5 to 10 minutes or until cherries are tender.

CHERRY FRITTERS

3/4 cup well drained pitted sour red cherries
2   tablespoons sugar
1   tablespoon brandy, kirsch, or rum (optional)
1   cup sifted enriched flour
1/4 teaspoon salt
1   teaspoon baking powder
1   beaten egg
About 1/2 cup milk
1   tablespoon melted butter or margarine
Confectioners' sugar

Mix cherries, sugar, and liquor.

Sift together flour, salt, and baking powder.

Mix egg, 1/2 cup milk, and butter. Add milk mixture to dry ingredients and stir only until smooth. Add and fold in cherry mixture. Add additional milk if batter is too thick.

Drop by tablespoonfuls into hot deep fat (365° to 375°F.) and fry until browned, turning as fritters rise to the surface.

Drain on absorbent paper. Sprinkle with confectioners' sugar and, if desired, serve with cherry sauce that has been flavored with the same liquor that was used in batter. Serves 4.

CHERRIES JUBILEE

- 1 **No. 2 can Bing cherries, pitted**
- 1 **teaspoon cornstarch**
- ½ cup **Cognac or kirsch**
- 1 **quart vanilla ice cream**

Drain juice from canned cherries. Cook 1 cup juice down to ¾ cup.

Make paste of cornstarch and 2 tablespoons of remaining cherry juice. Add to hot juice and cook, stirring until thick and clear. Remove from heat.

Add cherries. Pour into metal pan, heat-resistant casserole, or chafing dish.

Carefully pour Cognac on top. Ignite and spoon flaming cherries over individual servings of ice cream. Serve immediately. Serves 8.

CRANBERRY SAUCE
(Master Recipe)

- 1 **pound (4 cups) cranberries**
- 1½ **cups sugar**
- 2 **cups water**

Wash, pick over, and drain cranberries.

Put berries, sugar, and water in saucepan. Bring slowly to boiling point. Cover and cook slowly about 10 minutes, or until skins burst. Skim and cool. Makes about 4 cups.

Cranberry Sauce Variations

Molded Cranberry Sauce: Increase sugar to 2 cups. Cook until a thin syrup is formed, about 20 minutes. Pour into mold; chill.

Glazed Cranberries: Prepare as in master recipe. Do not drain thoroughly.

Measure and mix equal parts sugar and berries in the top of double boiler.

Cook over hot water until sugar forms thick syrup, about 1 hour, and berries are glazed. Stir carefully a few times at the start.

Minted Cranberry Sauce: In master recipe, stir in teaspoon chopped fresh mint or few drops mint extract.

Cranberry Taffies

CRANBERRY TAFFIES

- 2 **tablespoons butter or margarine**
- 6 **tablespoons brown sugar**
- 4 **pineapple rings**
- 4 **cut-outs made from 1-pound can jellied cranberry sauce**

Crumble brown sugar and butter together. Arrange cranberry cut-out on top of each slice of pineapple.

Carefully sprinkle sugar-butter mixture over top. Place in shallow pan.

Bake in moderate oven (350°F.) for 30 minutes or place on broiler pan and broil with tops of cranberry pineapple taffies about 3 inches from broiler flame. Taffies will take about 10 minutes to broil.

CRANBERRY STRAWBERRY COMPOTE

Cook 1 pound cranberries, in water to cover, in covered pot about 5 minutes.

Add 1 cup sugar and 2 cups strawberries. Cook 5 to 8 minutes. Serve cold.

BAKED CRANBERRY SAUCE

Wash and pick over berries. Place in a baking dish. Add 1¾ cups sugar and 1 cup water for each quart of berries.

Cover and bake in slow oven (325°F.) 30 minutes, or until berries are tender.

CRANBERRY APPLE SAUCE

Combine 2 cups each of cranberries and sliced, pared apples, ¾ cup water, and 1 cup sugar.

Cover and cook slowly until tender, about 20 minutes. Cool slightly. Beat until fluffy.

Raspberry Meringue Cupcakes

TO SERVE FRESH CURRANTS

Wash, drain, and remove stems from chilled red or white currants. Sprinkle liberally with sugar, since these berries are sharply acid. They are particularly good when combined with other and sweeter berries.

If served with cream, serve the cream separately because the acid may turn the cream.

Ripe black currants are decorative but not as flavorful as the red or white.

GOOSEBERRIES

These small sour berries resemble currants but are larger. They are usually cooked before eating.

Wash, remove stems, add sugar and prepare in the same way as cranberry sauce, cooking 10 to 15 minutes.

OLD-TIME GOOSEBERRY DESSERT

1 pint green or ripe gooseberries
3/4 cup water
1/2 cup sugar
1 tablespoon butter or margarine
1/8 teaspoon salt
2 eggs, separated
1/4 cup sugar

Stem berries; wash in cold water and drain. Put into saucepan with water. Cover the pan and boil gently un-

til the berries are soft, 8 to 10 minutes.

Put through colander or food mill, making sure to push through all pulp. Return purée to saucepan; add sugar, butter, and salt; stir to mix.

Beat egg yolks well; stir into purée.

Beat egg whites to stiff foam; gradually add sugar and beat until stiff and shiny.

Place purée over heat; stir constantly until mixture bubbles and thickens. Quickly pour hot berry mixture over whites; cut and fold in until thoroughly blended. Cover; chill in refrigerator.

Serve in chilled dessert cups with a topping of whipped cream, a sliced strawberry, or finely chopped nuts. Serves 4.

LOGANBERRIES

Loganberries are a cross between the raspberry and the blackberry. These sweet berries are cooked and served like raspberries.

STEWED RASPBERRIES

1 quart raspberries
1 cup water
1/2 to 1 cup sugar
1 tablespoon lemon juice

Wash, drain, and hull raspberries. Heat water with sugar in a glass saucepan. (Use more sugar for red raspberries than for black.)

When the water-sugar mixture simmers, add berries, cover and simmer 10 minutes.

Add lemon juice and chill. Serves 4 to 6 as a sauce over ice cream, cake, and puddings.

RASPBERRY MERINGUE CUPCAKES

For a quickly prepared dessert, serve bakery cupcakes with a meringue into which fresh, canned, or well drained frozen fruit has been folded.

Slice the cupcakes into wedges, cutting only half way through; open gently, fill the cavity with the meringue and fruit.

MULBERRIES

Mulberries are very sweet and may be eaten raw, usually served with lemon juice or cream. In recipes they are prepared in the same way as raspberries.

CONTINENTAL STRAWBERRIES

2 3-ounce packages cream cheese
1/4 cup sour cream
2 tablespoons confectioners' sugar
1 pint strawberries

Whip mashed cream cheese with sour cream until smooth; add sugar and mix well.

Place cheese in small rinsed molds, the smaller the better; chill 2 hours.

Unmold and serve surrounded by washed, hulled strawberries. Serves 4.

BRAZILIAN STRAWBERRY COMPOTE

1 quart ripe strawberries
Powdered sugar, to taste
Grated rind of 1 orange
About 1/4 to 1/2 cup **Cointreau or Triple Sec**
1 tablespoon Kirschwasser

Stem and wash strawberries. Dust them with fine powdered sugar.

Grate in the orange rind. Moisten with Cointreau; point up with Kirschwasser. Toss well; chill for at least 4 hours.

Serve each portion with 1 tablespoon well chilled rose-tinted whipped cream on top, sprinkled with slivers of blanched almonds. Serves 4 to 6.

STRAWBERRIES SWISS

1 quart strawberries
2 3-ounce packages cream cheese
4 tablespoons or more cream
1/3 cup confectioners' sugar

Wash strawberries, drain and hull. Chill them.

Work the cream cheese and cream to a smooth paste. The mixture should be thin. Work in confectioners' sugar, then chill it.

Reserve a few of the finest berries to garnish the dish and, about 1/2 hour before serving, combine the remaining berries and cheese mixture. Fold one into the other until the strawberries are well coated. Chill them until ready to serve. Serves 6.

STRAWBERRIES ROMANOFF

2 quarts strawberries
Sugar
1 pint vanilla ice cream
1 cup heavy cream, whipped
Juice of 1 lemon
1/4 cup Cointreau or Curaçao
2 tablespoons gold label rum

Clean and hull strawberries. Sweeten with sugar.

Whip ice cream slightly and fold in whipped cream. Add lemon juice, Cointreau, and rum. Pour over berries. Spoon into chilled sherbet glasses to serve. Serves 8.

Note: To ripen flavors correctly, prepare the topping several hours before serving and store in refrigerator tray with temperature control at normal.

STRAWBERRIES À LA JEFFREY

1 pint strawberries
1/2 cup sweetened condensed milk
1/4 teaspoon salt
1 tablespoon lemon juice
3/4 cup canned pineapple juice
1 cup shredded coconut

Wash, drain, and hull strawberries. Slice and spread in shallow dish or bowl.

Whip condensed milk with salt, lemon, and pineapple juice. Spread this mixture over strawberries.

Chill 2 hours or longer. Just before serving, top with coconut. Serves 6.

FRUIT STACKUP

Alternate layers of French oven toast (see Index) with fruit and serve as a main dish.

Fresh strawberries, peaches, or hot green applesauce may be used.

Rhubarb

The rhubarb plant, sometimes referred to as pie plant, is classified as an herb and sometimes as a vegetable; however for cookery it is classed with fruits.

STEWED RHUBARB

Wash 2 pounds rhubarb. Cut off leaves and root ends. Peel only if stalks are tough.

Cut into 1-inch pieces. Add 1/2 cup hot water. Simmer, covered, 10 minutes.

Add 3/4 cup sugar and simmer 5 minutes longer, or until tender.

The amount of sugar necessary may vary with the tartness of the rhubarb. Add dash of cinnamon, if desired. Serves 6 to 8.

Steamed Rhubarb: Prepare as above and cook in top of double boiler until tender, about 1/2 hour.

RHUBARB WHIP

Whip 1 pint of heavy cream until stiff. Sweeten. Fold into 1 cup stewed rhubarb.

Place each serving in a sherbet glass which has been lined with lady fingers or pineapple spears. Chill. Serves 6.

STEWED RHUBARB AND BERRIES

Mix equal amounts of diced washed rhubarb and fresh berries. Add sugar to taste. Let stand 1 hour or more.

Heat slowly until sugar dissolves. Simmer without stirring until rhubarb is tender.

STEWED RHUBARB AND PINEAPPLE

Mix equal parts diced washed rhubarb and diced fresh pineapple. Sweeten to taste. Let stand 1 hour or more.

Heat slowly until sugar dissolves. Simmer until rhubarb is tender.

HONEYED RHUBARB AND PEAR COMPOTE

1 1/2 pounds rhubarb
1/3 cup liquid honey
1/3 cup sugar
1 No. 2 can (2 1/2 cups) pear halves

Cut off leaf and root ends. Wash rhubarb; do not peel. Cut in 2-inch pieces; place in shallow baking dish.

Mix honey and sugar; pour over rhubarb. Cover and bake in moderate oven (350°F.) 40 minutes or until tender, stirring after 20 minutes. Chill.

Arrange in serving dish. Drain pears; place on rhubarb. Serves 4 to 6.

RHUBARB BANANA DESSERT

Cook fresh or quick-frozen rhubarb; sweeten to taste. While rhubarb is still warm, add sliced bananas. (3 bananas to 4 cups cooked rhubarb.) Chill. Serve with cream if desired.

RHUBARB-CRUMB DESSERT

2 cups graham cracker or fine dry breadcrumbs
1 1/2 cups sugar
1/4 teaspoon salt
1/4 teaspoon cinnamon
2 tablespoons coarsely grated orange rind
1/3 cup butter or margarine
6 cups rhubarb, cut in 1-inch pieces (1 1/2 pounds)

Combine crumbs, sugar, salt, cinnamon, and orange rind. Melt butter; mix with crumbs.

Alternate layers of rhubarb and crumb mixture in greased 8x8x2-inch baking dish. Press crumbs down firmly with spoon.

Bake in moderate oven (350°F.) until rhubarb is tender, about 40 minutes. Cut in squares. Serve warm or chilled with whipped cream. Serves 8.

BAKED RHUBARB

Arrange alternate layers of cleaned diced rhubarb and sugar in baking dish. Sprinkle top with sugar.

Bake in slow oven (300°F.) until rhubarb is deep red in color, about 1 hour.

RHUBARB COMPOTE

1½ pounds rhubarb
1   cup sugar
1   2-inch stick cinnamon

1   orange
Mint sprigs

Cut off and discard leaf and root ends. Wash rhubarb; do not peel. Cut in 4-inch pieces; combine with sugar. Place in baking dish.

Break cinnamon in small pieces; add. Cover and bake in moderate oven (350°F.) 40 minutes, or until tender, stirring after 20 minutes. Chill.

Arrange in individual serving dishes. Peel orange, slice and use as garnish with mint. Serves 4.

Prunes and Raisins

STEWED PRUNES
(Master Recipe)

½ pound dried prunes
3   cups hot water
1   to 2 tablespoons sugar
Slice of orange or lemon

Wash prunes and soak in hot water 1 to 2 hours. Simmer in same water until tender, about 30 minutes.

Add sugar and lemon or orange slice last 5 minutes of cooking.

If syrup is very thin, remove prunes and boil down syrup. Serve hot or cold.

Variations:

Stewed Prunes and Apricots: Use ¼ pound each of dried prunes and dried apricots. Double the amount of sugar.

Stewed Prunes and Peaches or Pears: Use ¼ pound each of dried prunes and dried peaches or pears. Increase sugar slightly.

PRUNE WHIP

1½ cups unsweetened cooked prune pulp
⅓   to ½ cup sugar
Grated rind and juice of ½ lemon
⅛   teaspoon salt
2   egg whites

Drain the cooked prunes before pit-ting so that the pulp is not too moist.

Place all ingredients in deep bowl and beat until mixture is thick and holds its shape. Electric mixer may be used. Place in serving dishes. Chill. Serve with cream or custard sauce. Serves 4 to 5.

Variation: Fold in ¼ cup chopped nuts or coconut after mixture is beaten until stiff.

Prune Whip

PRUNE PUDDING

To 1½ cups pitted stewed prune pulp and juice add a mixture of ¼ cup cornstarch, ¼ teaspoon cinnamon, and ¼ cup cold water.

Cook until clear and thick, stirring constantly. Chill. Serves 4 to 5.

PRUNE PURÉE

1 pound prunes
2 cups water
⅔ cup sugar

Wash prunes; cover with water and soak 2 to 3 hours. Then cover pan and cook in the same water until tender, about 35 minutes.

Add sugar for the last 5 minutes of cooking. Drain off liquid and put prunes through a sieve. Makes about 2 cups purée.

SPICED OR PICKLED PRUNES

1 pound prunes
Whole cloves
3 cups water
1 cup dark brown sugar
1 cup vinegar
4 3-inch sticks cinnamon

Wash prunes. Stick 2 cloves in each prune. Soak in water for 2 hours.

Add sugar, vinegar, and cinnamon. Bring to a boil. Simmer 30 minutes. Chill overnight in syrup. Makes 1 quart.

CLARET PRUNES

1 jar (about 1 pound) stewed prunes
⅔ cup claret wine
⅓ cup prune liquid
¼ cup brown sugar
¼ teaspoon powdered cinnamon
⅛ teaspoon powdered allspice
6 whole cloves

Remove lid from jar; set lid aside. Drain liquid from prunes; save liquid.

Place wine, prune liquid, sugar, and spices in saucepan. Cook, stirring occasionally, until mixture comes to a boil. Reduce heat and cook gently 5 minutes.

Remove from heat and cool slightly before pouring over prunes. Recap jar tightly. Store in refrigerator until ready to use.

STEWED RAISINS

Wash raisins. Add 1 cup water for each cup of raisins. Cover and simmer 10 minutes. Add ½ tablespoon sugar for each cup of raisins and cook 5 minutes longer.

PLUMPED RAISINS

Wash raisins, cover with boiling water and let stand about 15 minutes or until cool. Drain, cover again with boiling water and soak 15 minutes. Drain and use in recipes.

Peaches, Apricots, Plums, and Nectarines

SPICED PEACHES

1 No. 2½ can peach halves
1 tablespoon vinegar
1 to 2 sticks cinnamon
1 teaspoon whole cloves

Combine ingredients in saucepan and heat to boiling. Simmer 5 minutes. Chill.

Drain before serving. Stud peaches with whole cloves.

FRIED PEACHES OR APRICOTS

Cut fruit into halves and remove pits from unpeeled peaches or apricots.

Melt butter in a skillet; sauté the fruit soft side down until brown, about 5 minutes, basting frequently with the drippings.

Turn and cook the other side. Sprinkle with sugar and cook fruit until sugar is melted.

PEACH MARY ANNS

Place one peach half, cavity side up, on each Mary Ann shell. Fill cavity with nuts.

Combine whipped cream and vanilla. Top each peach half with whipped cream.

Combine preserves and peach juice and spoon over top of each peach Mary Ann. Chill until ready to serve.

PEACH MELBA

5   to 6 fresh peaches
1   cup sugar
2   cups water
Dash of salt
Fresh raspberry sauce

Dip peaches in boiling water for a few seconds and slip off skins.

Combine sugar, water, and salt; bring to boil. Simmer peaches in this syrup 10 to 15 minutes or until tender.

Dip syrup over fruit as it cooks. Chill in syrup. Drain before serving with raspberry sauce. Serves 5 to 6.

Fresh Raspberry Sauce: Sprinkle 3/4 cup sugar over 1 pint fresh raspberries. Let stand 2 hours. Put fruit through sieve.

BAKED PEACHES

Peel, cut in halves, and remove pits from firm juicy peaches. Place in baking dish.

Fill each hollow with 1/2 teaspoon butter, 1 teaspoon sugar, a sprinkling of lemon juice, and a dusting of nutmeg or cinnamon.

Place 2 tablespoons water in the bottom of dish. Bake in moderate oven (350°F.) 20 minutes.

STEWED DRIED PEACHES

Rinse peaches; cover with water and boil 5 minutes. Drain and remove skins.

Cover with fresh water and boil 35 to 45 minutes. Allow 1/4 cup sugar for each cup of peaches and add for last 5 minutes of cooking.

Peach Mary Anns

FLAMING FRESH PEACHES

6   large fresh peach halves, peeled
6   tablespoons brown sugar
2   tablespoons butter or margarine
6   maraschino cherries
1/3 cup brandy
Whipped cream or chilled custard

Place peach halves in baking dish. Sprinkle hollows with brown sugar and dot with butter. Broil until sugar crusts, about 3 minutes.

Place cherry in each peach hollow. Pour brandy over all. Ignite and serve while flaming. Serve with whipped cream or chilled custard. Serves 6.

PEACHES WITH BRANDIED CREAM

1/2 cup heavy cream
1   tablespoon brandy flavoring
Few grains salt
3   tablespoons powdered sugar
Few grains mace
8   fresh peaches

Whip cream slightly. Add flavoring, salt, 1 tablespoon sugar, and mace. Whip until cream is thickened.

Peel and slice peaches. Add remaining sugar and mix well. Arrange in serving dishes and top with cream. Serves 4.

BROILED PEACHES

Place fresh or canned peach halves, cut side up, in a buttered shallow pan. Place 1 teaspoon butter in each cavity. Sprinkle with brown sugar.

Place under broiler about 3 inches from heat until lightly browned.

Curried: To above, add a dash of curry powder.

With Coconut: Before broiling peaches, sprinkle with brown sugar, then with shredded coconut, and dot with butter. Broil until coconut is delicately browned.

BAKED PEACHES AND MINCEMEAT

Drain canned peaches. Fill each half with mincemeat.

Place peach halves in a shallow pan with enough peach juice to keep them from scorching.

Bake in slow oven for 25 or 30 minutes. Serve with roast poultry or ham.

FRESH APRICOTS

Fresh apricots may be used in most dishes calling for peaches. Cooked and

Orange Apricot Porcupines

pureéd, they may be used in any dishes calling for applesauce.

To Peel Apricots: Drop raw apricots into boiling water. Remove from heat and let stand ½ minute.

Plunge into cold water for a few minutes. The skin will pull off easily.

APRICOT-APPLESAUCE

¼ pound dried apricots
2 cups water
5 cooking apples
⅔ cup sugar

Wash apricots in cold water; cover with water and soak 4 hours.

Drain; add 2 cups water and cook 10 minutes.

Wash, pare, core, and slice apples very thin; add to apricots and cook 10 minutes.

Add sugar, stir to mix thoroughly, and cook 1 or 2 minutes longer. Put through a coarse strainer or serve unstrained. Serves 4 to 6.

ORANGE APRICOT PORCUPINES

32 whole firm apricots
¼ cup blanched almonds slivered
2 cups sugar
½ cup white vinegar
½ cup orange juice
½ teaspon salt
½ teaspoon almond extract

Scald apricots 1 minute in boiling water; plunge into cold water; drain and peel. Press about 3 pieces of almond into each apricot.

Combine sugar, vinegar, orange juice, salt, and almond extract in a 1½-quart saucepan; bring to boil on high heat.

Lower apricots, studded with almonds, carefully into hot syrup; cook on high heat about 3 minutes. Remove from heat.

Lift apricots into hot sterilized, wide-mouthed pint jars, using slotted spoon. Pour on syrup, working out bubbles by running a spatula down sides of the jars. Seal. Makes 4 pints.

Plums in Port Wine

NECTARINES

There is a mistaken impression that the nectarine is a cross between a peach and something else. As a matter of fact, it may be simply classified as a smooth-skinned peach, with an especially rich, aromatic flavor all its own.

It can be served in exactly the same ways as the peach and substituted in any recipes given for peaches.

STEWED PLUMS

    4   cups plums
    1½ cups boiling water
    ½   to 1 cup sugar

Cut into halves and remove pits from plums, or use whole plums.

Drop into boiling water. When they are nearly tender, add sugar. Cook a few minutes longer.

PLUMS IN PORT WINE

    2   pounds fresh prune-type plums
    1½ cups port
    ⅔   cup sugar
    2   inches stick cinnamon
    ½   lemon, sliced

Cut plums in half. Remove stones.

Cook wine, sugar, stick cinnamon, and lemon slices 5 minutes. Add plums. Cook 3 to 5 minutes. Chill and serve. Serves 6.

Pears

STEWED DRIED PEARS

Wash 1 cup dried pears. Remove remaining parts of core. Cover with water.

Cover and simmer until tender, about 25 to 35 minutes. Add ¼ cup sugar and simmer 5 minutes.

STEAMED DRIED PEARS

Add ¼ cup sugar and ⅓ cup water to 1 cup dried pears and steam until tender.

CRUMBED CRANBERRY PEARS

    1   can pear halves
    1   cup corn flakes
    Melted butter or margarine
    1   1-pound can whole cranberry sauce

Roll cereal fine. Dip cut side of pears in melted butter, then roll in crushed cereal and place cut side up in open baking pan.

Bake in moderate oven (350°F.) until lightly brown. Add a spoonful cranberry sauce to each. Serve with ham slices.

STUFFED CANNED PEARS

    ¼   cup heavy cream, whipped
    ¼   cup chopped nuts
    ½   tablespoon sugar
    ¼   teaspoon vanilla
    6   canned pear halves

Combine stiffly whipped cream, nuts, sugar, and vanilla.

Pile lightly into hollows of pear halves placed in chilled sherbet cups. Serves 6.

STUFFED PEAR BUFFET PLATTER

3 Anjou or Comice pears
Juice of 1 lemon
3 dates
3 walnut halves
1/2 (3-ounce) package cream cheese
2 tablespoons toasted coconut
Mayonnaise
3 bananas
1/2 cup chopped walnuts
1 1/2 cups pineapple cubes
1/3 cup maraschino cherries

Cut pears in half and remove the core with a 1/2-teaspoon measuring spoon. Pour lemon juice in shallow bowl and let pears stand cut side down while preparing other fruits.

Stuff dates with walnuts. Make balls of cheese and roll in the toasted coconut. Spread mayonnaise on bananas which have been cut in half lengthwise. Roll in nuts.

Arrange fruits on platter and add stuffing of dates and cheese to pears. Serve at once or allow to stand in refrigerator a half hour. Serve with honey dressing. Serves 6.

SPICED PEARS

1 No. 2 1/2 can Bartlett pears
1 stick cinnamon
8 to 12 whole cloves
1/4 cup vinegar or lemon juice

Drain syrup from pears. Heat it with stick cinnamon and cloves for 5 minutes.

Remove from heat and add vinegar or lemon juice. Pour back over pears and let stand overnight in refrigerator.

STEWED FRESH GINGER PEARS

3 winter pears
1/2 cup firmly packed brown sugar
1/4 to 1/2 cup granulated sugar
Grated rind and juice 1/2 lemon
Dash of salt
1 teaspoon ground ginger
1/8 teaspoon ground cinnamon
1/2 cup water

Peel, core, and dice pears.

Combine remaining ingredients in saucepan; bring to boil. Add pears. Simmer, covered, for 20 minutes, or until pears are tender. Serves 4.

Stuffed Pear Buffet Platter

PEARS BAKED IN PINEAPPLE JUICE

4　winter pears
1　teaspoon grated orange rind
Juice of 1 lemon
½ cup canned pineapple juice
¼ cup sugar

Cut pears in half, peel, and core. Put in 1½-quart casserole. Mix remaining ingredients and pour over pears.

Cover and bake in hot oven (400°F.) for 45 minutes, or until pears are tender. Baste pears every 15 minutes with some of the syrup in bottom of casserole. Chill. Serves 4.

SOUTHERN BAKED PEARS

6　canned pear halves, drained
6　whole cloves
⅔ cup firmly packed light brown sugar
3　tablespoons pear juice
2　teaspoons lemon juice
3　tablespoons orange juice
¼ teaspoon grated orange rind
1　tablespoon butter or margarine
2　tablespoons chopped nuts

Arrange pear halves, with cored side up, in greased baking dish. Stick a clove in each pear.

Mix light brown sugar, fruit juices, orange rind, and butter in a saucepan. Bring to a boil and boil for 10 minutes, stirring occasionally.

Add nuts. Pour syrup over pears. Bake in moderate oven (350°F.) about 30 minutes. Serve hot with meat course or use as a dessert. Or serve cold with whipped cream. Serves 6.

BAKED HONEY PEARS

4　fresh pears
½ cup liquid honey
4　teaspoons minced candied or preserved ginger
½ cup hot water

Halve pears, core, and place in baking dish. Add honey; sprinkle with ginger.

Add water; cover. Bake in moderate oven (350°F.) 45 minutes or until tender. Serves 4.

PEARS IN PORT WINE

3　large fresh pears
1　cup water
½ cup brown sugar
2　cups port wine

Stew pears, halved, peeled and cored, in 1 cup water and brown sugar, until tender, taking care not to break them.

Drain; add port wine. Chill in refrigerator after they are cold. Serve cold.

Pineapple

When buying fresh pineapple, select firm fruit, free of specks and soft spots. Rounded, plump pineapples have more flesh than the tapering ones. The aroma of ripeness is noticeable at the leafy end when one or two leaves are pulled out. A pineapple weighing 2 pounds yields about 2½ cups cubed or 4 cups grated fruit.

PREPARATION OF FRESH PINEAPPLE

Wash pineapple. Cut off leafy end and a slice from stem end. Stand pineapple upright and cut off skin in strips from top to bottom. Remove eyes with pointed knife or special pineapple knife.

Prepare as below. Sprinkle with sugar and chill. Sugar will dissolve as it stands.

Shredded Pineapple: Cut very thin slices. Shred with a fork.

Pineapple Slices: Cut into thin serving slices. Cut out round core.

Pineapple Spears: Cut prepared pineapple into wedges with core removed. Cut into strips.

Pineapple Wedges or Cubes: Cut slices into wedges or cubes after core is removed.

Pineapple Ambrosia: Cut prepared pineapple into slices or cubes. Add 1 cup each of orange and grapefruit sections and ½ cup shredded coconut. Chill 1 hour or more before serving.

PINEAPPLE COMPOTE

Pare and cube or shred 1 medium-sized pineapple.

Make syrup by combining 2 cups sugar and 1 cup water and stirring over low heat until sugar dissolves. Bring to boil and cook 5 minutes.

Add pineapple. Cover and cook 10 minutes. Chill.

PINEAPPLE GLAZED WITH CRANBERRY SAUCE

Drain pineapple slices and place on broiling rack.

Beat cranberry sauce until smooth and spreadable. Add just a little of pineapple juice to make it spread more readily, if necessary. Spread each pineapple slice with sauce.

Place in preheated broiler under moderate heat. Broil until heated through and glazed, about 10 to 15 minutes. Serve with poultry.

BROILED PINEAPPLE

Drain slices or sticks well. Brush with melted butter. Sprinkle with sugar. Broil under moderate heat until lightly browned.

SAUTÉED PINEAPPLE SLICES

Drain pineapple well. Dip slices in flour. Sauté in hot fat, turning to brown on both sides.

PINEAPPLE (LUAU STYLE)

Cut thick slices from top and bottom of pineapple. Run knife around inside of pineapple, close to rind. Remove center in one piece.

Cut center in half lengthwise, then

again. Continue cutting lengthwise until 6 or 8 wedge-shaped sticks are formed. Refill shell to serve.

Note: If center core of pineapple is hard, cut this off before placing pineapple sticks in the shell.

PINEAPPLE FLUFF

1 fresh pineapple
¼ cup sugar
½ pound marshmallows, cut in small
    pieces
1 cup heavy cream, whipped
Sliced maraschino cherries

Pare and cut pineapple into fine pieces. Place in bowl in layers, sprinkling each layer with sugar and marshmallow pieces. Cover and let stand several hours.

To serve, fold in whipped cream and spoon into serving dishes. Garnish with maraschino cherries. Serves 8.

SPICED PINEAPPLE CHUNKS

¼ cup vinegar
1½ cups sugar
8 whole cloves
Small piece whole ginger
Grated rind of 1 lemon
½ large, ripe pineapple, cut in small
    chunks

Combine vinegar, sugar, spices, and lemon rind in saucepan. Bring to boil.

Add pineapple and boil until transparent, about 15 minutes. Serve as accompaniment to meat. Makes about 2 cups.

PINEAPPLE IN SPICED WINE

1 cup Port or Madeira
1 cup sugar
18 whole cloves or 1 4-inch stick cinnamon
12 slices fresh or canned pineapple

Simmer wine, sugar, and cloves or cinnamon in a saucepan for 5 minutes.

Add pineapple slices and simmer 5 minutes. Turn the slices several times. Serve as a dessert. Serves 6.

Serve frozen pineapple chunks semi-frosty for a quick and easy appetizer or dessert.

GLAZED PINEAPPLE

Method #1: Drain canned pineapple slices or spears; dip in brown sugar. Brown by cooking in hot bacon fat, pan drippings, or butter.

Method #2: Drain canned pineapple slices. Place in shallow buttered baking pan. Do not let the slices overlap.

Dot with butter or margarine. Bake in slow oven (325°F.) 1 hour. Serve with a maraschino cherry in each slice.

Method #3: Sprinkle drained canned pineapple slices or spears with grated cheese. Season with a few grains red pepper. Broil or bake in moderate oven to melt cheese.

PINEAPPLE AND BACON STICKS

Drain pineapple spears and wrap bacon around them.

Fasten the slices with toothpicks. Broil the bacon under moderate heat.

PINEAPPLE TRIFLE

1 cup canned crushed pineapple, drained
10 marshmallows, cut in pieces
1 cup macaroon crumbs
1 cup chopped dates
¾ cup heavy cream, whipped

Combine pineapple, marshmallows, macaroon crumbs, and dates in a bowl.

Fold whipped cream into above ingredients. Chill. Serves 6 to 8.

Dates and Figs

TO SERVE FRESH FIGS

Fresh figs (green ripe figs or black figs) are highly perishable; therefore buy only for immediate use. They must be handled with great care because they are easily bruised. When bought, spread out on a flat surface so they do not touch each other and place in refrigerator. The skins are thin and may be removed or not before eating.

Serve sliced fresh figs with cream, or with lemon or orange juice. If they are thoroughly ripe they need no sweetening.

Use them in practically any other way that you make use of other fresh fruits—in fruit cups, salads, etc.

SPICED CANNED FIGS

1 No. 2½ jar figs
½ cup sugar
¼ cup cider vinegar
⅛ teaspoon salt
1 stick cinnamon
¼ teaspoon whole allspice
Whole cloves

Drain fruit. Combine syrup, sugar, vinegar, salt, and cinnamon. Add allspice in cheesecloth bag. Bring to full rolling boil and boil 2 minutes.

Stick 2 cloves in each fig and add to hot syrup. Simmer 10 minutes. Do not boil.

Remove spice bag. Cover. Chill 24 hours before serving.

SPICED DRIED FIGS

1   pound dried figs
2   cups cold water
Sliced lemon peel
1   1-inch piece ginger root
½   cup sugar
2   tablespoons lemon juice

Wash figs and remove tough stems. Combine with water, lemon peel, and ginger root in a saucepan. Simmer until figs are tender, about 30 minutes.

Add sugar and simmer 10 minutes. Remove from heat and add lemon juice. Stir and chill. Serves 6 to 8.

FRESH DATES

To serve fresh dates, wash carefully, remove stems, and serve as part of a fruit salad or platter.

SPICED FRESH DATES

3   pounds fresh dates
Shelled walnuts or almonds
4   cups sugar

1½   cups vinegar
½   cup water
½   teaspoon salt
Few drops extract or oil of cinnamon and cloves

Pit dates and stuff with large pieces of nuts; the almonds may be blanched or not, as preferred.

Pack into small jars, standing dates on end.

Make a syrup of remaining ingredients, simmer for 5 minutes, and pour over dates in jars. Seal while hot.

STEWED DRIED FIGS

Rinse figs; cover with water and boil 20 to 30 minutes. For each cup of fruit add 1 tablespoon sugar for the last 15 minutes of cooking.

Stewed Figs with Oranges: Cook as above, adding ½ slice orange for each 6 figs for the last 5 minutes of cooking. Serve room warm. Sugar may be added if desired.

Citrus Fruits

ORANGE COMPOTE

2   seedless oranges
1   cup water
¾   cup sugar
⅛   teaspoon salt
3   additional oranges
1   tablespoon rum or liqueur (optional)

Cut yellow rind off 2 oranges. Cut rind into thin slices and add water, sugar, and salt. Boil 20 minutes.

Skin and remove membrane from the 2 oranges and from 3 additional oranges. Place the sections in a serving bowl. Pour the hot syrup and rind over them. Chill the compote. If desired, add rum or liqueur before serving. Serves 4.

BROILED ORANGE SLICES

12   slices orange, ¼-inch thick
2   tablespoons brown sugar
½   teaspoon cinnamon
6   maraschino cherries

Slice oranges; nick edges into eighths. Spread slices with a mixture of brown sugar and cinnamon. Put a half cherry in center.

Broil 4 minutes, or until hot and bubbly. Serve with meat. Serves 6.

BROILED ORANGE SLICES #2

Before broiling, dip large orange sections or thick slices in French dressing. Serve with duck or ham.

Orange Banana Ambrosia

ORANGE BANANA AMBROSIA

2 medium-sized oranges
2 ripe firm bananas
2 tablespoons sugar
1/2 to 3/4 cup shredded coconut

Peel oranges and cut crosswise into thin slices, removing seeds and fibrous portions. Peel bananas and slice about 1/4 inch thick.

Arrange alternate layers of orange and banana slices in large shallow dish, sprinkling each layer with sugar.

Use orange slices for bottom and top layers. Sprinkle top generously with coconut. Chill about 1 hour before serving.

Just before serving, garnish with additional ripe banana and orange slices, if desired. Serves 4 to 6.

TANGERINES IN KIRSCH

Peel the tangerines and separate the segments. Arrange in glass serving dish and sprinkle with powdered sugar.

Sprinkle with kirsch and refrigerate 2 hours before serving.

BAKED SPICED ORANGES

3 seedless oranges
Whole cloves
1 cup sugar
1 cup water
1/3 cup light corn syrup
1 teaspoon grated lemon rind
Few grains of salt

Grate a very thin layer of yellow rind from the oranges. Drop the oranges in boiling water to cover and boil gently for 1/2 hour. Remove from water and drain.

Cut large oranges in half crosswise, into thick slices, or into quarters. Small oranges may be left whole. Stick each piece of orange with whole cloves. Place close together in a shallow baking pan.

Combine remaining ingredients. Stir over low heat until sugar is dissolved. Bring to a boil and boil gently without stirring for 5 minutes. Pour over oranges.

Cover and bake in moderate oven (350°F.) about 1 1/4 hours or until glazed, basting once or twice. Serve with meat or poultry. Serves 6.

STEWED ORANGES

Peel 6 seedless oranges, removing all the white membrane and cut oranges into sections. Do the cutting over a bowl so that all juice is collected.

Cut thick white part off some of the peel and cut peel into fine slivers. You'll need about 2 tablespoons of these slivers.

Cook slivered peel with 1 cup sugar and ½ cup water, over a medium heat without stirring, for about 8 minutes or until mixture looks as thick as maple syrup.

Then pour this hot syrup over the uncooked orange sections, give it a good stir and chill in refrigerator. Serves 4.

POACHED ORANGES

```
6   seedless oranges
2   cups sugar
2   cups water
```

Cut oranges in half crosswise. Cover with water; bring to boil. Pour off and discard water.

Combine sugar and 2 cups water; bring to boil. Add oranges; cook gently until skins can be easily pierced with wooden pick (20 to 30 minutes). Chill.

TANGERINE SURPRISE

```
8     medium tangerines
1½  cups water
½   cup sugar
5     2-inch cinnamon sticks
6     whole cloves
2     tablespoons lemon juice
```

Wash, peel, and section tangerines, placing rind from 3 tangerines in saucepan. Remove all white fiber from fruit; add fiber to rind, along with water, sugar, spices, and lemon juice. Bring to full, rolling boil; boil, uncovered, 10 minutes.

Remove rind, add tangerine sections and bring to boil again. Boil 1 minute, then cool. Refrigerate. Serve with cream cheese and crackers. Serves 4.

KUMQUATS

The kumquat is a very small citrus fruit, orange in color, with a flavor somewhere between that of orange and lemon. The entire fruit, rind and all, is edible if it is fully ripe.

To serve, wash and dry kumquats. Slice very thin and use in salads. The large seeds should be removed.

Stuffed Kumquats: Slice in halves. Remove the large seeds. Stuff the fruit with cream cheese or chopped nuts and use to garnish salads.

BOILED KUMQUATS

Wash 1 pound kumquats. Cover with cold water; bring to a boil, then cover and simmer 30 minutes.

Add 2 cups sugar and, if desired, ¼ teaspoon powdered cinnamon, and boil 5 minutes.

The kumquats may be served whole or they may be cut into halves, in which case remove the large seeds. Chill thoroughly and use as a garnish for a meat platter or in salads.

Note: Kumquats may also be cooked in water to cover (without sugar) until the skin is clear and tender, about 20 to 30 minutes.

BROILED OR BAKED GRAPEFRUIT

Wash grapefruit and cut in halves. Remove seeds, core, and loosen segments. Sprinkle each half with 1 tablespoon brown sugar, then pour 1 tablespoon sherry or brandy over each.

Put under the broiler until the sugar melts, or bake in moderate oven. Serve at once as a dessert.

Broiled Honeyed Grapefruit: Prepare grapefruit as above. Spread with honey and sprinkle with cinnamon and mace instead of other ingredients. Brown lightly under moderate broiler heat.

Grapefruit with French Dressing: Use French dressing instead of above ingredients. Spoon 2 tablespoons over each prepared grapefruit half, being careful that all is covered. Bake or broil as directed. Serve hot as a first course.

BAKED GRAPEFRUIT

    2   cups crushed corn flakes
    1/2 cup brown sugar, firmly packed
    1/2 teaspoon cinnamon
    1/4 cup melted butter or margarine
    2   grapefruit, halved and cored

Combine corn flakes, sugar, cinna-

mon, and butter. Fill and top the halves of grapefruit in which the sections have been loosened.

Bake in hot oven (400°F.) about 10 to 12 minutes. Serve at once. Serves 4.

SHADDOCK

The shaddock is a large, yellow, coarse-grained, pear-shaped fruit resembling a grapefruit. It is frequently imported from Cuba and may be used as other citrus fruits.

Melons and Miscellaneous Fruits

Chilled berries and melon combine to make this fruit delight.

MELONS

Melons are fruits of the gourd family, one that includes many trailing or climbing plants such as the squash and pumpkin. There are many varieties of melons; the watermelon, cantaloupe or muskmelon, honeydew, and honeyball are perhaps the best known.

Hints on Buying Melons

Melons of all types are at their best when fully matured. Ripeness in al-

most all kinds of melons is indicated by the softening at the part of the fruit which surrounds the "eye" or stem end and should yield to pressure of the finger. In some melons a change of color to a more or less yellowish tinge is also a sign of ripeness. Usually the fragrant aroma that most melons diffuse becomes stronger and is most perceptible when a melon is fully ripe. No one indication is infallible. Sometimes one, and sometimes a combination of indications must serve as a guide. If melons have soft spots on them, they are overripe and may not taste or look right.

Watermelon is tested for ripeness by thumping with the knuckle; if ripe, it gives a resonant, hollow sound.

Unripe melons should never be chilled, because they do not then fully ripen. In quantity, melons are stored at a temperature of 70°F. until ripe, and then chilled just before serving. An unripe melon will ripen in 1 or 2 days on a sunny window ledge.

A cut melon should always be wrapped in waxed paper or the cut section covered with moistened waxed paper before placing in refrigerator to prevent its odor permeating other foods.

To Serve Melons

Melons should be washed and chilled thoroughly before serving fresh in the shell or cut into various shapes and

Persian Melons

Make a basket by cutting wedges from both sides of upper half of honeydew melon, leaving a ¾-inch strip between wedges for a handle. Be sure handle is not cut but remains attached to lower half of melon. Remove seeds carefully.

With a melon ball cutter, form balls from the meat of the lower half of melon, hollowing out entire lower half, and from the cut-out wedges.

Cut balls from halves of cantaloupe. Trim some of the meat from inside the melon handle with a knife.

Return the balls to basket, arranging them to show contrasts in color between honeydew and cantaloupe balls. Pour wine over balls. Chill thoroughly. Serves 6.

GUAVAS

This tropical fruit is pear-shaped, somewhat like a peach in texture. Some guavas are sweet, some sour; the sweeter types are best for eating out of hand, for using fresh in salads and desserts, and for cooking or canning. The sour ones are best for making jellies and jams.

To be served fresh, the guava should be washed and served unpeeled. The peel is not eaten.

served in fruit cups, salads, etc. Lemon or lime wedges are usually served with melons in the shell such as cantaloupe, honeydew, honey ball, or casaba because the citrus juice emphasizes the melon's flavor. If desired, melon may be served on ice, but the cavity should never be filled with ice because that injures the fruit and dilutes the flavor.

BAKED CANTALOUPE

    2   cantaloupes
    3   cups sliced peaches
    ½ cup sugar
    Few grains mace
    Mint sprigs

Halve cantaloupes; remove seeds. Combine peaches, sugar, and mace. Fill cantaloupes with peaches, arranging slices in radiating pattern on top.

Bake in hot oven (425°F.) 15 minutes. Garnish with mint. Serve at once. Serves 4.

MELON BALL BASKET WITH WINE

    1   ripe honeydew melon
    1   ripe cantaloupe, halved and seeded
    ½ cup sweet wine (marsala, muscatel,
          or port)

Cranshaw Melons

CRYSTALLIZED GRAPES

Select perfect red or purple grapes. Wash and drain well. Cut into small clusters.

For each pound of grapes, use $\frac{1}{2}$ cup water and 1 cup sugar. Combine water and sugar and boil 5 minutes.

Dip each cluster of grapes separately into hot syrup. Let excess syrup drain off. Sprinkle grapes at once with granulated sugar.

Place on cake rack to harden and place rack in refrigerator.

FROSTED GRAPES

Select perfect red or purple grapes. Wash and dry well. Cut into small clusters.

Beat egg white until slightly frothy. Sprinkle it over the grapes. Dust with granulated sugar. Let dry.

PAPAYAS

The papaya is a large, yellowish-orange fruit like a melon which grows on a tropical tree (the papaya or papaw tree). It is much used in Hawaii and the Philippines, and is now grown in some parts of the United States. It has a thick flesh ranging from yellow to deep salmon pink.

The papaya is ready to eat when it is soft enough to yield to slight pressure with the thumb. It is served raw. The small fruit may be served at room temperature, on a fruit plate, with a fruit knife.

The large papayas are chilled, cut into wedges or halves, seeded, and served with lime or lemon wedges as a breakfast or dessert fruit. Salt or sugar may be added, if desired.

It is also excellent cut into balls or cubes, dressed with a little lemon juice and sugar, plus a little sherry, if desired, then chilled for an hour or two, and served as a fruit cocktail.

Or it may be combined with pineapple, mangoes, oranges, grapefruit, or other fruits for salad; or it may be made into jam, pickles, or ketchup, or into sherbets and other desserts. In Hawaii, green papayas are steamed or baked with a little water until tender, seasoned and served as a vegetable.

PERSIMMONS

The persimmons which are usually available in fruit stores are large, beautiful fruits, ranging from rosy orange or salmon pink to yellow, about the size and texture of tomatoes, and round or oval in shape. A number of varieties are available, including the smaller, puckery ones native to many parts of the United States and the large ones grown on the Pacific coast.

The most common use is as a dessert fruit; it should be thoroughly chilled.

To serve, wash the persimmon, set it stem end down on a plate, and cut off a bit of the top, so that the fruit may be eaten out of the skin with a spoon. Or cut in quarters, beginning at the top, cutting to the stem end, but not quite through the bottom. Spread out the sections petal fashion.

MANGOES

The mango is a yellow-red, oblong tropical fruit with a thick rind, somewhat acid and juicy pulp, and a hard stone. It is eaten when ripe, or preserved or pickled when unripe.

The type grown in this country are usually the size of a large apple. They may be chilled, but are also delicious at room temperature.

To serve, wash them and cut in halves. Remove the pit and eat the soft pulp with a spoon. Or peel and cut the flesh from the pit; slice and eat with a fork with or without cream and sugar. A sprig of mint and a half lime makes a pleasant garnish for each serving.

Mangoes are good also when cooked like any other stewed fruit, or used in pies, puddings, sherbets, or ice cream, or made into preserves, jelly, sweet pickles, or chutney.

POMEGRANATES

The pomegranate is about the size of a large orange, or larger. The color varies from light yellow to deep purplish red. Most varieties have a thick, leathery skin. The enclosed seeds and crimson juice are used in salads, cocktails, punches, and fancy dishes. Or pomegranates may be eaten out of hand, as one eats an orange. The juice has long been the basis of grenadine syrup.

To serve pomegranates, wash, cut in half, and remove seeds with a spoon. Mix the seeds with powdered sugar or honey, chill and serve as a dessert.

QUINCES

The quince is a golden yellow or greenish-yellow fruit with a hard flesh and, when fully ripe, has a distinct flavor and delightful aroma. The shapes vary from round to pear shape. Quinces are most frequently used in making preserves, although they may be stewed or baked, used in pies, tarts, and other desserts.

Unripened quinces will ripen in a few days if kept on a sunny window ledge. When buying quinces, select fruits without specks or dark soft spots.

BAKED QUINCES

6   medium quinces
1½ cups water
1   cup sugar

Pare, core, and slice the quinces into a casserole. Add water and sugar. Cover and bake very slowly until the fruit is tender and deep red in color.

If the water evaporates, add a little from time to time to insure enough syrup to surround the fruit when it is served.

CHERIMOYAS

Other names for this tropical fruit grown in parts of California are custard apple, sweet sop, and sherbet fruit.

Cherimoyas are tree-ripened, but must stand several days before they become soft and edible.

The perfumy flesh, creamy smooth in texture, has a flavor suggesting a mixture of strawberry and pineapple. To serve, chill the soft fruit thoroughly, then cut in halves if small, quarters or wedges if large, and serve on plates, to be eaten with spoons. The seeds are discarded as one does cherry pits.

The fruit may also be peeled and sieved and used in ice creams and custards. It is especially good combined with bananas.

SAPOTES

The white or golden sapote is a fruit of the evergreen tree sometimes referred to as the "peach of the tropics." The soft, pale yellow flesh has an appealing flavor and may be used in any of the ways you like to serve peaches.

LOQUATS

The loquat is a delicious plumlike fruit of an ornamental fruiting tree, very popular in parts of California. Fruits of the better varieties grow as large as eggs.

Loquats may be used as table fruits, in preserves, pickled, or in pies. For loquat pie, follow ordinary fruit pie recipes, allowing 2 to 3 cups of pitted loquats for a pie.

JUJUBES

The jujube is a datelike fruit of any of a number of trees and shrubs of the buckthorn family growing in warm climates. It is gaining favor as a home fruit in the drier sections of the West. The fruit varies considerably in size and is shaped somewhat like a plum, has a pit, and is brownish or reddish brown in color.

It may be eaten fresh or the dried fruits may be chopped and added to breads, cakes, and cooked cereals. The fresh fruit is sometimes made into jujube butter or skinned and pickled.

GAME COOKBOOK

Game is the term applied to any wild or partially wild animal or bird, commonly used as food. Most game is protected by game laws and may be taken only during certain open seasons, and in definitely stated numbers and limitations.

GAME COOKERY HINTS

Wild game is prepared and cooked in much the same manner as domestic meats and poultry.

The flesh of game usually has a characteristic wild flavor which is highly prized and should not be disguised with strong seasonings. Despite some beliefs to the contrary, soaking in water or diluted vinegar is usually unnecessary. This does not necessarily lessen the "gamy" flavor. It just draws out all the rich juices which give flavor to all meats and poultry, domestic or wild.

For added flavor it is, however, sometimes advisable to soak tougher cuts of the meat of older animals in wine or a French dressing. This is especially true of caribou.

In general, before being cooked, freshly killed game should hang at least two days to ripen and tenderize the flesh, otherwise it may be tough and tasteless. Select a cool place with good circulation of air and protected from flies and insects. Cut pieces of venison may be kept in the refrigerator to ripen.

The actual length of time to allow game to hang is best determined by preference and experience. For example, the English like their birds "high" and let them hang for 10 days or longer in a cool place. This is not practical in our climate and, as a matter of fact, the flavor which is thus developed is not well liked in this country. Two days is usually sufficient ripening time for most game. Ducks must never be allowed to hang until "high."

The most commonly used wild birds are grouse, pheasant, quail, and wild duck. When purchased in the market, they are dressed, drawn, and if desired, cut up ready for use. Like other game, birds are lean and require generous use of extra fat during cooking to prevent drying out. The light meated birds such as partridge and quail should always be cooked until well done. Dark-meated birds may be served rare.

Because game is somewhat less tender than domestic meats, in some cases it must be larded with strips of fat salt pork. This is done by drawing the strips through the surface of the flesh with a larding needle. Most game may be broiled or roasted without the addition of liquid.

If the animal is no longer young or if the cuts are tough, it must be braised or stewed by moist heat. Game is parboiled only when the recipe specifically suggests it.

Any of the stuffings used for domestic fowl may be used for game; however, wild rice stuffing is the favorite for game birds. The addition of tart apple or orange to bread stuffing is an improvement in strong-flavored game.

Drippings are made into gravy with a little wine frequently added, or a wine sauce may be made from the pan drippings.

Serve game in the same manner as other meats and poultry. A tart jelly is a good accompaniment for roasted or broiled meat or birds. Broiled game birds are generally served on toast.

Game Birds

HOW TO DRESS BIRDS

Ducks, geese, grouse, and turkeys are usually dry picked. To do this, hang the bird up by one leg. Pluck the pinion and tail feathers first, then the small feathers from shanks and inside of thighs. Then pluck the remaining body feathers.

To pluck and avoid tearing the skin, grasp only a few feathers at a time and pull downward in the direction the feathers grow.

Game birds are drawn (entrails removed) in the same way as with domestic fowl.

FISH EATING GAME BIRDS

The flavor of birds depends upon the type of food they eat. Birds that eat fish have a "fishy" flavor which some people find objectionable. This flavor may be eliminated by parboiling the birds for 10 to 20 minutes, depending upon size of birds.

Add to enough water to cover 2 birds 1 teaspoon baking soda and 1 teaspoon black pepper, then parboil.

Drain well and rub with salt and pepper. Tie a piece of bacon over breast. Brown the birds in melted butter in heavy kettle. Cover tightly and cook over low heat until tender, about 1½ hours. Add giblet stock during last part of cooking. Serve with gravy.

BROILED WILD DUCK

Use young mallards and canvas backs. Cut off tail, removing oil sack. Split down the back. Draw and wipe well with a damp cloth. Do not wash.

Rub with salt and pepper and then with melted butter or oil, or spread with slices of bacon.

Spread open and lay skin side down on broiler rack. Broil under moderate heat until tender, 15 to 20 minutes, turning at least once. Take care to avoid overcooking.

Serve with melted butter seasoned with a little lemon juice and chopped parsley. A tart jelly is a natural accompaniment.

BROILED WOODCOCK

Woodcock is not drawn. The entrails shrivel up when cooked and are easily removed at the table. If one is finicky about this, the lower end of the trail (intestines) may be removed.

Clean birds and wipe with damp cloth. Rub with butter. Wrap completely in bacon slices or thin strips of fat salt pork. Broil under very moderate heat about 15 minutes, turning frequently.

BROILED PARTRIDGE, PHEASANT, QUAIL, OR GROUSE

Clean birds and split them down back. Sprinkle with salt and pepper. Dust with flour to keep juices in.

Broil on wire rack, laying the inside first toward the fire. Length of broiling time will depend upon size of bird and how well done you like the meat. Allow 10 to 15 minutes for quail, 15 to 20 minutes for grouse, and 20 to 30 minutes for young partridge and pheasant.

When done, place on warm platter and butter or oil well on both sides. If the breasts are quite thick, use very moderate heat.

PARTRIDGES WITH CABBAGE

2 or 3 partridges
3 small strips fat salt pork
2 or 3 small cabbages
1 carrot
1 onion
3 cloves, if desired

Prepare the partridges for cooking. Sear with the strips of salt pork.

Dip the cabbage in boiling water for a minute, remove the core and pull the leaves apart. Drain well. Place a layer of cabbage leaves in the bottom of a small roasting pan.

On top of this, place the partridges together with the crisped pork, then a layer of cabbage to cover.

Or the partridges may be wrapped individually in cabbage leaves.

Add the carrot, the onion (with the cloves stuck into it), salt, pepper, and enough boiling water to cover with an inch to spare. Cook, covered, for 1 to 1½ hours in moderate oven (350°F.). Serve with the cabbage.

ROAST PARTRIDGE

Wipe cleaned birds with a damp cloth. Rub with melted butter or oil. Sprinkle inside and out with salt and pepper.

Bake in roasting pan in slow oven (325°F.) until tender, 30 to 40 minutes.

ROAST QUAIL

Wipe the cleaned bird with a damp cloth. Brush inside and out with butter. Rub with salt. Place a large mushroom inside the bird.

Place in pan. Cover with buttered parchment paper. Roast, uncovered, in slow oven (325°F.) 25 to 30 minutes. Remove paper after first 20 minutes.

ROAST GROUSE OR PRAIRIE CHICKEN

Wipe inside and out with damp cloth. Rub inside and out with salt.

Fill with bread or wild rice stuffing, or if preferred, put a strip of bacon or salt pork inside. Do not fasten opening.

Cover breast with strips of bacon or salt pork. Bake in slow oven (325°F.) until tender, about 30 minutes.

Roast Duck and Orange—A Favorite Flavor Combination

ROAST WILD DUCK OR WILD GOOSE

Cut off tail, removing oil sack. Draw and wipe with damp cloth. Rub inside with salt and pepper.

Fill with savory stuffing or wild rice stuffing or omit stuffing and put a small stalk of celery, or a whole apple or a whole onion in the cavity. If desired, add 1 tablespoon wine and 1 tablespoon melted butter. Close openings with small skewers. Truss wings to body.

Cover breast side with strips of fat salt pork or bacon, or rub skin with butter or oil. Sprinkle with salt and pepper.

Bake, uncovered, breast side up in slow oven (300°F.) until done. Allow 15 to 20 minutes per pound or ½ to 1 hour, depending upon size of bird. Duck should be served rare; therefore take care to avoid overcooking. Baste frequently with drippings from pan. Serve with gravy made from drippings and giblet stock.

ROAST PHEASANT

Use young hens weighing about 3 pounds each when dressed. Draw and truss as for chicken.

Rub inside with butter or oil. Sprinkle with salt. Fill lightly with a bread or wild rice stuffing. Cover with strips of bacon or fat salt pork or rub skin with butter or oil.

Bake, uncovered, in slow oven (325°F.) until tender, about 1 hour. Baste often with butter or drippings. Serve with gravy made from drippings.

ROAST WILD TURKEY

The wild turkey is the largest of American upland game birds; it is a highly prized and delicious meat. Young hens average 8 pounds; young toms, 12 pounds, undressed.

Follow method used for preparing, stuffing, trussing, and roasting domestic turkey (see Index).

PHEASANT BAKED IN SOUR CREAM

Cut bird into serving pieces. Roll in flour and sprinkle with salt and pepper. Brown in melted butter in heavy skillet. Add 1 cup light cream.

Cover and bake in moderate oven (350°F.) 30 minutes. Turn occasionally. Serve with gravy made from cream in pan.

QUAIL EN CASSEROLE

4 quail
Salt
1/3 cup salad oil
1 carrot, finely chopped
1 small onion, minced
1 tablespoon minced green pepper
3/4 cup sliced fresh or canned mushrooms
2 tablespoons flour
2 cups stock (or 4 bouillon cubes dissolved in 2 cups boiling water)
1/3 cup white wine

Rub the whole birds lightly with salt, then brown them in oil (or in part oil and part butter, if you like). Remove quail to a heated casserole.

In the same oil, sauté carrot, onion, green pepper, and mushrooms slowly for about 5 minutes. Blend in flour, then gradually stir in heated stock. Season to taste with salt; pour this sauce and wine over quail.

Cover and bake in moderate oven (350°F.) about 1/2 hour or until birds are tender. Serves 4.

SAGE HENS

Use young hens. Dress immediately after killing to prevent too strong a sage taste. Fry or roast as ordinary chicken.

COOT OR MUDHEN

Skin the birds. Cut off legs and breast. Discard remainder of carcass. Split breast in half.

Wash all parts thoroughly in cold water. Roll in seasoned flour.

Fry in hot bacon fat until well browned on all sides. Cover and let steam until tender. Make milk gravy in the skillet.

Rabbit, Hare, and Squirrel

RABBIT OR HARE

Domestic rabbit is a meat that is becoming increasingly available in retail markets. Fresh or frozen, it is sold all year 'round.

Rabbit meat can be used in most of the ways in which chicken is used. It is fine-grained and mild-flavored, and practically all of it is white meat. Like other lean meats, poultry, and lean fish, rabbit meat is a good source of high-quality protein.

BUYING RABBIT

Rabbits are sold live or ready-to-cook. Like poultry, ready-to-cook rabbits may be government inspected for wholesomeness.

Most commercially produced rabbits are marketed when they are 8 to 12 weeks old. These young rabbits are known as "fryers" and weigh not less than 1 1/2 pounds and rarely over 3 1/2 pounds, ready-to-cook. Rabbits known as "roasters" usually weigh over 4 pounds, ready-to-cook, and are ordinarily 8 months or older.

A large volume of the ready-to-cook rabbit is marketed in frozen form—usually pieces of one rabbit are packaged and frozen together. The giblets—heart, kidneys, and liver—are often included.

THAWING FROZEN RABBIT

A 2 1/2-pound frozen rabbit packaged in pieces needs about 3 hours to thaw under cold running water, about 6 hours at room temperature (75°F.), or 8 to 10 hours, or overnight, in the refrigerator.

Large rabbits—over 3 pounds—should not be thawed at room temperature unless they are to be cooked immediately.

POINTERS ON COOKING RABBIT

Small young rabbits (fryers, 1½ to 2 pounds ready-to-cook) may be fried satisfactorily in much the same way that chicken is fried. Or they may be stewed and the meat used in various recipes.

Large fryers and roasters need long, slow cooking in a covered pan to make them tender. Best methods of cooking them are stewing—that is, simmering in a small amount of water—and braising—first browning in a little fat and then cooking slowly, with or without added liquid, on top of the range or in the oven. Liquid used in braising may be a sauce that adds flavor to the dish.

For most recipes, the rabbit is cut in serving pieces before it is cooked. Dealers usually cut large rabbits into 9 or 11 pieces—the 2 forelegs, 4 pieces from the 2 hind legs, and 3 or 5 sections of back.

The kidneys are usually attached inside the lower back and are cooked and served with this piece. The liver and heart may be cooked with the rest of the rabbit in any recipe you are using, or stewed separately and used in gravy.

Yield of Stewed Rabbit Meat

From a small rabbit 1½ to 3½ pounds, ready-to-cook, you may expect 2 to 4½ cups of cooked meat. From larger rabbits you may count on about 1½ cups of cooked meat per pound of ready-to-cook weight.

HOW TO SKIN A RABBIT, HARE, OR SQUIRREL

Hang up by hind legs in cool place for several days. To skin it, leave it hanging. Carefully cut up the front from tail to throat with a sharp knife. Take out entrails. Cut out bile sack from liver, saving liver and heart. Discard other parts.

Cut fur around each of the 4 ankles, pulling legs through. Cut off ears.

Strip the fur skin, separated from the inner skin, from the hind legs down and over the head.

Cut off the head, throat, and paws and discard these parts together with the skin from the belly. Remove small waxy kernels directly between body and forelegs.

Wipe thoroughly inside and out with a cloth dipped in a mixture of 1 cup water and 1 tablespoon vinegar. Serving portion: ¾ to 1 pound.

IRISH POT ROASTED RABBIT (Braised Rabbit with Gravy)

Young rabbit (2 to 2½ pounds ready-to-cook) cut in serving pieces
Flour, salt, pepper
3 tablespoons cooking fat or oil
¼ cup hot water
2 tablespoons flour
2 cups milk

Roll rabbit in mixture of flour, salt, and pepper. Heat fat or oil in a heavy fry pan and brown the rabbit slowly, turning to brown on all sides. Add water and cover pan tightly.

Reduce heat and cook slowly until meat is tender (about 1 hour), adding a little more water if needed. Uncover and cook 5 minutes longer to recrisp surface. Remove rabbit from the pan and keep it hot.

Remove fat from pan and pour back 2 tablespoonfuls. Stir in the 2 tablespoons flour and cook until mixture bubbles. Add milk slowly, stirring constantly. Cook until thick, stirring occasionally, then cook a little longer. Add salt and pepper if needed. Serves 4.

To braise a large rabbit (about 4 pounds), use ⅓ cup fat or oil for browning and ⅓ cup water. Cook about 1½ hours, or until tender. Make gravy with 3 tablespoons flour, 3 tablespoons fat and 3 cups milk. Serves 8.

BROILED RABBIT OR SQUIRREL

Squirrel meat is similar to rabbit but more delicate in flavor. Clean and wipe young animals with damp cloth. Rub inside and out with melted butter.

Lay on side and cover with strips of bacon. Broil under moderate heat until well browned on all sides.

FRIED RABBIT

Small young rabbit (1½ to 2 pounds ready-to-cook) cut in serving pieces
Flour, salt, pepper
Cooking fat or oil

Roll rabbit in mixture of flour, salt, and pepper. Heat fat or oil about ¼ inch deep in a heavy fry pan large enough to hold the pieces without crowding.

Use moderate heat for frying. Put in the large meaty pieces of rabbit first and cook about 10 minutes before adding the smaller pieces and giblets. Turn the pieces often for even cooking, and cook until well browned and tender (30 to 35 minutes total time).

Serves 3 to 4.

FRIED SQUIRREL

Use only young, fresh squirrels that are free of any strong, unpleasant odors. Follow method for frying rabbit. If animal is old, add a little water, cover and cook until tender.

RABBIT STEW

2 cups dried lima beans
1 small rabbit, dressed and cut in serving-size pieces
Boiling water
2 teaspoons salt
⅛ teaspoon pepper
1 teaspoon Ac'cent
1 bay leaf
1 medium-sized onion, sliced
1 bunch carrots, sliced
2 large green peppers
2 tablespoons butter or margarine

Soak beans overnight in 1½ quarts cold water; drain.

Wash rabbit; place in large kettle with drained beans; cover with boiling water; add salt, pepper, Ac'cent, bay leaf, and onion; simmer ½ hour.

Add carrots; cook 1 hour longer or until rabbit is tender. Add more boiling water as needed.

Cut seeded green peppers in rings; add during last 15 minutes, with butter or margarine. Thicken gravy if desired. Serves 6.

Rabbit Stew

HASSENPFEFFER

½ cup vinegar
2 cups water
2 teaspoons salt
¼ teaspoon pepper
½ teaspoon whole cloves
2 teaspoons sugar
4 bay leaves
1 medium onion, sliced
Small rabbit (about 2½ pounds ready-to-cook) cut in serving pieces
Flour
3 tablespoons fat
2 teaspoons Worcestershire sauce
3 tablespoons flour

Make pickling mixture by combining the vinegar, water, salt, pepper, cloves, sugar, bay leaves, and onion in a glass or enameled-ware bowl.

Add pieces of rabbit and sliced giblets and cover the bowl. Let stand in refrigerator 8 to 12 hours, turning the pieces occasionally so that they will absorb the flavor evenly.

Remove the rabbit pieces. Save liquid and onions but discard bay leaves and cloves.

Roll the rabbit in flour. Heat fat or oil in a heavy pan and brown the rabbit in it, turning to brown all sides.

Pour the pickling mixture over the rabbit. Cover pan and cook over low heat about 1 hour, or until rabbit is tender.

Take rabbit from pan and keep it hot. Add Worcestershire sauce to the liquid. Mix the 3 tablespoons flour with a little cold water, add a few tablespoons of hot liquid to it, and pour the mixture back into the pan. Stir and cook until the sauce is thick and smooth, then cook a little longer.

Pour sauce over rabbit. Serves 4.

To use a large rabbit (about 4 to 5 pounds ready-to-cook), double the amounts of ingredients for the pickling mixture. It is important to have enough to flavor all of the meat.

Use ⅓ cup fat to brown the rabbit and ⅓ cup flour to thicken the sauce. It may be necessary to skim off part of the fat before thickening the sauce. Serves 8 to 10.

ROAST RABBIT OR SQUIRREL

Rub inside of cleaned, dressed rabbit or squirrel with salt.

Fill with desired stuffing. Sew up and truss. Brush with melted fat or bacon drippings. Sprinkle with salt and pepper. Place on side in roaster.

Roast, uncovered, in slow oven (325°F.) until tender, about 1½ hours. Turn at least once while cooking. Baste frequently with melted fat.

RABBIT PIE

¼ cup butter or margarine
¼ cup chopped onion
½ cup chopped green pepper
¼ cup sifted flour
2 cups rabbit broth (or water with 4 chicken bouillon cubes)
3 cups coarsely cut cooked rabbit meat
Salt and pepper to taste
Pastry (basis 1 cup flour)

Heat butter or margarine in a large fry pan. Add onion and green pepper and cook about 5 minutes over low heat.

Blend in the flour and cook until the mixture bubbles. Pour in the broth gradually, stirring constantly. Cook until thick and smooth, stirring frequently. Add salt and pepper.

Add meat to the sauce and heat thoroughly. Pour mixture into a shallow baking dish or pan.

Roll out the pastry and cut slits for steam to escape. Fit to top of dish or pan, crimping the edges of the crust.

Bake the pie in hot oven (425°F.) 15 to 20 minutes, or until crust browns and sauce bubbles. Serves 4 to 6.

Variations: Use 1 cup of cooked diced vegetables (potatoes, carrots, celery) with 2 cups of rabbit meat. Make the topping of tiny baking powder biscuits.

RABBIT OR HARE FRICASSEE WITH VEGETABLES

Rabbit (about 3 pounds ready-to-cook) cut in serving pieces
Flour, salt, pepper
1/3 cup cooking fat or oil
2 cups hot water
4 cups raw vegetables (peas and coarsely chopped carrots, onions, and celery)
1 teaspoon salt
1/4 cup sifted flour

Roll rabbit in mixture of flour, salt, and pepper.

Heat fat or oil and brown the rabbit slowly, turning often. Add water and cover pan.

Cook slowly on top of range about 1 hour, or until rabbit is almost tender. Add water if needed during cooking. Add vegetables and salt and cook about 20 minutes longer, or until vegetables are done.

Or, after browning, bake the rabbit in slow oven (325°F.) about 1½ hours, add vegetables, and bake about 30 minutes longer.

Mix the 1/4 cup flour with a little cold water, add a few tablespoons of hot liquid from the pan, and stir the mixture into the liquid in pan. Cook 15 minutes longer, or until sauce is smooth and thick. Serves 8.

To fricassee a smaller rabbit (about 2 pounds ready-to-cook), use 1/4 cup fat or oil for browning, and half the quantity of the other ingredients in the recipe above. Cooking time on top of range before adding vegetables is about 30 minutes; in oven, about 45 minutes. Serves 4.

RABBIT CASSEROLE, WESTERN STYLE

6 slices bacon, cut in squares
1 young rabbit, cut in serving portions or 2 packages frozen rabbit
1/4 cup flour
1 teaspoon salt
1/4 teaspoon pepper
1/4 teaspoon marjoram
1/2 teaspoon Ac'cent
4 medium potatoes, pared and thinly sliced
2 small onions, sliced
2½ cups hot water
2 bouillon cubes

Fry bacon slowly until lightly browned. Remove from pan and pour off half the fat.

Dip rabbit pieces in a mixture of flour, salt, pepper, marjoram, and Ac'cent. Brown in the bacon fat. Transfer rabbit to casserole.

Cover meat with potato and onion slices. Sprinkle lightly with remaining seasoned flour. Add hot water to which bouillon cubes have been added.

Cover and cook in moderate oven (350°F.) 2 hours. Remove cover for last 15 minutes to brown. Serve with bacon squares on top. Serves 4.

RABBIT WITH PRUNES (Belgium Style)

1 rabbit
2 cups claret wine
1 cup vinegar
1 teaspoon salt
8 whole black peppers
1 bay leaf
1/4 teaspoon thyme
1/4 teaspoon marjoram
1/4 teaspoon fennel
3 tablespoons salad oil
1 tablespoon flour
Salt and pepper
1/2 pound prunes

Have rabbit cut into serving-size pieces. Make a marinade of the claret, vinegar, salt, whole black peppers, bay leaf, thyme, marjoram, and fennel. Add rabbit, let stand for 24 hours.

Remove and dry pieces of rabbit. Put salad oil in large saucepan, add rabbit, brown lightly. Blend flour into salad oil, season with salt and pepper.

Cover rabbit with marinade, add soaked prunes. Cover, simmer until meat and prunes are tender. Usually served with gooseberry preserves. Serves 4.

JUGGED HARE

1 large rabbit, disjointed
1 medium-sized onion, sliced thin
1 cup burgundy wine
3 ounces bacon or salt pork
Flour
Salt and pepper
1 garlic clove
1 bay leaf
A bit of thyme
2 sprigs parsley

Place rabbit in a deep bowl with onion and wine. Cover and marinate several hours, turning once or twice to marinate all parts thoroughly. Remove meat and reserve marinade for gravy.

Fry bacon or salt pork in a deep, heavy kettle, then remove it. Sprinkle rabbit meat with flour seasoned with salt and pepper.

Sauté meat in hot drippings until nicely browned on all sides. Add bacon or salt pork, the marinade, and herbs tied in a piece of cheesecloth.

Cover tightly and cook over low heat until tender, 2 to 3 hours. Remove meat and keep hot while preparing gravy.

Skim fat from sauce. Blend 6 tablespoons of this fat with 6 tablespoons flour. Add enough water to cooking liquid to make 2½ cups liquid. Stir this slowly into the flour-fat mixture and cook over low heat until gravy is thickened and smooth.

Pour gravy over rabbit or serve in separate bowl. Serves 6.

Venison

Venison actually means the flesh of any antlered game animal such as deer, caribou, elk, moose, and reindeer; however, in popular usage it generally refers to the deer, when used as a food.

Venison is cooked in much the same manner as domestic meats, particularly lamb or mutton. Because the meat is considered somewhat of a "treat," an attempt is usually made to give it extra attention in preparation by the addition of wine, cream, mushrooms, etc.

The texture is very similar to beef. Tender cuts of young animals are cooked by dry heat: broiling or roasting. Tough cuts such as the shoulder are cooked by moist heat: braising or stewing.

Venison tends to be lean, therefore bacon, butter, or other fat has to be added generously to keep moist and juicy.

Large herds of Alaskan reindeer are making considerable quantities of frozen reindeer meat available for tender steaks, roasts, stews, etc. Allow it to thaw slowly at room temperature before cooking. While the flavor is somewhat "gamy" it is not strong. It has an excellent texture and is usually tender.

VENISON STEAKS, CHOPS, LOIN CUTLETS

Use tender cuts from loin or leg, about ½ to 1½ inches thick. Sprinkle with salt and pepper. Brush with butter or oil.

Place on greased broiler rack in moderate broiler. Cook 5 to 10 minutes on each side or until well browned, turning once during cooking.

To pan-broil: Place in hot frying pan which has been brushed lightly with fat. Cook over moderate heat.

If desired, rub both sides with cut clove of garlic before broiling. If desired, steaks may be marinated in French dressing for 1 hour before cooking.

Serve with fresh mushrooms which have been sautéed in butter or with melted butter seasoned with lemon juice, or with a mixture of half butter and half currant jelly.

ROAST VENISON

Use thick loin or upper leg cuts from young venison. Rub with butter. Sprinkle with salt and pepper.

Place in roasting pan. Cover with strips of fat salt pork. If desired, stick a few cloves of garlic deep into flesh.

Roast in moderate oven (350°F.) until done, allowing about 25 minutes per pound. Baste frequently throughout roasting period with melted butter.

Make brown gravy from the drippings. Serve with a tart jelly.

BRAISED VENISON

Use a 4- to 6-pound cut from shoulder or leg. Lard lean side with strips of fat pork, drawing them through with a larding needle. Rub with softened butter. Coat well with seasoned flour.

Brown on all sides in ½ cup hot fat, turning often. Add ¼ cup hot water. Cook, covered, over low heat until tender, about 2 to 2½ hours. Add small amounts of water if necessary and turn frequently.

If desired, add 2 medium-sized sliced carrots, ½ cup chopped celery, 1 medium-sized onion, sliced, and 1 tablespoon lemon juice during the last half hour of cooking.

STEWED VENISON

Do not lard. Cut the meat into 1½- to 2-inch cubes. Otherwise prepare in the same manner as braised venison.

A full cup of water may be added instead of the half cup after the meat is browned.

Stewed Venison

Miscellaneous Game Animals

ROAST RACCOON

Skin and dress, being careful to remove scent glands under each front leg and on either side of spine in small of back. Wash in cold water.

Parboil in freshly boiling water ½ hour, repeating if animal is not young. Drain and dry carefully.

Stuff with bread stuffing to which a quartered tart apple has been added. Place in baking pan.

Roast in moderate oven (350°F.) until tender and delicately browned.

WOODCHUCK (GROUND HOG)

Woodchuck must be parboiled because of its extremely strong flavor. The red scent kernels between forelegs and body must be removed when the animal is skinned. Parboil 20 minutes in fresh boiling water.

Drain. Rub with salt, pepper, and sage. Place in baking pan. Roast in moderate oven (350°F.) until tender and richly browned. Or, brown in hot fat, then add ¼ cup water, cover and cook over low heat until tender.

ROAST OPOSSUM ('POSSUM)

The flavor of 'possum is improved if the animal is caught alive and fed for a week or longer on persimmons, apples, berries, etc. Some 'possum fanciers insist that mashed persimmons and warm water is the best diet. The 'possum is then killed and dressed in much the same way as a suckling pig.

The animal is at its best when it is fat; however as much fat as possible should be removed. The head and tail may be left on or removed.

Rub the cleaned cavity with onion or sage. Sprinkle with salt and pepper. Fill with apple or onion stuffing.

In many parts of the South a herb-seasoned mixture of persimmons, sweet potatoes, and breadcrumbs, moistened with beef stock, is a favorite stuffing.

Truss and place on rack in shallow pan underside down. Add 2 tablespoons water and roast in slow oven (300°–325°F.) until well done, 2 to 2½ hours, basting occasionally with drippings from pan. Skim fat from gravy and serve with sweet potatoes and stewed persimmons.

If desired, small parboiled sweet potatoes may be placed around the 'possum when it's nearly done and basted with drippings from time to time.

PORCUPINE

Skin in the same manner as a rabbit. Dress and wipe with damp cloth.

Roast, whole or cut up depending on size, in an open roasting pan. Add no water. Bake in moderate oven (350°F.) until tender and richly browned.

BEAR

Bear meat is very dark, and usually dry and tough. The meat should be marinated before cooking and, like pork, it must be very thoroughly cooked before eating.

The use of a pressure cooker is advisable. Cub bear meat is tender when very young.

MOUNTAIN GOAT

Mountain goat is tough, dark, and usually dry meat. It should be marinated and the use of a pressure cooker is advisable.

MOUNTAIN SHEEP

This highly prized meat should be roasted in the same way as lamb. The fell from the legs is not removed but it should be removed from chops.

Roast in open pan, basting frequently with a little water in pan. If the meat is dry, use a little butter in the pan with the water. Serve with a mint jelly or sauce.